THE SCOTTISH GOVERNMENT
YEARBOOK 1979

The
Scottish
Government
Yearbook
1979

Edited by
H. M. DRUCKER
*Department of Politics and Unit for
the Study of Government in
Scotland,
University of Edinburgh*

and

N. L. DRUCKER
*Department of Social Administration,
University of Edinburgh*

Paul Harris Publishing
Edinburgh

Rowman & Littlefield
Totowa, N.J.

First published in the United Kingdom 1978
by Paul Harris Publishing
25 London Street
Edinburgh

ISBN 0 904505 53 7
ISSN 0141-0482

First published in the United States
by Rowman & Littlefield
Totowa, N.J.

ISBN 0-8476-6114-8

British Library Cataloguing in Publication Data:
The Scottish government yearbook.
    1979.
    1. Scotland — Politics and government —
20th century
    I. Drucker, Henry Matthew   II. Drucker, N. L.
    320.9'411'0857   JN1187
    ISBN 0-904505-53-7

Printed in Great Britain by The Shetland Times Ltd., Lerwick, Shetland

CONTENTS

REFERENCE SECTION

Reference section prepared with assistance of
Richard Parry

PREFACE

The *Yearbook* is edited by H. M. Drucker and N. L. Drucker of the University of Edinburgh. The Unit for the Study of Government in Scotland acts as an editorial board. Additional copies of the *Yearbook,* back-copies of the two previous volumes, and further information about the Unit's activities can be obtained from the editors, at 31 Buccleuch Place, Edinburgh EH8 9JT, Scotland.

We are grateful to several previous contributors and to other friends for suggestions for papers for this volume. We would welcome suggestions from our readers too about subjects or authors for papers. We are indebted to the *Glasgow Herald* and to several other Scottish newspapers and broadcasting organisations for permission to reprint public opinion polls they originally sponsored. We also wish to record our thanks to Helen Ramm, Hazel Plenderleith and Judy Adams for typing large sections of the text.

HMD
NLD
June 1978
Edinburgh

NEIL WILLIAMSON

It is with great regret that we record the death on October 17, 1978, of one of our contributors, Neil Williamson.

1

INTRODUCTION

TOWARDS A SCOTTISH POLITICS

This is the third volume in our series of *Yearbooks of Scottish Government*. It is jointly dedicated to Professor John P. Mackintosh, MP, and to Councillor Geoff Shaw. John Mackintosh was the Chairman of The Unit for the Study of Government in Scotland for the six months before his untimely death. Those of us who worked with him in Edinburgh University were delighted with the way John put his back into the work of the Unit. He gave it some of his great vitality and now he is gone. We are pleased to dedicate this *Yearbook* to John and to include a brief appreciation of his work both as politician and academic, prepared as we went to press by Professor Bernard Crick. The *Yearbook* is also dedicated to Councillor Geoff Shaw who was Convener of Strathclyde Region, and one of the most respected and well-liked public servants in Scotland until his death in 1978. We are happy to publish an appreciation of Geoff Shaw by his friend the Secretary of State for Scotland, the Rt. Hon. Bruce Millan, MP. Either John Mackintosh or Geoff Shaw could have led the Scottish Assembly with distinction. Our public life will be diminished without them.

This volume in our series is also the book for the year — 1979 — which will, very possibly, be the most significant in Scottish political and constitutional history for a long time. Perhaps it is appropriate then, to reflect here on the nature and direction of Scottish politics.

The main thing which strikes us, as observers of Scottish politics and government, and as editors of this *Yearbook,* is the discontinuity within Scottish politics. Despite the arguments of James Kellas (*The Scottish Political System,* 1973) "system" is precisely what Scottish politics lacks. Perhaps it is foolish to expect system in British institutions; but Scottish political life carries the normal British flair for *ad hoc* arrangements to an extreme. Scottish politics find expression in a series of practices and institutions some of which have been thought out in relation to each other, but most not. It is a collection of parts of governmental agencies which operate *in* Scotland (such as the Scottish Region of British Rail); and governmental agencies *for* Scotland (such as the Scottish Arts Council); and governmental agencies which *include* Scotland in their remit (such as the Department of Energy). Some of these agencies are directly controlled by the British government (like the last named); many are directly controlled by no elected body but rather by an appointed board (like British Rail or the Board of Governors of the BBC); some are local governments of parts of Scotland. Sometimes these institutions are distinctively Scottish (like the Scottish legal system) and sometimes they are unique to Scotland (like the Highlands and Islands Development Board). But often they are simply Northern copies of an English agency. The operations of too many of these agencies are unknown — if not secret — and one of the things we are trying to do in our *Yearbooks* is open them up to scrutiny.

Sometimes the British government, which directly controls some of the agencies of government in Scotland and which importantly affects them all, has the same political colour as the majority of Scottish MPs; but sometimes it does not. Opinion polls tell us that the Scottish people don't particularly like this state of affairs; they like it rather less than people from other parts of Britain; but on the other hand they don't seem to want to increase their own control over government very much. They don't want it nearly so much as they want lower rates of unemployment or inflation. In 1979, Scotland may get a form of devolved government which will go some way towards tying the various parts of government in Scotland and the wishes of the Scottish electorate more closely together. If this change has the desired effect, then Scotland will be substantially closer to having a political system.

It would be wrong for us to use this introduction to argue in favour of or in opposition to the Government's proposals. We have published papers in the *Yearbooks* both for and against the plans. But it would be remiss of us not to draw attention to the changes which the preferred Assembly will bring about if, as we have consistently expected, it is created. It is more than conceivable that the first elections to the Assembly will occur in the autumn of 1979, and that the newly elected Assembly members will take office shortly thereafter. It is unfortunate that no definite description of the Assembly's powers has been published nor even a list of those parliamentary seats which will have three Assemblymen. We have given our own estimates on these two questions in the Reference Section.

One effect of the Assembly will be to call into question the need — or if one likes, the continued need — for so many *ad hoc* and appointed agencies of government. The existence and powers of such agencies (quasi-autonomous non-governmental agencies or QUANGOs as they are often called) has been mentioned by us before. We have argued that at least some of the powers given to such bodies as the Scottish Development Agency, the Housing Corporation and the Countryside Commission for Scotland, might have been given to elected local authorities. One argument against our previous position has always been that these agencies operate on an all-Scottish basis. No one local authority represents all of Scotland. The new all-Scottish Assembly will undermine that argument.

Nevertheless, it is not denied that at present there are a large number of *ad hoc* and appointed bodies and they exercise considerable power. We publish this year a paper by Sir Douglas Haddow in which he discusses some of them. So little is generally known about them that we hope Sir Douglas's piece will help to guide discussion. As this paper demonstrates, the tasks of the agencies differ considerably. Of itself this will make the job of democratisation — if that is what the Assembly chooses to do — complicated and difficult. On the other hand, Sir Douglas's paper points to some features of the *ad hoc* agencies which could certainly do with public scrutiny. They tend, amongst other things, to acquire a life of their own and to be impossible to abolish even after their tasks have been completed or outmoded. Professor Flinn's paper about *The Scottish Arts Council* raises other questions. Flinn points out that the Scottish Arts Council is required to make public reports of its activities each year. To this extent it is publically accountable. But some public bodies in which the public has a legitimate interest (he mentions, for example, the Convention of Scottish Local Authorities) operate under no such requirement.

Last year's book noted the fear of many in local government that the Assembly would take an uncomfortably close interest in the affairs of local councils to the point where the councils would lose what initiative they currently retain. Professor Flinn indicates that some *ad hoc* agencies harbour a similar fear. It is a real enough possibility. The Assembly was not created in order to make life intolerable for existing agencies, but once created it may look around for things to do. Public finance for the arts is difficult enough to handle when those responsible for handing out the money are sympathetic people. How could less well informed people make judgements between the various proposals? Would less well disposed people put a high priority on arts spending at all? Certainly the job of the Scottish Arts Council has been made more difficult recently by the refusal of some local authorities to maintain the value of their grants. Democracy has its drawbacks — with the coming of the Assembly we may be about to see some of them.

Both Sir Douglas, and Dorothy Bochel and Morag Mac-Laran in their paper on *Local Health Councils,* mention the complexity of the present organisation of the health service in Scotland. But they come at the problem from different points of view. Bochel and MacLaran are concerned that the local health councils, the voice of the consumer in the health service, have so little authority. They point out that this part of the recent reform of the health service has had limited success.

John Waterhouse's paper on *Penal Policy in Scotland* makes an interesting contrast. He argues for the creation of an appointed body of experts to advise the Secretary of State on penal policy and argues convincingly that the dearth of innovation in penal policy for Scotland owes something to the lack of such a panel to lobby the Secretary of State. But if we have to create appointed bodies of experts to generate the political will for reform, is that not a considerable indictment of public politics and existing interest groups?

In our last *Yearbook,* Robin Cook, MP, suggested that the liberalisation of Scottish law — in relation to divorce, homosexuality, and so on — had been impeded not so much by the inherent failures of the Westminster system, as by the feebleness and ineptitude of the Scottish pressure groups. In this volume Peter Gibson takes issue with him. Using the passage of the *Housing (Homeless Persons) Act 1977* as an example, Gibson shows that one needs to distinguish between the operations of various Scottish pressure groups. There are some, like those built around the Churches and established professional groups, which are well organised and financed. Others, including most of the

newer voluntary groups such as Shelter and Scottish Women's
Aid, find the going hard. They are simply not in a position to
finance a London office or meet the cost of sending a representative — let alone a team of representatives — to London to work
on the administration or Parliament. Another way of putting
this, of course, is that some interest groups are powerful enough
to have some of their leaders co-opted into the system as members of *ad hoc* or appointed agencies. It is those which are not
— like Shelter and Women's Aid — which need help.

Jim Hunter is the author of *The Making of the Crofting
Community* (1976). This background gives his account of
the recent change in crofting legislation special authority.
Hunter's verdict on the effects of the *Crofting Reform (Scotland)
Act 1976,* is not flattering to its creators. He argues that it was
ill conceived and has had almost no effect. The interesting and,
for anyone who feels strongly about this, supremely emotional
issue, the infuriating thing about this Act, was that it was framed
by the Scottish Office for a Conservative administration.
It was passed into law by the succeeding Labour government
in the face of a decision by the Scottish Council of the Labour
Party, that crofting land should pass into public ownership.
Hunter thinks that the Government should have listened to its
party. The failure of the Government to respond to the wishes
of its party — and the response in this case is not unique —
shows one of the weaknesses of the discontinuous sort
of government we now have in Scotland. Whether the parties
will receive a more positive response from their governments
if an Assembly comes, remains to be seen.

If, however, we are to place any confidence in the democratic process — as opposed to the appointment process — we
need high votes at elections. One of the strongest complaints
against the old system of local government which was replaced
in 1975 was that too few seats were contested and that the
turnout of voters in the contested seats was very low. In the
years immediately preceeding the reform, the average vote in
Scotland in contested wards could be as low as 35%. In the first
elections under the new system higher turnouts were achieved.
But, as John Bochel and David Denver point out in their paper
on *The Regional Council Elections of May 1978* we seem to be
returning to the bad old days. The proportion of people who
voted at these recent elections was noticeably down from the

previous (1974) Regional elections; and it was lower than for the 1977 District elections. If the electors refuse to vote — for whatever reason — the Councillors or Assembly members elected will have less weight when they attempt to stand up to the appointed officials of *ad hoc* agencies.

It is perhaps as well to remember that we do not yet have an Assembly. This is no mere quibble, for the Conservative Party in Scotland has at last come out unequivocally for a "No" vote in the referendum on devolution. If a Conservative government is returned at the next General Election that government might delay the referendum or otherwise contrive to dampen expectations such that the Assembly never comes to be. Jim Naughtie points out in his paper on *The Scotland Bill in the House of Commons* that the Conservatives' slow shuffle away from their previous commitment to devolution was one reason for their lackluster performance against the Bill in the House of Commons. Naughtie's paper makes an interesting contrast with the paper by John Kerr we published last year about *The Scotland and Wales Bill.* Kerr spoke of the lack of will on the Government's side; this year Naughtie shows that, led by John Smith, the Government knew what it wanted and got it. It was the anti-devolutionists, particularly the Conservative anti-devolutionists, who knew what they were against but not what they were for, who lost out. Naughtie is able to point to the increasing confidence and authority of John Smith, Minister of State in the Privy Council Office, as the debate wore on. He won the respect of many — just as, indeed, Lord McCluskey won much respect for his championing of the same Bill through the House of Lords. This makes quite a change from last year when all the arguments were being won by the anti-devolutionists.

All of the papers in this year's *Yearbook* which concern themselves with specific public policies relate to policies over which the Assembly will have much control. As it happens, we have no papers this year about the Scottish economy and the Government's attempts to control it. In this year of the Assembly, however, that gap is perhaps justified. The Assembly will have no influence over the Scottish economy. It will have no tax-raising powers and will need the consent of the Secretary of State for every money borrowing decision it makes.

It remains for Neil Williamson who has written a paper for us, *Ten Years After — The Revolutionary Left in Scotland* to raise the questions of unemployment and inflation. In his paper Williamson points out that the revolutionary Left has failed to take advantage of the anguish created by these problems just as surely as governments have failed to deal with them. One thing one can normally expect from the Left, however, is a critique of the operations of government. Thus, the fact that the Left are interested in the economic failures of government, rather than, say, the problems of QUANGOs is a reminder that government machinery is there to provide services for the country; not simply to operate smoothly. It is also revealing in this context to repeat Williamson's observation that there is hardly a Scottish Left — but rather that there is a Left in Scotland. The Left is not devolved; neither does it think devolution an important problem.

The Assembly's lack of economic powers points to the fact that this addition to the political machinery of Scotland will still leave gaps. Scottish politics will be less fragmented than once they were; but they will hardly form a fully developed system. The Assembly will have no power over those government subjects which, as opinion poll after opinion poll shows, are of greatest interest to the citizens. It will have no control over inflation or unemployment. If Scottish politics is becoming more systematic, it is still very far from being a distinct or — to use a loaded word — a separate system.

In this edition of the *Yearbook* we have made a special effort to make our Reference Section more useful. We are presenting here a series of both factual and analytical appendices on the operation of government in Scotland. In particular, we have tried to indicate which of the Scottish Office's present responsibilities will be devolved and which will not. We are grateful to Richard Parry who has taken on the task of editorial assistant and prepared these Appendices for us. We are also, as always, grateful to Chris Allen for the patient and careful labour he has put into the preparation of the Bibliographical Appendix, *Recent Publications in Scottish Government and Politics*. W. J. A. Macartney has also provided us with a valuable guide to the results of major political opinion polls in Scotland since the October 1974 General Election.

When the first *Yearbook of Scottish Government* was launched by Edinburgh University's Unit for the Study of

Government in Scotland, we were determined to keep it broadly based. One of the advantages of politics in a small country is that it is possible for people to talk to each other across the boundaries of profession and party. Thus we are particularly proud of the fact that of this year's nine papers, three are written by people who practise what they are preaching; three are written by academics who have made a special study of the area they are writing about; and three are written by journalists who are experts in their subjects.

When the *Yearbook* was launched it was edited by Michael Clarke and Henry Drucker. Shortly before this, Michael Clarke had left Edinburgh University for the Policy Planning Unit of Lothian Region and we were very pleased to have his help as someone uniquely able to bridge the gap between the academic world and the world of public administration. Unfortunately, the demands on his time inside Lothian Region have made it impractical for Michael to continue editing the *Yearbook*. He will, however, remain in close touch with the book and has advised us on this year's selections and already produced some suggestions for next year. We wish to record our thanks to him for helping to launch the series. Careful readers of past *Yearbooks* will remember that Nancy Drucker was referred to as a copy editor. In fact she was a full participating editor in all but name. It seemed only fair to end this exclusion. The Scottish Government Unit has agreed to make her a full editor of the *Yearbook*.

<table>
<tr><td>Edinburgh</td><td>H. M. Drucker</td></tr>
<tr><td>September 1978</td><td>N. L. Drucker</td></tr>
</table>

2

JOHN MACKINTOSH — AN APPRECIATION

BERNARD CRICK
Professor of Politics, Birkbeck College, University of London

John Mackintosh died on the 30th of July 1978 at the tragically early age of 48 when at the height of his remarkable powers, and while enjoying vastly his two roles of professor and of politician. I knew the book before I knew the man. *The British Cabinet* was at first warmly praised by most academics, then it became a universal target for critical exercises, from thousands of student essays to scores of learned articles; but even before his death, it had entered a third phase of recognition as a classic work on the British Constitution. No other book has pulled together so much historical knowledge and showed so well how Britain is governed. Students tend to believe that the book is primarily about whether the Prime Minister or the Cabinet governs. John never posed so crude a dichotomy. The real thesis of the book is far broader: that cabinet government is limited in its use of power not merely by Parliament, or even the parties, but by public opinion and politics in its broadest sense.

This is the clue, I think, to his character and career. Deeply as he believed in the House of Commons, yet he saw that it too was only a part of politics; and that there were more politics and political education "out of doors" than "in-doors" — as the eighteenth century had put it. His journalism, his broadcasting and his peripatetic, persistent and stimulating lecturing were neither venal nor just an excess of adrenalin: he was deeply radical in the sense that he believed primarily in public controversy out-of-doors, outside Parliament to rouse public opinion to influence government, as being the heart of politics. Thus he did not seek high office and was judged too "independent" and "reckless" for it, though it might have come with time as with Dick Crossman; and he refused offers of junior office simply as an attempt to muzzle him. He valued his chair and a column in *The Times* more than being Minister of this or that — there

B

was a certain arrogance in this maybe, but a definite truth too: his way carried more political influence — we are short of political ideas, not of administrators. There was pith in his joke to friends, "I am the Enoch Powell of the Left". He was deeply radical and had the common touch as well as the academic graces (as an English friend, I was always astounded by his mixture of reckless vulgarity in a *fight* and of academic graces in a *controversy* — was it Glasgow and Edinburgh combined in one character?). But this radicalism, though of the Labour movement, did not imply specifically left-wing sympathies: there are a few Tories of that ilk, and all Liberals (save one) who go out to the people, but to the actual people, not the left-wing myth, at times. John was a realist. Perhaps too much of a realist. Politics *is* the art of the possible. But *what* is possible? He asked for a positive theory of a mixed economy in the last major article he published before his death in the July number of the *Political Quarterly* which we edited together; but the mix might have been suspect to many in the Parliamentary Labour Party — although he called their bluff in talking about the mixed economy at all. One thinks of him mainly, however, for his honesty rather than his theoretical clarity. I do not think that he was reckless, he was simply courageous and no respecter of persons. So many are self-seekingly prudent. Orwell once wrote that "liberty is telling people what they do not want to hear". John was a master of that, and a "bonnie fechter" right down the line — whether over Scottish devolution or trade union reform. When he wrecked the Government's majority over the passage of the Dock Labour Bill by his deliberate abstention, no one claimed that his action was motivated by any reason other than that he did not believe in it in principle.

He excited jealousy as well as admiration. As he took strong blows himself without bearing any grudge, he was naively surprised that some other politicians didn't like the ring — unless the fight was fixed. But the admiration was greater. Two days after he died saw a memorial meeting in the largest committee room of Parliament which was crowded with MPs from all parties and many, many others. All the tributes pointed to his independence. If British politics had a hundred Mackintoshes it would be unworkable; but if it does not have a few still in the House, it would not be worth having. Above all, he showed that the academic and the political can, when the sincerity, scholarship and honesty of a man are clear, be bridged. He believed that they should be bridged. He would listen politely for a few moments when friends advised him to concentrate his energy — but if one went on too long, he would say, "What, and become like so and so! " — and laughter of self-knowledge swept all away in merriment. He had to be twice as large and active in two fields as most of us ever hope to be in one. One loved him for the enemies he has made. One loved him for the impossible example. He irritated one every time one met him that he was also dealing with something else. But there are so many like that. Who can one think of in the whole of the United Kingdom like John?

A last word — who can one think of who brought so many Englishmen, like myself, to see that the Scottish national spirit needed and would be incomplete without political forms? The Scotland Bill ground through the House of Commons as if it were a weary political necessity: John treated it as a matter of the deepest principle. So it was. And so was he a man of principle — though he never denied that a fight could be enjoyed.

GEOFF SHAW — AN APPRECIATION

THE Rt. Hon. BRUCE MILLAN

Geoff Shaw himself would have been embarrassed and confused by the tributes that have been paid to him since his death on 28 April 1978. He never sought publicity for himself, for he was an unassuming and genuinely humble man. He was also motivated by very clear social and political ideals which left no room for anything that might have been interpreted as a cult of personality. Geoff Shaw nevertheless provided in his life and work an inspiration to all who knew and worked with him, and played the key role, as first Convener of Strathclyde Region, in setting up that Authority and determining the manner and tone in which it operated. His practical achievements and the memories he leaves behind him will continue to influence Scottish politics for a long time to come. However, Geoff was not just a "practical" politician who helped to launch Strathclyde. He was a deeply committed Socialist with a strong sense of social justice. He threw himself with vigour and commitment into everything he took up — whether the needs of the deprived areas of Glasgow or in his international concerns, for example his longstanding involvement in CND.

Geoff Shaw was born in 1927. His background was Edinburgh and professional middle class, and he was educated at Edinburgh Academy from 1933 until 1944, when he was Dux Gold Medallist. He went the same year to Edinburgh University to study Arts, but his studies were interrupted by two years National Service in the Royal Navy. Typically, he was concerned to emphasise that most of this service was spent at a land base in Malta. He returned to Edinburgh University in 1948 to study philosophy and moral philosophy, and graduated Master of Arts in June 1950. After three further years studying theology at New College, Edinburgh, he graduated Bachelor of Divinity. He then undertook a year's post-graduate study at the Union Theological Seminary in New York. It was during his period of theological study that Geoff first became involved in community work, first in Pilton, Edinburgh and then in New York, where he worked with the East Harlem Protestant Parish. This worked outside the traditional religious style and attempted to take the Church out into the world to share the social and economic circumstances of the community in which it found itself. It was while in Harlem that he became particularly aware of the conflicts facing the under-privileged young, between the values of home and family and the values of the street and of gang culture. Support for the young therefore became a key part of Geoff's thinking, and his Harlem experience was an important influence on what he did later.

He returned to Scotland in 1955 and spent the next two years as a boys' leader in Church House, Bridgeton, a youth club attached to the Church of St Francis in the East.

In 1957 Geoff Shaw and a number of like-minded friends moved to the Gorbals and persuaded the Glasgow Presbytery — after initial hesitation — to support them in a new form of ministry. The Gorbals Group is still perhaps the initiative for which Geoff Shaw is best known. The Group's object was to live among the people with whom it was concerned, identify their needs at first hand (and indeed share in them) and so be able to respond and help them. An important part of the thinking was that people should be helped to develop their own capabilities to help themselves. The Group lived a communal life, sharing a house in the early years, pooling their resources, and sharing a common Christian witness which was self-evidently important to them all. The key point in their week was their regular Thursday evening meeting when they gathered together for discussion and communal worship, and all members of the Group regarded attendance at this meeting as an overriding obligation. In line with his earlier interests, Geoff Shaw's particular concern within the Group was to establish informal group activities with boys of the neighbourhood. He also played an important role in setting up the *Gorbals View,* an influential local paper which was eventually taken over by a local tenants' association (itself a product of the Group's activities) and which is still published as *The View.*

Members of the Group came and went until it was formally wound up in 1973. Geoff Shaw himself remained in the Gorbals beyond that, retaining his links with the community and providing a temporary home for a succession of boys in need. By then he was deeply involved in local politics in Glasgow Corporation, to which he was elected in 1970 to represent Govanhill, and where he quickly became sub-convener of the Social Work and Health Committee (1971) and leader of the Labour Group (1973-1974). It was typical of Geoff that he still lived in the Gorbals until fairly recently before his death.

In 1974, having played an important role in the preparatory work for local government reorganisation, he was elected to Strathclyde Regional Council, and it was during the last period of his life, as the Region's first Convener, that I got to know him best. Strathclyde Region is, I believe, a major success story of local government reorganisation in Scotland, and it has produced many able men. But I think that none of them would grudge or dispute the assertion that the Region today is Geoff Shaw's monument. As Convener he combined the roles of chief public representative of the Region and, as Chairman of the Policy and Resources Committee, the effective political leader as well, in partnership with Dick Stewart as leader of the Labour Group. The burden of these two roles was ultimately too great and the Regional Council has now sensibly decided to split them. But in the first years Geoff carried out both these with distinction and dedication, and it is difficult to imagine the Region turning out as it has, had the arrangements been different. The representational role was particularly important in the early days and he made great efforts to get out and about to the more distant parts of the Region and demonstrate that the new system could work as much to their advantage as to that of the Glasgow conurbation area. His enthusiasm in those early days for the concept of regionalisation, and his conviction that Strathclyde could be made to work to everyone's advantage, was persuasive. Within the new Council the ruling Labour group took a clear view on priorities, and worked out coherent policies for dealing with them.

Geoff Shaw also provided for Strathclyde an important leavening of humanity and concern for the individual. This was particularly clear in the development of the Region's policies on social deprivation. These policies need money but they also need to develop community initiatives and build up the self-confidence of the community and its capacity to care for itself. Geoff Shaw never lost sight of the simple fact, all too easily forgotten, that the primary object of local government is to provide services for individuals. And he was in no doubt as to which individuals he was most concerned about.

There was thus an essential continuity — a wholeness — in Geoff's life, from his time in New York to his involvement in community work in Glasgow and on to the major political role of his later years, in pursuit of the principles and objectives that moved him. He believed in looking for the goodness in people even when in his social work he was dealing, as he often was, with the hardest of hard cases, in prison and elsewhere.

One aspect of Geoff Shaw that must be emphasised (though others are no doubt more competent to speak of it than I am) was the foundation of his social and political views in his religious beliefs. Having qualified as a Minister, Geoff never, as is well known, had charge of a conventional parish. But the witness he bore in other ways was nevertheless an essentially Christian witness, as the Thursday night meetings of the Gorbals Group confirms. Geoff often described the work he did in the Gorbals as "gossiping the Gospel" — a phrase that needs no expansion, and that certainly speaks volumes for anyone who ever knew him.

It is also worth reflecting on the relatively few years he spent in elected politics, and the heights to which he rose in those years. By the time he was elected to Glasgow Corporation Geoff was already forty-three, the greater part of his active adult life having been spent in vigorous but unassuming Christian commitment. His Socialist commitment was also well known but his rapid rise to political prominence thereafter is an amazing achievement. It is itself a comment on the respect in which he was generally held, but his values and even his personal lifestyle remained manifestly unaltered in the transition from a private to a very public man.

I think in fact Geoff never really adjusted completely to his role as Strathclyde Convener. Practical politics require some compromise. Geoff was always uneasy about compromise. The atmosphere of tight public expenditure control in which local government reorganisation in Scotland was launched was particularly painful to Geoff. There was so much to do and not enough money to do it with. But he was committed to the Labour Party and to Strathclyde Region and as Secretary of State I found him a loyal and steadfast colleague.

Geoff was an idealist of the best kind, one who was prepared to stand up doggedly for what he believed in and not to shrink from personal sacrifices to achieve it. Idealists in politics are, of course, not always a comfortable experience, either for themselves or for others. They do, however, provide a clear vision which allows them to get through the necessary day-to-day changes of direction without losing sight of the longer term objectives. Geoff's own ideals shine through all that he did, and much of what Strathclyde Region did under him. I had hoped that the man and his ideals would have remained available perhaps for the new Scottish Assembly. That is sadly not to be. But the legacy of his achievements, and the memory of his integrity, dedication and gentle kindness remain to inspire all who knew him. We shall remember too his great charm — I'm sure he would have hated that word — wit and good humour, with none of the priggishness and intolerance often associated with men of high ideals. It was always a happiness to meet Geoff, especially with his delightful wife Sarah, and we shall miss that too.

3

THE SCOTLAND BILL IN THE HOUSE OF

COMMONS

JAMES NAUGHTIE
The Scotsman

On 22 February 1978, exactly a year after delivering the
death-blow to the little-lamented Scotland and Wales Bill, MPs
settled down to give a third reading to the more robust of its
offspring, the Scotland Bill. A casual observer might have been
forgiven for supposing that nothing had changed. There were
more speeches against devolution than in favour, as before.
It was said that the heart of the Commons was not in the Bill,
as before. Mr Tam Dalyell, on the Labour side, was rising from
his mound of papers like a jack-in-the-box, as before. Across the
chamber, Mr Enoch Powell was lounging, sphinx-like, as if he had
not moved since he helped to check the guillotine twelve months
before. Yet the truth is that everything had changed, except the
House of Commons.[1]

The Bill had changed, and so had the Government's tactics.
The odd coalitions of supporters and opponents had shifted a
little. The unionists were more determined, and so were the
Nationalists. Above all, the stakes were higher. But maybe the
most important change was that the Bill was actually discussed
at some length and not subjected to filibuster (at least, not
successfully). The question is: why did the anti-devolutionists
fail to stop the Bill and fail to change the structure of the
Assembly as envisaged by the Government? The story of the
committee stage is the story of the failure of the "antis" to
turn their natural majority against devolution into victory.[2]

It is easy enough to explain this by Government arm-
twisting and the spectre of a General Election, but that is not
good enough. The Conservatives, Ulster Unionists and assorted
Labour rebels should have been able to use the committee

stage to cripple the Bill. Yet what did they manage? The only clauses removed from the Bill were declaratory, and did not affect the arrangements for setting up an Assembly. One (Clause 1) declared that the proposals which followed did not affect the unity of the United Kingdom, and the other (Clause 40) stated that the Assembly would "have regard" to national pay policy. The Government hardly noticed they had gone.

What the opponents of the Bill did achieve was the imposition of the 40% test in the referendum which would follow Royal Assent and the addition of an opt-out clause for Orkney and Shetland. So the Secretary of State will be required to lay before Parliament an order repealing the Act unless at least 40% of the Scottish electorate vote "Yes", and to set up a commission to consider the future of Orkney and Shetland if the islanders vote "No". Thus the case put by the antis will be decided outside the House: during the long days of debate they made no significant internal changes in the Bill. Given the frequent assertion that the Commons were solidly against devolution, that needs some explanation. Whips, for all their power, are not enough to account for it.

To begin at the beginning, Scotland and Wales were dealt with in separate Bills, as all the antis (and the Liberals) had said they should be from the start. Wales, where the fervour for devolution was muted, was promised an executive body only: Scotland held on to its "Parliament". Thus the Government were guaranteed the votes of some Labour rebels who had voted down the combined bill because of their passionate belief that Wales did not want devolution. Not surprisingly, most of them were Welsh.

The second crucial concession was the referendum. Towards the final days of the Scotland and Wales Bill, as it hung in parliamentary limbo, Government Ministers began to espouse the notion of shifting the last responsibility for the Bill to the people themselves, hoping to give the Commons a hefty shove. The introduction of the referendum was necessary to buy votes: some anti-devolutionists would be happy to have it both ways, voting for their Government in the lobbies and reserving the right to campaign for "No" in the country. The referendum would allow a kind of controlled schizophrenia in the Labour Party which might ensure that the Bill passed its third reading, leaving the Government to fight another battle, an easier one, on the hustings. Assuming that the rush to devolve began with the belief that the people wanted it, this at least seemed logical.

The splitting of the Bills and the introduction of the referendum were the moves which gave devolution a new lease of life, but parliamentary arithmetic demanded more. The Liberals, who had split against the first guillotine, had to be brought round. The new Bill which emerged in November 1977 could scarcely be said to be bristling with Liberal fire, but it was cheerfully admitted in Government circles later that they had won "more than 50% of their battles", quite enough to keep them happy.

In the lengthy (and secret) talks which preceded publication of the new Bill, the Liberal banner was carried by Mr Russell Johnston, MP for Inverness-shire, and by Lord Mackie of Benshie, a grand old man of the party if ever there was one, and a formidable fighter. They faced Mr John Smith, Minister of State in the Privy Council Office and argued for proportional representation in Assembly elections; a relaxation of the powers of the Secretary of State to override Assembly decisions; a quasi-constitutional court to settle questions about the scope of its powers on legal rather than political grounds; tax-raising powers for the Assembly and provisions which would end the proposed annual haggle between Westminster and Edinburgh over the block grant.

The talks were amicable. The Liberals knew they could not hope for a Government committment on PR; but they got a promise of a free vote on the Labour side. On the question of a constitutional court, the Liberals were satisfied with the role assigned to the judicial committee of the Privy Council, giving it pre- and post-enactment powers of review on Assembly legislation and removing the more offensive aspects of the override powers enjoyed by the Secretary of State which had aroused such opposition in the original Bill. They dropped their tax-raising demand when the Government said they would introduce a proposal if they could find a workable system. They could not, and did not, but honour was satisfied on both sides. On the block grant, there was to be no new clause in the Bill, but a promise that the Government would consult with the Assembly about the possibility of four-yearly rather than annual negotiations.

So the Liberals were brought in. However, the Lib-Lab

talks should not be seen simply as a Government surrender to some sort of blackmail from a crucial voting block. After the stalemate of the Scotland and Wales Bill, there is evidence that the Government rethought their whole approach to devolution. Some of the major changes might have come without Liberal pressure — the apparent loosening of the over-ride powers, for example — because the most important thing was to produce a Bill which would be reasonably attractive to the electorate who were to be given the chance to seal its fate in the referendum. Any concession to popular feeling which did not increase parliamentary opposition made political sense.

In redrafting the Bill, Mr Smith and the civil servants in the Devolution Unit strengthened considerably the position of the Assembly. While the UK Parliament would remain sovereign — the keystone of the Government's fight against the SNP — at several key points the word "shall" in relation to the Assembly was changed to "may". Even in such an apparently uncontroversial section as that dealing with standing orders, the Government argued that the precise nature of the rules by which the Assembly would conduct its business were a matter for the elected members and should not be imposed from outside. Such a defence of the Assembly's right to some freedom of action was hardly likely to calm the frenzy of the die-hard antis and could be seen as a hindrance to the passage of the Bill through a reluctant House. But nonetheless it was done.

So there was considerable progress in the constitutional arrangements during the months after the first guillotine defeat. But on the economic front there was almost none. The main reason for this was the hostility of the Government's "supporters" from North-East England, Merseyside and parts of the West Midlands who bitterly resented what they feared would be economic "weighting" in favour of Scotland's problems, while their own areas of deprivation were left to fester. Pleas for wider Assembly control over trade and industry might have been logical or even necessary, but concessions would probably have meant another fiasco on guillotine night, and that would have been the end of the story. So the Government gave no ground.

Mr Smith demonstrated in the run-up to the second attempt to get a Bill through the House that he was a master of the balancing act needed to placate those who were offended by the limited extent of devolution and at the same time those who would resist any attempt to devolve significant economic powers. The committee stage was to prove that this strategy — at least as a realistic assessment of what was possible — was right.

The guillotine vote came on the night of 16 November 1977, and as the majority of 26 for the Government was announced, the faces on the Front Bench were a picture. Mr Smith wore a very broad grin, the broader for having gone through the trauma of that vote nine months before when he saw, not only his Bill in ruins, but maybe his promising Ministerial career as well. He had no illusion that the Commons approved of devolution any more than it had done before, but he guessed that the Government had found a formula which would link most of his party, the Liberals, the SNP and a couple of stray Tories in a fragile coalition which could stagger through the hours of committee debate on the floor of the House and emerge with a Bill more or less intact. The proposals were far from perfect — for *anybody* on the devolution side — but they might at least become law.

In his closing speech on the debate on the guillotine — imposing a strict timetable for the discussion of amendments which would prevent a filibuster — he said: "The House of Commons must have the capacity to act as well as to argue. We are not a talking shop to embark on endless discussion on interesting points about Bills. We are a legislative chamber and we have an obligation to come to decisions and to act upon them. It is not as though devolution was hurried into the House of Commons last week and was being rushed through in some fleeting way."[3]

That simple argument was the strongest card. There was no such thing as devolution in principle, the Government seemed to say, only a workable scheme for an Assembly. Ten years had passed since Edward Heath made the "Declaration of Perth" at the Scottish Tory Party conference and delay was no longer acceptable. So Mr Smith had the argument ready, and the political instinct and intellectual capacity to drive it home from the dispatch box. He was assisted in his task by the fact that the Tories did not have *their* argument ready.

The difficulties in which they were to find themselves during the 91 hours of debate by the committee are epitomised by the predicament of Mr Francis Pym, their chief devolution spokesman, in that guillotine debate. As a former Chief Whip in the Heath Government, he had supervised the application of a guillotine on the European Communities Bill and was thus in a difficult position to argue that there should be no curbs on the discussion of a major constitutional Bill. Indeed Mr Pym was on record — outside the Commons — as saying that the Government were right in claiming that it was impossible to steer a constitutional measure through the Commons without a guillotine if there was organised opposition to it. The power of a small group of backbenchers to stop legislation in its tracks increases as one night of debate follows another and the faint-hearted lose their appetite for the struggle. It was precisely what had happened to the Scotland and Wales Bill and everyone knew it would happen to the Scotland Bill. The Tories objected to the term "filibuster", but to most observers it was the first word which sprang to mind.

So Mr Pym's righteous indignation about Government bully-boy tactics seemed more like traditional political fencing than serious concern about the constitutional implications of curtailing debate. The Government were proposing it, so it must be opposed. The soft underbelly of the Tory attack was showing on the first night and it was not long before the pro-devolutionists would be putting the boot in.

Strangely enough, the Tory problem was laid bare on the first night of the committee stage, not by a devolution supporter but by the indefatigable Tam Dalyell, Labour MP for West Lothian, whose opposition to the Bill was to be expressed in an unending series of questions and declarations at every stage of the discussion, turning him into a kind of chorus to the debate, pulling every argument back to his firm belief that devolution would lead to a separate Scotland and the end of the United Kingdom. He demanded from Mr Pym a statement of his devolution policy. It was a question which would be put night after night. Mr Pym rested on the Tory promise of all-party talks to come up with a workable devolution scheme, and would not (for the moment) go further. But it was clear to the whole House that the consensus on devolution was shaky, to say the least, and that all-party talks would almost certainly produce nothing. So why not say so? Why not come out wholeheartedly against legislative devolution?

There is a view among some of the staunchest antis on the Tory side that it was this weakness which reduced their effectiveness in the debate. Mr Dalyell would agree. In the debate on Clause 1, Mr Pym moved an amendment to soften the effect of the Bill's declaration that none of the provisions affected the unity of the UK. It was, said Mr Dalyell, "a fudging amendment". Tory criticism of the Government's scheme — that it would lead to constant bickering between Edinburgh and Westminster which in turn would lead to separation — would apply to any scheme for legislative devolution, would it not? No, said Mr Pym, but not very convincingly, since many of those on the benches behind him clearly agreed with Mr Dalyell. He ended with a defiant, but lame, statement: "That is what I think."

On that first night, the Government lost Clause 1. Having failed with his amendment, Mr Pym led his side into the "No" lobby against the motion, "that the clause stand part of the Bill" and found himself alongside the SNP and thus defeating the Government. Ministers were embarrassed by the shaky start, but unconcerned. The clause did not have to be saved. But for the Conservatives the division had been embarrassing too. Although SNP jibes accusing them of voting against the unity of the UK were clearly unfair, there was a sense of unease among the Tory backbenchers who realised that maybe the votes had set the pattern for what would follow.

Behind Mr Pym during his vigil on the Bill was an assortment of dedicated opponents of devolution in any form. One of their leaders was Mr George Gardiner, MP for Reigate, an articulate right-winger and close associate of Mrs Margaret Thatcher. Round him sat Iain Sproat (South Aberdeen), Ian Gow (Eastbourne), Tim Raison (Aylesbury), Graham Page (Crosby) and a collection of antis with less stamina. They were ready to bring each debate back to one simple proposition: that legislative devolution was not only expensive and unnecessary but would lead to tension which would ultimately destroy the UK. It was no secret that some of them suspected Mr Pym of being "soft" on devolution and hedging his bets about any future Tory policy. For them, that was just not good enough. They were happier with his sidekick on the Front Bench, Mr Leon Brittan, barrister and ex-President of the Cambridge Union, who seemed more offended by the principle of the Bill than Mr Pym and was better equipped to challenge the intellectual agility and rhetorical skill of the Minister of State, Mr Smith.

This Tory weakness had implications for their strategy. It was clear from the early debates that the subject of the guillotine was to be brought up at every turn, thereby preparing the ground for the hordes of Tory Peers to argue over every detail which had not been discussed in the Commons and justifiably give the Bill a mauling, safe from any Government steamroller, in a House where a few phone calls to the shires could bring in the Tory vote. Mr Pym and his colleagues regularly warned the Government of the consequences of curtailing debate. They would not like it in "another place", and we all knew what that meant. But did we? Perhaps there was a misreading of the Lords' intentions. After all, their Lordships were very keen on PR, which was scarcely close to the heart of Mrs Thatcher and her followers in the Commons. Certainly some of the backbench Tories were nervous that the Lords would not wreck the Bill — for the rather obvious reason that they were nervous about their future as legislators — and that therefore the Tory Front Bench strategy in the Commons was misconceived.

Before considering what the official opposition achieved in their fight against the Government's plans, it is worth looking at the other members of the anti-devolution coalition. As with the "pros", the net was spread wide, and traditional party loyalties were, for the moment, forgotten. The Tories' best friend and worst enemy was Mr Dalyell. When he expounded his theory of break-up he did so with more diligence (and often better research) than most, though not all, of the Tories. Yet when he pressed Mr Pym on his policy he was no less diligent, and caused a few embarrassing moments. A more reliable friend was Mr Enoch Powell, speaking on nearly every clause, and carrying the break-up argument to its logical extremes night after night. It was impossible, he said, to devolve power to a subordinate legislature in a unitary state. He argued simply that the devolution exercise could not be carried through in the United Kingdom.

Among the Labour antis there was less diligence. Mr Eric Heffer (Liverpool Walton) argued the case against any advantage for Scotland at the expense of deprived areas in England, and Mr George Cunningham (Islington South and Finsbury) prepared for his triumph in the referendum debate with a string of procedural points in an attempt to mitigate the effect of the guillotine.

In the Scottish contingent on the Labour side, those who were most active were the MPs suspicious of the Assembly, particularly Mr Robert Hughes (Aberdeen North) and Mr Robin Cook (Edinburgh Central). They took the standard left-wing line that devolution would contribute nothing to the economic regeneration of the British economy and threw in some biting attacks on the narrow philosophy of the SNP, with Mr Hughes sparking off a furious row when he described the Nationalists as "allies of Dr Goebbels". If they were, their propaganda was not very effective in the House.

The Nationalists kept a low profile during the committee stage. Their bench was often occupied by only one or two members and many of their interventions were ritual denunciations of English members who, they claimed, did not understand the problems of Scotland. They provided an easy target for Mr Dalyell when he launched into one of his dissertations on the "slippery slope" argument, nodding their heads vigorously when he said the Assembly would be a vehicle for the drive to independence. However embarrassing this may have been for the Government, the Nationalists trooped dutifully into the right lobby on the crucial votes. The same is true of the Liberals, and they embarrassed the Government not at all. Mr Johnston acted as a kind of extension of the Government Front Bench, articulating, in his woolly way, the principles of devolution. He was the most active of the pro-devolutionists.

Indeed, many of those supposed to be in favour of devolution were distinguished only by their silence. But that did not annoy the Government too much. Had every anti speech been matched by one in favour, the number of amendments discussed would have been even lower and the frustration might have triggered off more Government defeats. The burden of supporting the Government fell on members like Mr Johnston, Mr Jim Sillars (SLP, South Ayrshire), Professor John Mackintosh (Labour, Berwick and East Lothian), Mr Alick Buchanan-Smith (Conservative, North Angus and Mearns) — a brave heretic — and, as often as not, Mr Norman Buchan (Labour, West Renfrew).

These were odd coalitions, for and against, but how much did they influence the course of events after the Government's victory on the guillotine motion? Once the votes had been garnered by careful surgery on the Scotland and Wales Bill, much of the political battling became counterproductive, and the Government were reasonably happy to leave the antis to make the running.

The guillotine vote was won just before the start of the committee stage. From then on the debate went the Government's way until the two hammer blows on 25 January — the imposition of the 40% requirement on the referendum and the Orkney and Shetland option clauses. In the heart of the Bill, the opposition coalition had little effect, and it was almost as though most speakers were determined to extend the second reading debate for three months, but do no more.

Second reading is the occasion for general speeches on the principle of a piece of legislation and is intended to pave the way for line-by-line examination of each clause at the committee stage. But on the Scotland Bill the same general arguments were heard again and again. The opponents argued that each clause drove them back to the principle. Mr Sproat would refer to the "irreducible conundrum" that was the Bill, others would talk of "the very heart" of the legislation, and there was a general drift away from the detail of pre-enactment review, or PR or tax-raising powers, to the principle of legislative devolution. Dominating it all was "the West Lothian Question", posed by Mr Dalyell and gratefully seized upon by all his temporary allies.

The argument is now well known. Mr Dalyell argued that after devolution a Scottish MP would be able to vote on English matters such as education and local government — matters for which he had no responsibility in Scotland because the Assembly would have legislative competence in these areas. He said Scottish MPs would be "mongrel" members. The Government's answer to this was, in effect: "So what?"

Mr Smith admitted he had no direct answer to the question as posed. Time and time again Tories would return to the disruptive effect in England of a Government kept in power by "mongrel" Scots legislating on subjects in England which were devolved in Scotland. The Government's answer was that this was a problem, but not a sufficient reason for blocking devolution. Perhaps Mr Powell realised this. He habitually referred to the Dalyell argument not as a question but as "the West Lothian Proposition". It fitted nicely into his argument that it was impossible to maintain the sovereignty of Parliament with a

C

subordinate legislature, but the argument found no converts among those who had decided they wanted devolution and that the Bill was as near to a satisfactory solution as they could get. The West Lothian debate enlivened the Bill's opponents because it was an eloquent statement of a situation they found offensive. To the pro-devolutionists (apart from the SNP) it was a secondary concern — an anomaly which they were prepared to live with to accommodate what they saw as a vital constitutional change.

The Government adopted a similar posture in response to the constant warnings about "the recipe for conflict" in the Bill. If there was a prize for the most-repeated phrase, "the recipe" would probably win hands down. Mr Smith based his reply on the assumption that the Scots would elect an Assembly which would behave responsibly and would demonstrate political maturity. Even if there was a Tory Government in London and a Labour Executive in Edinburgh — the most frequently-used scenario — he said he had no reason to suppose that most problems would not be tackled in a spirit of co-operation. He repeated this many times, and opponents said many times that it was not true. As soon as the committee stage started it was clear that there could be no agreement on the extent to which the Assembly would fight with Westminster, and it was the theme which lay behind most of the debate.

The twice-weekly sessions revolved around this dispute and the dispute over the relevance of the West Lothian Question. Until the coalition of antis turned to the referendum and Orkney and Shetland, they sang the same song over and over again. The amendments moved by the Tory Front Bench reflected this overriding concern, but they failed to amend the Bill in the way they wanted. Mr Pym and his colleagues tried to reduce the number of Assembly members; to strengthen the control of the Commons over Assembly legislation; to restore some of the power of the Secretary of State for Scotland which he had had in the Scotland and Wales Bill and to remove some of the devolved areas from the Assembly's control. But through it all there seemed to be no coherent plan. Mr Pym seemed equivocal on the desirability of the Assembly. He refused to say whether he thought *some* kind of devolution would work, only that he knew *this* scheme would not. So the opposition chipped away at the structure of the Bill, succeeded in knocking out the two declaratory clauses, but failed to present an alternative which could persuade some waverers to oppose the Government.

In the eleven days of debate between the guillotine vote and the insertion of new clauses on the referendum and Orkney and Shetland, the main provisions of the Bill emerged unscathed. The House approved the mechanics of the Assembly: two members for each Westminster constituency with extra members for some large seats; first-past-the-post-elections; the power of the Assembly to dissolve itself in case of deadlock; technical details of membership qualifications.

The powers of the Assembly were also untouched. The structure of the ruling executive and its rights to legislate — circumscribed by the ultimate authority of Parliament, the powers of the Secretary of State and the Judicial Committee of the Privy Council — built up as the guillotines fell regularly at 11 p.m. and the Government notched up the marks on its timetable, and looked hopefully for Royal Assent before the summer recess.

During the debates on the extent of the Assembly's powers and the ways in which they would be exercised, two attempts were made to introduce a new dimension into devolution. One was a proposal for proportional representation and the other for tax-raising powers for the Assembly, both moved by Professor John P. Mackintosh. The PR amendment, predictably, fell by 209 votes to 107 and the tax-raising proposal by a crushing 301-61 margin. It seemed there was no possibility of extending the Assembly's powers in any way: the House was reluctant to go even as far as the Government had proposed, and that only after a display of fine arm-twisting and the threat of a vote of confidence leading to an election to which some of the rebels could only look forward with a shudder.

But the reluctance to experiment changed dramatically on 25 January 1978, a night which revived in Ministers' minds the memory of the guillotine vote a year before. In retrospect it is possible to see the ground being laid weeks before the ambush in the referendum debate. During his speech on second reading, Mr George Gardiner promised that he and his fellow objectors would be looking very carefully at the question of what constituted a decisive majority in the referendum. At the time, it seemed a cloud no bigger than a man's hand, but the Government's problems multiplied from the moment Mr George Cunningham put down his new clause, requiring the Secretary of State to lay before Parliament an order repealing the Act unless at least 40% of the electorate (*not* just of those voting) voted "Yes" in the referendum.

It is now known that Tory anti-devolutionists were keen to have the new clause moved by a Labour member, in the hope of picking up some extra support. In Mr Cunningham — himself a Scot — they found a formidable ally. He argued persuasively that if the Government were so certain that a majority of Scots were in favour of the devolution scheme, why did they oppose his plan which would only ensure that the question was decided by a reasonable proportion of the people of Scotland?

His argument simply served to polarise the feelings of the pros and antis. Those who had been in the middle, persuaded to support the Bill, perhaps out of loyalty to their own government, tended to go the Cunningham way. For those with fixed views on the principle of devolution the argument was either a logical test of the Government's premise for drawing up legislation or an attempt to fix the result of the referendum, and an insult to the Scottish electorate. It was the touchstone. The argument brought out some of the passions which had often been dormant in earlier stages. There were predictions that the 40% test would be seen as an affront by Scots voters and, from the other side, claims that a constitutional issue of such importance should have a built-in test to guard against a freak result.

By the time Mr Smith rose to reply to the debate, passions in the House were running high. There was a complication which had heightened the tension. Earlier in the day the anti-devolutionists had accused the Leader of the House, Mr Michael Foot, of attempting to prevent debate on "the Grimond amendment" by imposing an extra guillotine in mid-evening, thereby splitting up a group of amendments. They suspected a "fix" — since the new time allocation would probably mean the Orkney and Shetland amendment would not be reached. All amendments not moved before the appropriate guillotine would fall, never to be revived.

The Government's intention had been to alter the guillotines to allow time for a debate on a proposal from Mr Norman Buchan for a third question — on independence — in the referendum. But their opponents were in no mood to believe that. Mr Foot withdrew the offending guillotine. Now, after winning that fight, the antis realised that if the vote on the Cunningham amendment was not over and the Grimond amendment moved before 11 p.m., the chance to build the Orkney and Shetland complication into the Bill would be lost. So, as the Minister of State struggled manfully to prolong the debate and answer the points made by Mr Cunningham, the jeers and shouts began and he looked rattled for the first and last time in all his sessions at the dispatch box. Under pressure, he wound up a short speech.

He sat down at 10.27 p.m. and the rush to vote began. First came a paving amendment by the Labour MP, Mr Bruce Douglas-Mann — to build in a 33⅓% test — and when that was won the antis knew they could romp home on the Cunningham amendment. The question was whether it would be over in time to move the Grimond amendment on Orkney and Shetland, which they felt would follow in the wake.

What came next was a parliamentary caper worthy of a Feydeau farce. It involved the Serjeant-at-Arms and his sword, a folding opera hat and the redoubtable Sir Myer Galpern, a deputy speaker. As members trickled back into the Chamber to wait for the result of the Cunningham amendment — counting can take anything up to 15 minutes after an important vote — a teller for the "Ayes", Mr William Hamilton, reported to Sir Myer (in a loud voice) that he had seen some members deliberately obstructing the "No" lobby, presumably in an attempt to delay the count until the magic hour of 11 p.m. Sir Myer, his face suffused with indignation, sent the Serjeant-at-Arms to the lobby to flush out the offending members with his sword, while the Tories — with Mr Teddy Taylor as cheerleader — began to chant "cheat, cheat" at some very white-faced Government Ministers opposite. During all this furore, several members who were anxious to make points of order had to call for the collapsible opera hat, specially kept under the Serjeant's chair for use when members wish to "rise, covered" to make a point of order during a division. The Tory jeers and Labour laughter grew louder as Mr Foot plucked at his mane and looked around as if nothing had happened which should concern a mere Leader of the House.

When the loiterers were cleared from the lobby, the result was announced amid scenes of excitement which belied the belief in some quarters that devolution was a bore. The 40%

test was accepted by 168 votes to 142, a majority against the
Government of 26. To keep the drama going, Mr Jo Grimond
rose to propose his amendment with the comment: "A damned
close-run thing, if I may say so." Indeed it was, with members
filing into the lobbies just one minute before the guillotine fell. As
expected, his amendment was carried, by 204 votes to 118.

The Government had resigned themselves to defeat on the
40% test some days before, but had hoped to avoid a similar
fate on Orkney and Shetland. However, the apparent reluctance
of some Shetlanders to accept the proposed devolution settlement
had caught the imagination of many English members, thanks
to some assiduous lobbying by a team from the Shetland Islands
Council and a few trips north for the enthusiasts. MPs like
Eldon Griffiths, Tim Raison and Ian Gow had seized on the
subject and lost no opportunity to bring it up. So, although
there was no debate on the amendment itself, the word had
got around. The antis saw in the Grimond amendment — which
proposed only that a commission should examine the position of
Orkney and Shetland if they voted "No" — a chance to wreck
the Government scheme and also to embarrass the SNP, whom
they accused of arguing for autonomy for Scotland while
opposing autonomy for a self-contained community because they
feared the loss of oil revenue. The fact that the SNP were
indeed sensitive and looked on the consequences of the amendment with some trepidation, is emphasised by the fact that two
of the loiterers in the lobby were Nationalists, Mr Hamish Watt
and Mr Douglas Henderson.

The Government's response to those who favoured an opt-
out clause for Orkney and Shetland was that it would discuss
with the Islands Councils their problems, but would also point
out that there was little danger of oil revenues disappearing into
an Edinburgh coffer for use in central Scotland because energy
was not a devolved subject, and the Assembly had no direct right
to the revenue. The moment the Grimond amendment was
carried they gave up hope of removing it at report stage: the
emotional appeal of the Shetland case had been too great. On
the 40% test, the fact that they doubted their ability to delete it
from the Bill was demonstrated when at report stage the
necessary motion was put, not by a Government Minister, but
by Mr Dennis Canavan, a Labour backbencher. They did try
a compromise figure of 33⅓%, but this fell along with the

Canavan amendment after a debate dominated by a powerful speech from Mr Cunningham, during which he held a crowded House silent and attentive.

The only other significant Government defeat was on an amendment from Mr Dalyell imposing a statutory three month gap between the referendum and any General Election. Despite assurances from Mr Smith that the Government would not confuse the two campaigns, the new clause was inserted. For Mr Dalyell and others — loyal to the Labour Party — the prospect of arguing against their Government (on devolution) and for it (on everything else) was too much to be expected of anyone on the same day.

So at the back of the Scotland Bill which trundled into the House of Lords in the Spring were three new clauses, the result of the committee and report stages in the Commons. But the kind of Assembly they would be considering in their own scrutiny of the Bill would be precisely that envisaged by the Government.

The victories for the antis in the Commons came when they were able to reduce the argument to its fundamental principles, and rely on a groundswell of feeling against legislative devolution. That happened in the run-up to the vote on the 40% test. No one in the Chamber believed some supporters of the 40% test who said that it did not reflect their antipathy to devolution and was not a wrecking amendment: its supporters were seen to be the antis, and vice versa. Similarly, in the earlier debates, those who had said the Assembly would not work — a purely practical argument — were seen to be those who also found the principle of devolution a worrying one. The two arguments tended to blend together, but at the heart of the opposition lay not practical arguments but strong feelings for the unity of the UK and suspicions of the links between devolution and nationalism.

These feelings extended to the break-up argument, but always seemed to come from those who were dissatisfied with the prospect of a non-legislative "talking-shop" in Edinburgh. The conflict which resulted in the Government defeats at the end of the committee stage and in report stage came when the argument was reduced to the fundamental divide between those who believed that democratic progress lay in devolution, however tentative, and those who believed that any tinkering with the constitutional framework was a "recipe for confusion and conflict".

On each devolution night at the Commons, through the winter, the divide seemed to open further as if in preparation for the 40% vote. There were the confident assertions of the die-hard unionists that there was no demand for devolution, such as that from Mr John Stokes, Tory MP for Halesowen and passionate defender of union and the Empire, who said: "On a recent visit to Scotland I could hardly find one Scotsman there who wanted the Bill. I tried to speak to everyone I saw."[4] How Mr Stokes explained the presence of the SNP in the House, or the Labour Party's conversion to devolution, or, for that matter, the nearly-forgotten "Declaration of Perth", no one knows. Many members appeared to be confident that devolution would be thrown out in the referendum, although some would doubtless admit that there was the 40% test, just in case.

The contrasting view came from the convinced reformists like Mr Buchanan-Smith, men who had not adopted a devolution-ary stance for the sake of peace in the Party but because they actually believed in it. In his third reading speech, Mr Buchanan-Smith said that if the House failed to pass the Bill, it would be failing democracy itself.

With such conflicting views, it was inevitable that much of the debate would be repetitious and often tedious. Indeed, there were times when the devolution debate was raging in Scotland while, at the centre of the argument on the floor of the House, there was a still and awful calm. Fifteen MPs might be stretched on the green leather benches — their colleagues some-times peeping in and scurrying off again — while Mr Dalyell quoted from his book or Mr Graham Page lectured on the history of the Judicial Committee of the Privy Council, or Mr Douglas Crawford talked about "the Scottish pound". Interest in the Bill was limited, both amongst MPs and, alas, in the Press. To be sure, there was a rush to the lobbies (or the typewriters) when the division bells began to clang, usually at 11 p.m., but for the debates themselves a large number of political aficionados took a break.

However, it would be unfair to denigrate those who took part (or most of them, anyway). Mr Dalyell took on a lonely fight, and fought it with a spirit which won him the admiration of everyone in the House, however frustrating he may have been when he announced such earth-shattering news as his tally of letters from constituents: after the first guillotine, he said, more people had written to him about the price of canary seed than about devolution, presumably proving that the British public cared not a whit about constitutional change but were getting very upset about whether they would be able to feed their budgies.

Towering over the debates was Mr Smith, who won glowing compliments, not only from his supporters on devolution but from the Tory Front Bench, for his handling of the Bill. His grasp of the complex detail of the Bill never faltered, and he never failed to defend the right of the Scots to elect the kind of Assembly they wanted, with freedom to act over a wide range of issues within the framework of the UK. His constant theme was that the Assembly would be composed of reasonable people and that "the recipe for conflict" argument was scaremongering. Conflict there would be but it would be controlled in the political apparatus included in the Bill.

Mr Smith gave the impression of enjoying himself thoroughly, even when the debate was straying into the further reaches of the imaginations of some Empire Loyalists. Above all he relished the fight with Mr Teddy Taylor on the Tory Front Bench, whom he called "the urban guerilla" of Scottish politics. Mr Taylor it was who was the most effective member of the Tory Scottish team. He would leap to his feet with a savage attack on the guillotine or a brilliantly quick calculation of the cost of a particular measure, always reduced, in the populist way, to a simple (and quotable) phrase. It was gut politics and the Tory attack always seemed more fiery when the urban guerilla was on form.

For much of the time, the dedicated opponents or supporters of devolution traded scenarios for the conduct of Assembly business without getting anywhere. It is the view of some Government Ministers that the opposition could have achieved much more, given the shaky state of the devolution coalition, if they had succeeded in curtailing debate on some amendments and packing more into the time allowed by the guillotine. Seldom was there a debate which did not drag on longer than was necessary.

On one occasion the Tories were attacking the cost of the Assembly — about £4½ million in capital expenditure and £13

million a year in running costs. Speech after speech covered the
same ground, straying into the West Lothian Question and what
was claimed to be the lunacy of different laws in Scotland and
England on uncontroversial subjects. Mr Sproat was moved to
bring up the question of dog licences, only drawing a retort
from Mr Johnston to the effect that there were different regulations for the control of dogs in the various cantons of Switzerland and he had not noticed a constitutional crisis there.
Sometimes the debate seemed to miss the point.

But it would be unfair to suggest that the members who
took part regularly did not take their role seriously: they did.
Some of them (on both sides) were certainly misguided, and
some hopelessly confused about the provisions of the Bill. But
most of them tried, and several — like Mr Smith, Mr Dalyell,
Mr Brittan, Mr Johnston, Mr Powell and Professor Mackintosh
— distinguished themselves at different stages of the debate.

But what did the exercise achieve? A Bill was passed,
slightly amended. The extent to which the devolution argument
penetrates the most deeply held political attitudes was clearly
shown in the collision between the unionists and the devolvers.
The fragility of traditional party loyalty on the issue was
demonstrated night after night.

The form of the debate was controlled by one important
factor. The guillotine took away the chance of a fiilibuster and
with it the chance for the antis to drive a steamroller through
the Bill, building up frustration in all-night sittings and in long
expositions of well-known attitudes. Their task was made more
difficult by the fact that many Labour antis were "softer" than
they had imagined, and trooped dutifully into the Government
lobby to vote for the guillotine. It was also made more difficult
by their doubts about the dedication of Mr Pym to their cause.
With a more coherent Tory strategy they could perhaps have
achieved more.

For the Government, it was a relief. With confidence in
the result of the referendum, they could be happy with the
outcome of the Commons stages of the Bill. While they might
have been looking forward to the battles in the House of Lords
with some trepidation they could reflect that they had steered
through a hostile Commons a Bill which at one time seemed
unpopular enough to be guaranteed instant defeat. The sad
thing is that it was not done simply by winning the argument,

because winning the argument could not be enough for the House. They *did* present the better case, and they got the votes, but it was not the merits of the case which filled the Government lobby. The House of Commons just does not work that way.

REFERENCES

1. For a discussion of proceedings in 1976/7 see "The failure of the Scotland and Wales Bill: No Will, No Way" John Kerr in *The Scottish Government Yearbook 1978.*

2. The chronological sequence of events was:

4 November 1977	Scotland Bill published.
14 November	Scotland Bill given second reading, 307-263.
16 November	Guillotine motion carried, 313-287.
22 November	Committee stage began. Committee stage taken on floor of House so that all MPs could attend and vote.
22 February 1978	Bill given third reading in Commons, 297-257.

    For a full chronology of devolution 1885-1978 see reference section at the end of the book.

3. Hansard, Col. 646, 16 November 1977.

4. Hansard, Col. 1665, 23 November 1977.

HOW SCOTLAND GOT THE HOUSING (HOMELESS PERSONS) ACT

PETER GIBSON

Formerly Director of Shelter (Scotland) and currently
Director, Scottish Consumer Council*

I intend here to look at how Scotland was included in the Housing (Homeless Person) Act of 1977 against the wishes of both the Scottish Office and Scotland's housing authorities. In so doing, I will examine the role of the Scottish Homeless Group, an alliance of mainly voluntary bodies, some of its problems and achievements in lobbying at Westminster, and some of the general problems of Scottish pressure groups.

This case study should be of interest to those concerned with the formulation of housing policy in Scotland, and to those who might like to be assured that anomalies in public policy, so widely predicted for post-devolution Scotland, are not totally unknown under the present constitutional framework which combines substantial administrative devolution and a separate legal system in Scotland with a single legislature for the whole United Kingdom at Westminster. For those who would like a detailed appraisal of the contents of the Act, and its effectiveness in operation, this piece may prove somewhat disappointing because I wish to concentrate mainly on what was involved in extending it to Scotland rather than on its content. Nevertheless, some background is essential.

On tackling homelessness, as on many other social issues in recent years, experience in England and Wales has been ahead of that in Scotland. Early in 1974, the Department of the Environment and the Department of Health and Social Security issued Joint Circular 18/74 recommending that responsibility for the homeless be transferred from social services departments of local authorities to housing departments in England and

*Mr Gibson writes in his personal capacity.

Wales. Though 18/74 was non-binding, it had considerable political weight behind it, having been drawn up while the Conservatives were still in office, and having been issued by the new Labour Government.

Implementation of 18/74 by housing authorities was patchy. Many refused outright to take on responsibility for homelessness, and others made purely token gestures. But enough councils implemented the letter and the spirit of the circular to show that it was indeed workable, given the necessary commitment. Certainly there were found to be problems; but it was shown that the ingenuity of housing officials could be applied just as readily to finding solutions as to finding excuses for not tackling the problems of homelessness. Moreover, the wild claims by some local politicians that such a transfer of responsibility would lead to "the end of civilisation as we know it" were exposed as absurdly alarmist. One very real problem posed by the circular, however, was that progressive authorities found themselves receiving homeless families from adjacent authorities which refused to implement the circular. This was not an argument against the transfer of responsibility: it was an argument in favour of legislation to make the transfer universal.

By November 1975 the late Secretary of State for the Environment, Anthony Crosland, conceded the need for legislation, in the face of evidence that half of the housing authorities outside London had failed to implement the circular. The Bill which his civil servants went off to draw up became, in time, the Housing (Homeless Persons) Act, but its progress was a slow and chequered one. Though a Bill had been prepared by the following autumn it did not, contrary to general expectation, feature in the Queen's Speech in November 1976. The English charities and voluntary bodies working on behalf of the homeless were furious, and denounced the Government's dropping of the Bill as "a cynical betrayal". However, the Minister of Housing Reg Freeson, let it be known that if one of the Members of Parliament who had come out near the top of the Private Members' Ballot were to take over the Bill he or she would receive the active support and co-operation of Freeson's department. For the campaigning organisations, England's peril was to be Scotland's opportunity.

Having set the scene south of the border, it is now necessary to do the same for Scotland. Here, under the Social Work

(Scotland) Act 1968, a general obligation to provide temporary accommodation for the homeless was imposed on all social work authorities. However, "homelessness" was not defined and neither was "temporary accommodation", so that practice varied greatly. In the early 1970s fewer than half of the social work authorities in Scotland had temporary accommodation of their own. Instead, they had to rely on the good will of housing departments, friends and relatives of the families, and, increasingly, bed and breakfast hotels.

Scotland's problems were highlighted in a Shelter Scotland report, "No Place to Call Home" (1973), but no equivalent to the 18/74 circular was planned for Scotland. Instead, after the shape of reformed local government had been decided in 1973, with social work going to the new Regions and housing going to the district councils, a government committee was set up under the chairmanship of Mrs Morris to study and make recommendations on links between social work and housing.

The Morris Committee reported in Spring 1975, and recommended, amongst many other things, that statutory responsibility for homelessness should be transferred from social work to housing.[1] This was welcomed by voluntary organisations, by those in the social work field, and by a few housing managers. But, on the whole, housing authorities, and the housing committee of COSLA (the Convention of Scottish Local Authorities) were highly critical. The idea of *housing* departments in Scotland having a responsibility to help those without a *house* seemed dangerous and new, and the Morris Committee, in spite of its carefully balanced membership, was characterised as being in some way "anti-housing" and "pro-social work".

Mrs Morris herself had been, seemingly, an ideal choice to help bridge any gap between social work and housing. Apart from her personal abilities, Mrs Morris had been chairman of a local authority housing committee, she was at the time chairman of a housing association, and she was also a professional social worker. She spoke on her committee's report at the Scottish Conference of The Institute of Housing in the Spring of 1975 and at many other conferences and seminars around Scotland for the next year. But, with a few honourable exceptions in some places, it was largely to no avail. Only social work authorities and the social work committee of COSLA accepted and supported the report's main proposals and this merely confirmed the worst fears of those on the housing side.

One would have expected that the Scottish Office, which had after all set up the committee and whose civil servants had serviced it from start to finish, would have taken the lead in trying to gain general acceptance. One would have been wrong.

The report was not given full ministerial endorsement or backed up with a circular. Caution was the order of the day, and consensus was still earnestly hoped for even after battle lines had been drawn. It was not until eighteen months after publication, on 9 November 1976, that the Secretary of State for Scotland, Bruce Millan, took the bold step of announcing that the Scottish Office accepted that primary responsibility for the homeless *should* be passed from social work to housing, but that this could be better achieved by "voluntary agreement" than by a change in the law — at the very time when legislation for England and Wales was ready to be put forward.

The reaction to the Secretary of State's announcement by those of us in Shelter Scotland was glum, the more so because the announcement came a few days before the Queen's Speech and we did not know that the Government was about to drop its Bill for England and Wales. What we did know was that the Scottish Office was proposing a course of action which was bound to prove inadequate, not least because experience in England and Wales had shown that a voluntary transfer of responsibility for the homeless had been most unsuccessful in non-metropolitan areas, where housing was a district function and social work a county responsibility, the same split as occurs in all of mainland Scotland. In England and Wales, there had been some consolation from the fact that the bulk of the population lived in Greater London or the metropolitan areas, where both functions were handled at either borough or district level, and where the transfer was somewhat smoother: in Scotland only the new Island Councils were in that happy position.

Why, we asked, could Scotland not learn from the hard-won experience south of the border, that a voluntary transfer of responsibility was not workable, and that legislation would prove necessary? As things turned out, of course, this is precisely what happened, but not as a result of the Scottish Office changing its mind.

When the Liberal MP for the Isle of Wight, Stephen Ross, came near the top of the Private Members' Ballot, voluntary organisations in England immediately appealed to him to take up Reg Freeson's offer and to sponsor a Bill on homelessness. At first he toyed with the idea of producing a catch-all Bill, covering compulsory penal rating for empty property and the exemption of landlords of single properties from the provisions of the Rent Acts, as well as homelessness. But he soon came to realise that a Bill covering a number of topics had little or no chance of survival, particularly since penal rating on empty property would arouse the ire of the Conservatives and any amendment to the Rent Acts would be likely to be strenuously opposed by Labour. Homelessness was still a difficult and contentious issue, but when Ross took over the Government Bill he did manage to attract all-party sponsorship, which gave it a strong chance of eventual enactment.

The Housing (Homeless Persons) Bill becoming a private measure was something of an irritation to the English charities, but to those of us in Scotland it was a godsend. Immediately, Shelter Scotland urged Stephen Ross, both publicly and privately, to extend the Bill to include Scotland. Simultaneously we asked the English charities to press the case for Scotland's inclusion, which they did at the earliest discussions.

At that stage we had no idea what the problems would be in achieving our goal of having a Private Members' Bill supported by the Government south of the border, in the shape of the Department of the Environment, extended to Scotland in the face of Scottish Office opposition. It was not of course unusual to have different housing policies pursued by government north and south of the border: earlier in 1976, for example, a Bill on agricultural tied cottages, which was similarly opposed by the government in Scotland, had been passed for England and Wales. But that had been a Government measure. A Private Members' Bill was a different kettle of fish, and there had been no direct precedent in recent years.

In Scotland, Shelter recruited the active support of other organisations in the weeks over Christmas 1976 and the New Year. An impressive range of mainly voluntary bodies had soon lined up with Shelter in support of Scotland's inclusion in the Bill: these were the Scottish Legal Action Group, the Scottish Consumer Council, the Scottish section of the British Association of Social Workers, Scottish Women's Aid, the Scottish Council for the Single Homeless, and the Scottish Council for Single

Parents. These groups, who were later to form the Scottish Homeless Group, wrote to Stephen Ross, the Scottish Office, and to individual MPs pressing for Scotland's inclusion.

Stephen Ross's response from the start had been favourable, though, like the Scottish voluntary organisations themselves, he was unwilling to risk the whole Bill for the sake of Scotland. He received powerful backing for including Scotland from David Steel, MP, a former Chairman of Shelter Scotland, who was not totally without influence in the Parliamentary Liberal Party and who, more surprisingly, was not totally lacking in influence with the Labour Government from the start of the Lib-Lab pact in March 1977.

The initial response from other parties was also good. Labour and Conservative Scottish backbench support seemed reasonably strong, while the SNP Parliamentary Party took a group decision to allow Andrew Welsh, MP, their housing spokesman, to take what was for them the unique step of sponsoring a piece of legislation for England and Wales for the express purpose of extending it to Scotland.

From the Scottish Office, however, the response remained negative. The voluntary approach was characterised as being preferable, and it was explained that this was being pursued actively by COSLA, whose housing and social work committees were drawing up a voluntary "code of practice". It was further suggested, informally, that the Bill was badly drafted. Moreover, it was argued that since housing was a devolved subject under the Scotland and Wales Bill, it would be inappropriate for Westminster to legislate at this stage. As had happened in local government before reorganisation took place, those in power were able to use the impending shake-up as a justification for holding up some measures while rushing through others. Since both processes were unique, there was no precedent by which such claims could be judged, particularly by bodies lobbying from the outside. Most pressure groups are unwilling to be cast as unreasonable, but in this instance it seemed far from unreasonable to press ahead with Scotland's inclusion in the Bill, given the widespread support from most quarters. At the root of the Scottish Office's reluctance to budge was a commitment given to COSLA (which was itself divided and understandably reluctant to have these divisions exacerbated) that there would be no legislation until a voluntary code had been tried.

D

It must be conceded that the main advantage of this approach would have been that housing authorities would have had time to adjust their policies, train their staff, and learn from their neighbours' experiences. However, the lack of preparation for assuming this responsibility, and the shock at the sudden prospect of taking it on were both intensified by the shortage of properly qualified housing management staff in Scotland. This has been well described in the report "Training for Tommorrow", produced by a sub-committee of the Scottish Housing Advisory Committee in 1977. Had there been a well-qualified profession of housing management in Scotland, lessons from English experience could have been more readily drawn and applied by local authority housing departments. One irony is that many of the best-qualified housing staff in Scotland are employed by the Scottish Special Housing Association and by the New Towns, which under the Act do not have primary responsibilities for the homeless, only a duty to co-operate.

Thus, the Scottish Office maintained their opposition to Scotland's inclusion and this continued up to the second reading on Friday, 18th February. In this period, a couple of worrying technical points were thrown at Stephen Ross, which had everyone reaching for their Erskine May. One was the assertion that a Committee of the Cabinet would have to approve the Bill's place on an already cramped timetable, and that this approval could be witheld if Scotland was not taken out. Another was that the House of Commons would have to give a formal "instruction" for Scotland to be included. Bob Hughes, the Labour MP for Aberdeen North, and an ex-Scottish Office Minister, was an invaluable adviser at this stage. Having himself fought hard at the Scottish Office to have Scotland included in the Children Bill, he had solid experience of some of the procedural niceties.

On the first technicality, he pointed out that as the Cabinet legislative committee had already provided time for the Bill, and given the Department of the Environment's support for the measure, it was unlikely to be ditched out of spite. On the second point, concerning the alleged need for an "instruction" from the House, he had consulted with the Clerk of the House who said that this was simply not so. "They are just trying to frighten you," he told Stephen Ross. It thus became apparent that as long as Stephen Ross kept his nerve and formally included

Scotland in the Bill, there was little that the Scottish Office could do. The necessary re-drafting was therefore done, the Bill was published, and it was welcomed by the Department of the Environment, although its spokesman expressed the obligatory misgivings about Scotland's inclusion.

The timely advent of the Lib-Lab pact has been mentioned by some commentators as being the crucial turning point on Scotland's inclusion. Certainly, the listing of the successful passage of the Homeless Persons Bill, with Scotland in it, as one of the conditions of the first phase of the pact was most welcome to the members of the Scottish Homeless Group. But this mainly served to make explicit what had already been tacitly agreed: so, while the Lib-Lab pact was valuable, it was not necessarily critical.

During the second reading debate, Hugh Brown, the Parliamentary Under Secretary of State for Scotland with responsibility for housing, voiced the Scottish Office's unhappiness about what had come to pass, but neither he nor any of the other handful of critics of the Bill on the floor of the House voted against the second reading. He said that the Scottish Office would not now attempt to frustrate the Bill.

The organisations in the Scottish Homeless Group were delighted at having achieved their main aim. They little realised how many problems for the Bill there would be at the Committee Stage, problems which would be common to England, Wales and Scotland. Nor did they realise that when it came to implementing the Act in Scotland in 1977 problems would again arise with the Scottish Office's reluctance, in contrast to the Department of the Environment, to issue a proper "Code of Guidance" which is vital to the proper working of the Act. All that was yet to come, and there was a proper sense of what had been achieved since the early days of the previous November. Of course, it is arguable that even if the Scottish organisations had not lobbied hard through press releases, letter-writing, telephoning, and occasional individual visits to London, the Bill would have been extended to the whole of Britain anyway.

That is indeed arguable, but recent legislative history is littered with instances of reforms being passed for England and Wales and no action being taken for Scotland. The reasons for this are various.

Robin Cook, MP, mentioned the ineptitude and inactivity of

many Scottish pressure groups in last year's *Scottish Government Yearbook* as being a root cause.[2] This is undoubtedly a major factor, and the instances which he quoted were convincing as far as they went. However, a useful distinction can be made between two basic sorts of pressure groups, in Scotland or elsewhere. On the one hand there are the established interest groups like the STUC, the CBI, the NFUS, the local authorities and the traditional professions. On the other hand there are a variety of voluntary organisations, ranging from the local to the national and from the purely charitable to the highly political. There may be some problem of classification, notably with the Churches, which may be firmly established organisations but also have to rely heavily on the work of volunteers for many of their activities. Nevertheless, the distinction is a useful one, and most of the evidence in Scotland is that the established interests need few lessons from anyone. The Scottish Licensed Trade Association's performance over the reform of the licencing laws may provide a spectacularly risible exception to this: but an exception it is.

Voluntary bodies on the other hand have been traditionally weak in Scotland on matters of lobbying, though it is to be hoped that the campaigns on the Children Bill and the Housing (Homeless Persons) Bill will mark a significant shift. Lack of resources is one reason for this weakness. A British-wide body may be just able to scrape up enough money to fund a full-time worker to staff an office. A Scottish-level body, because of the much smaller population, has to fund-raise ten times as effectively from its public to fund that first, crucial, full-time worker. Faced with this problem, the tendency of many Scottish organisations is simply to leave any lobbying felt necessary to the London head office or to the equivalent organisation in England.

Secondly, while much administrative devolution exists already in Scotland, and voluntary organisations can consult fairly regularly with civil servants in the relevant departments, consultations with Scottish Members of Parliament are much more difficult for purely practical reasons. Even though one can sometimes arrange a meeting with one particular MP on a Friday, when Scottish MPs are usually back in Scotland on constituency business, if one wants to meet several MPs together on an issue, one generally has to go to London. This is both time consuming and costly for voluntary bodies. Thus, the relative ease of contact with civil servants and the relative difficulty of contact with legislators combine, in classic Skinnerian fashion, to condition the behaviour of the voluntary organisations.

Thirdly, in Scotland the concept of "politics" is commonly believed to be identical to "party politics". This misconception is reinforced, rather than dispelled, by commentators on TV who announce with a straight face that certain Regional Council election contests are "non-political". In this climate, voluntary organisations shy away from any activity like parliamentary lobbying which could, rightly, be construed as "political" in the real meaning of the word.

On issues which are highly contentious, and over which the political parties divide, any voluntary organisation which does not want to be caught up in party politics would certainly be wise to pronounce with caution, but caution and inactivity are not the same. In fact, many politicians would welcome greater levels of activity by special groups. Before the Scottish monthly *Focus* folded up at the end of 1976, its last editor was producing a special feature on mental health and he made enquiries by telephone to find out what the mental health policies were of the various parties in Scotland. In each case, after inconclusive shunting from one person to another, he was asked what sort of policy he thought they should adopt! Voluntary organisations should need no encouragement to fill this vacuum.

Thus, voluntary pressure groups in Scotland may, for a variety of reasons, have been weak in pushing their views onto legislators. But that is only half of the equation. While many Scottish Members of Parliament are able and hard-working, and unfailingly send a courteous reply or at least an acknowledgment to letters from lobbying organisations, a distressingly large minority fail to respond at all. When the Scottish Homeless Group was lobbying, the member organisations each wrote assiduously to MPs, and it was interesting to note the pattern of replies. Not surprisingly, many MPs preferred to reply at great length to some bodies, with which they presumably had more regular contact or great sympathy, and merely acknowledged receipt to other organisations. Fair enough. But it soon became evident that a core of MPs never reply to anything. Presumably they feel that this sort of correspondence is a dispensable part of the job. Now, these individuals may be "good constituency members" and much loved colleagues in the House, but their apparent lack of interest in a crucial issue like homelessness is hardly encouraging to campaigning organisations when they do take the trouble to send individual letters to MPs. Lobbying, to have any meaning must be a two-way process. Members of Parliament and equally importantly, councillors, have a duty to understand and to facilitate this essential democratic process.

There are signs that the number of voluntary bodies in Scotland willing and able to engage in campaigning is on the increase. Of the seven organisations originally involved in the Scottish Homeless Group, four, the Scottish Legal Action Group, the Scottish Consumer Council, Scottish Women's Aid, and the Scottish Council for the Single Homeless, had all been established within the previous three years, and BASW had only recently taken on a full-time Scottish organiser. If an Assembly is finally established in Edinburgh this will both facilitate and stimulate the work of pressure groups in Scotland, and the Scottish Council of Social Service is encouraging voluntary organisations to plan now for that eventuality.

Even though the Scottish Homeless Group was successful in its main aim of extending the Bill to Scotland, it was still dependent throughout on the active co-operation of the English charities, and during the Committee Stage of the Bill the logistical problems of a Scottish voluntary group lobbying in London were compounded. Amendments would be put down by MPs on the Committee the day before the next sitting, other amendments would suddenly be withdrawn as the result of private agreements made in the corridors of power: all normal practice no doubt. But it bears emphasising that the very speed and unpredictability of the changes makes it extremely difficult for any voluntary organisation to keep up with the passage of a complicated piece of legislation from nearly 400 miles away.

In the event, John Smythe of Shelter went down to London on behalf of the Scottish Homeless Group to attend some of the key sittings. His personal lobbying was far from unsuccessful: it resulted, for one thing, in an amendment being carried with the effect that homeless persons being turned away by a housing authority must receive reason in writing, and it nearly resulted in the right of appeal to the courts being written into the Bill — something which the English charities were reluctant to propose.

However, the problem of having only one representative on the spot in Westminster without much back up is that this person in turn tends to become isolated from those in Scotland whom he represents.

Of course, in principle, these logistical problems can be overcome — all one needs is an office in London, extra staff to run it, and couriers who can fly back and forward between London and Scotland with fresh drafts and lists of new amendments. But if the Civil Service finds this demanding at times, how much more so for the penny-pinching charity? Even a brief period of intensive lobbying at Westminster tends to make keen devolutionists of those involved. The prospect of being able to nip along to the "High School" about an issue seems most attractive. Whether this greater accessibility will result in genuine "open government" in a devolved Scotland, or in a new cosiness for the well connected, is a matter for conjecture. But the chances are that we will soon know the answer.

REFERENCES

1. "Housing and Social Work — a joint approach". The Report of the Morris Committee on links between housing and social work. Scottish Development Department, 1975.

2. "Parliament and the Scots Conscience: Reforming the law on Divorce, Licensing and Homosexual Reform", R. F. Cook, MP, in *The Scottish Government Yearbook 1978.*

5

THE CROFTER, THE LAIRD AND THE AGRARIAN SOCIALIST: THE HIGHLAND LAND QUESTION IN THE 1970s

JAMES HUNTER
The Press and Journal

The Highlands fit uneasily and insecurely into the British political system. As the underdeveloped, thinly populated periphery of a predominantly industrial state, north and north-west Scotland seem fated to suffer from governmental neglect of a kind which would be inconceivable in less heavily indus-trialised European countries such as Norway — where districts with problems not unlike those of the Highlands still exercise an occasionally decisive electoral influence. There are, to put the matter bluntly, few votes to be won in northern Scotland. And Britain's urban-orientated party structure has, moreover, developed in such a way as to ensure that while the Highlands' traditional ruling class, its landlords, have generally been able to count upon the Conservatives to defend their position, the mass of ordinary Highlanders have had no national political voice since the demise of the radical, rural-looking Liberalism personified by the young Lloyd George. For the greater part of this century, in other words, there has been no identity of interests between those Highlanders who favour reforming the region's landlord-dominated agrarian structure and the only political organisation likely to effect such a reform: the Labour and trade union movement.

What applies to the Highlands considered as part of Great Britain, remains applicable in an exclusively Scottish context — with one significant and slightly puzzling reservation. Scottish politics are predominantly urban politics also. And Scotland's most pressing requirement, as is all too apparent in the central belt, is the implementation of policies designed to regenerate an increasingly derelict industrial society. In such circumstances, it would be perfectly understandable, if a little regrettable, to find little or no attention being paid to the peculiar difficulties confronting the handful of Scots who still live and work in the Highlands. But that is very far from being the case. Highland problems, and the Highland land question in particular, remain capable of arousing more passion and fervour than just about any other Scottish political issue — not always excepting that relative newcover, devolution.

The origins of this phenomenon remain mysterious; and it cannot currently be explained in terms much more intelligible than those which assume the existence of some sort of collective guilt complex about the Highland Clearances and what caused them. But whatever its causes, there is no doubt as to the strength of Lowland concern about the Highland future. It is regularly demonstrated on the letter page of *The Scotsman* — that perennially fascinating index of Scottish obsessions. It is equally regularly observable in the House of Commons — where anxiety about the Highlands' agrarian structure has been expressed more frequently in this Parliament by MPs like Dennis Canavan and Margaret Bain, the Labour and Nationalist representatives of West Stirlingshire and East Dumbartonshire, than by many of the members sent south by Highland constituencies. It is presumably responsible for the fact that the editors of *The Scottish Government Yearbook 1979,* thought it worth requesting a fairly hefty slab of print about the Highland land problem. And because of the Highlands' peripheral status, it offers the only substantial hope of ever mounting the political pressure needed to solve that problem once and for all.

During the present decade, while the solution has been brought little closer, the nature of the problem has at least been more clearly defined: by the often embittered debate about the merits or demerits of the Crofting Reform (Scotland) Act 1976; by renewed attempts to probe the long-standing mystery of who precisely owns the Highlands; by the intrusion of foreign landowners into an area previously reserved for the native breed; and by The Highlands and Islands Development Board's belated, but nevertheless welcome, discovery that, in words used by board chairman Kenneth Alexander in his foreword to the HIDB's annual report for 1976, "a sound approach to land use can contribute more to the economic health of every part of the Highlands and Islands than any other single policy".

Traditionally, crofting has extended from Orkney and Shetland in the north through the crofting counties of Caithness and
Sutherland, Ross and Cromarty, Inverness and Argyll to its
heartland in the Western Isles. The 1976 reform of crofting
law was, in many respects, long overdue. Changing circumstances
had rendered the protection offered by earlier legislation
inadequate. To take one glaring example, in 1886 crofters had
won the right to security of tenure — thus terminating the era
of clearance and eviction. But that right applied only as long
as croft land was used for agricultural purposes. A change in
land use could still lead to a crofter losing all or part of his
holding. And though compensated financially for his loss, the
crofter was entitled only to a sum based upon the affected land's
agricultural value — development value accruing to the landlord. For a long time, that anomaly did not matter very much
— for the simple reason that non-agricultural developments were
few and far between. More recently, because of commercial
pressures associated with tourism and the beginnings of Highland
industrialisation, it came to matter a great deal. Individual
landlords profitted substantially from the sale of croft land;
while the crofters concerned had to be content with the pittance
awarded them by a Scottish Land Court which was bound and
fettered by an obviously outmoded law. The 1976 Act, by
entitling crofters to a share in their land's development value,
brought that situation to an end.

But it was not on account of such relatively minor benefits
that Parliament's most recent venture into the thorny field of
crofting legislation was described by the Crofters Commission,
in their annual report for 1976, as marking "the beginning of
what may possibly be the most important period in the evolution
of crofting since 1886". Nor was it on account of clauses relating
to development value and other essentially subordinate matters
that the reform measure became the cause of a good deal of
political controversy — controversy which was, admittedly, more
in evidence in the Highland press and within the Labour Party
than among crofters themselves.

The Crofting Reform Act was designed primarily to give
crofters the option of becoming the owners, rather than the
tenants, of both their homes and their holdings. This was, in a
sense, the logical conclusion to a process initiated 90 years earlier
— the process, that is, of enhancing crofters' legal rights at the

expense of those of their landlords. But it was also, despite the many conditions and restrictions imposed upon the subsequent resale of croft land, an undoubted step in the direction of exposing crofters to market forces from which they had previously been sheltered by their unique tenurial status. To the Act's advocates, notably the Crofters Commission, this seemed no bad thing. By deciding to buy their holdings, it was argued, crofters could free themselves from the restrictions which the old order imposed on enterprise and initiative — thus enabling the crofting community as a whole to take advantage of commercial opportunities made available by developments such as the expansion of the tourist trade and the arrival of oil-related industry.

An alternative analysis of the legislation's likely consequences was provided by the Act's Labour Party critics. It would, they declared, bring about the eventual demise of crofting and the crofting way of life by exposing crofting townships to the activities of holiday home purchasers, land speculators and other socially and culturally disruptive elements. The Act, in short, was condemned as a betrayal of socialist principles — a defect thought to be compounded by its being arguably a breach of party policy. Labour's own committee on crofting questions had come out in favour of public ownership of croft land. So had the party's Scottish conference. Harold Wilson's administration nevertheless refused to abandon its own reform proposals — proposals which, apart from minor changes designed to reduce the purchase prices likely to be paid by crofters who opted for ownership, were esentially those placed before Parliament by the previous Conservative government. This refusal to take cognizance of majority Labour opinion in Scotland predictably provoked angry resignations from the committee responsible for the public ownership policy — notably those of Inverness author Allan Campbell McLean and Skye-based journalist Brian Wilson, then prospective Labour candidate for Ross and Cromarty.

Which, if either, of these opposing views of the Reform Act's significance will prove to be correct is still impossible to ascertain. On present evidence, however, both the hopes and fears expressed at the time of the legislation's passage through Parliament seem decidedly exaggerated.

Purchase prices are nothing if not reasonable. A crofter can become the outright owner of his home for around £5 — a sum which appears derisory until it is realised that crofters, unlike tenant farmers, have always been responsible for providing their crofts with houses and other buildings. Prices for entire holdings, certainly those on the west coast, in the Hebrides and in Shetland, seem unlikely to greatly exceed £100. And while some estate managements have discouraged their tenants from taking advantage of the new Act by — in words used by Crofters Commission chairman James Shaw Grant — "tendering gratuitous advice of a questionable nature", landlords have made no general effort to resist reform.

Those crofters who have become owner-occupiers have done so for reasons anticipated by the Commission. In some instances, a small piece of a croft has been bought to provide a house site for a friend or relative — thus helping to ease the housing shortage which characterises many parts of the Highlands. Portions of other holdings have been acquired in order to initiate enterprises based upon the tourist trade. And some surplus croft houses have been bought and resold to raise capital for agricultural improvements. The Crofters Commission take some pride in such developments. But they cannot disguise the fact that there has been no rush to buy. No doubt, as the Commission point out, many purchases are still underway. Perhaps, as they maintain, interest in ownership should not be taken as the sole yardstick of the reform measure's effectiveness. There remains, however, a very awkward and undismissable set of statistics. The Highlands and Islands contain around 18,000 crofts. At the end of 1977, eighteen months after the Reform Act's implementation, the Crofters Commission had been notified of the purchase of only 78 whole crofts, ten part crofts and 48 house sites. In the Outer Hebridean heartland of the crofting community, the position was summed up thus by Western Isles Crofters Union secretary, Donald John MacQueen: "The Reform Act has made absolutely no impact here." And that, if present trends are maintained, may well turn out to be the controversial legislation's epitaph.

The causes of this state of affairs remain largely unexamined. They are unlikely, however, to differ fundamentally from those which brought about the failure of attempts made around 1900 to persuade a previous generation of crofters to become owner-occupiers or, in the jargon of the day, "peasant proprietors" — a transformation then being implemented in Ireland. The crofters of 80 years ago preferred tenancy to ownership because, given the security of tenure and low rents which were the major consequences of the original Act of 1886, tenancy was considerably more advantageous in financial terms; and because, for reasons rooted deep in Highland history, the very concept of private ownership of land was viewed with considerable suspicion and dislike. The present generation of crofters, though less steeped in Gaelic tradition than their grandfathers, have little incentive to adopt a radically different course of action. And, so far at any rate, they have not done so.

Whether as tenants or owner-occupiers, few crofters can make an adequate living from their crofts — their household finances being consequently dependent on the availability of employment additional to that provided by their holdings. By itself, therefore, no reform of crofting tenure can solve the crofting community's problems. More and better jobs are also required; and their creation depends upon the growth and diversification of the regional economy as a whole. That is not to say, however, that land reform has no part to play in the general development process. On the contrary, its role may eventually prove crucial — but only if reform measures are extended outwith the crofting sector and applied to the entire agrarian structure of which crofting is a relatively small and well-protected part. The keystone of that structure is the power of private landlordism.

The precise nature of Highland land ownership patterns remains uncertain — largely because successive governments have refused to establish a comprehensive system of land registration. But two recent books have demonstrated that, in the century which has elapsed since the last official enquiry into the Highland land system, that system's dominant characteristic has remained the concentration of ownership of northern Scotland's basic natural resource, its land, in the hands of a very small number of people and institutions.

The books in question are: *Who Owns Scotland?*, by retired forestry expert John McEwen[1]; and *Agrarian Change in the Scottish Highlands,* by George Houston, an agricultural economist, and John Bryden, head of the land division of the Highlands and Islands Development Board.[2] McEwen's work is that of a life-long Socialist committed to land nationalisation. Bryden and Houston adopt a more detached approach. But both assessments of current land ownership come to very similar conclusions — the general tenor of these conclusions being indicated by Bryden and Houston's finding that some 35 families or companies possess no less than one third of the Highlands' 7.39 million acres of privately owned land.

McEwen, whose cordial detestation of private landlordism and all its works has not been diminished by his 90 years, concluded that his discoveries implied a need for the prompt addition of those 7.39 million acres to the 1.60 million already in public ownership. The Duke of Buccleuch, with the authority lent him by his own 277,000 acres, reacted to this suggestion by describing John McEwen's book as a "joke" and people who adhered to John McEwen's views as "cranks". No public opinions were proferred by the Wills family, Lord Seafield or the Countess of Sutherland — the proprietors of estates weighing in at 263,000 acres, 185,000 acres and 158,000 acres respectively. But in the aftermath of the controversy caused by the publication of *Who Owns Scotland?*, that most effective pressure group, the Scottish Landowners Federation, felt it necessary to hold a press conference to proclaim that (despite contrary allegations made by what *The Scotsman* called Scotland's "somewhat strange band of agrarian socialists") all was fundamentally well with the existing land ownership structure — except, not unexpectedly, for the increasingly heavy capital taxation to which federation members were said to have been subjected by recent governments.

The "agrarian socialists" remained unconvinced. One of them, Danus Skene of the Scottish Labour Party, had previously written a discussion paper on SLP rural land policy in which he had commented: "No international agricultural aid programme in a developing country would contemplate investment or change without land reform as a prior condition if it was faced with a land tenure pattern as elitist as Scotland's". If Scotland were in a position to apply for international development aid, in other words, such aid would be refused until a land reform programme had been initiated. The statistics produced by McEwen, Bryden and Houston do nothing to discredit Skene's opinion — an opinion based, incidentally, on first hand experience of the position in the Third World. And there are plenty of examples of the type of abuse which might well bring about the aid refusal which Skene thought likely.

Suppose, for instance, it is decided to construct a publicly funded road in order to open up a previously underdeveloped locality. Suppose that the resulting highway gives access to derelict homes — originally abandoned because of the absence of such access. Suppose that, not content with the compensation received for the land occupied by the road and the overall benefit which his estate derives from its construction, the local landowner sells the newly available dwellings to people who have no connection with the district but who are prepared to pay high prices for the privilege of holidaying in a remote and scenically beautiful area for three or four weeks each summer. The landlord and the holiday-home purchasers thus benefit substantially from the new road. The local population, inevitably outbid for the houses in question, benefit not at all; and the cycle of decline is scarcely even interrupted. Such occurences would not be tolerated in Africa or Asia by the far from revolutionary gentlemen who run the World Bank and kindred agencies. But they can and do happen in the Highlands — and for reasons identical to those underlying the mass evictions of 150 years ago. As long as the Highlands and Islands are parcelled out among a tiny minority of monied men there will be an irresistible tendency for the pursuit of private profit to take precedence over the interests of the community as a whole.·

The most generally evident example of this tendency is to be found in the declining level of Highland agricultural production. This decline, particularly marked in the sheep farming sector, has no simple cause. But it cannot be divorced from the landownership system — especially since that system is characterised by the possession of land for purposes which are essentially unrelated to its agricultural potential. Among such purposes might be included the ownership of land for reasons relating to sport, financial speculation or mere social aspiration — the latter being a far from minor consideration in a Highland context. Any or all of those influences on estate management policies operate to the disadvantage of sound husbandry — as well as to the disadvantage of communities which might otherwise possess comparatively favourable economic prospects. And while there is nothing new about this situation, as is confirmed by even the most rudimentary acquaintance with the facts of Highland history, it has been the subject of renewed controversy of late — largely as a result of the purchase of substantial tracts of the Highlands by foreign companies and individuals.

The nature and extent of external involvement in the Scottish land market is the subject of a recent study by two Scottish academics — Tony Carty of Glasgow University's law department and Strathclyde University sociologist, John Ferguson.[3] Some of the transactions which Carty and Ferguson examine are frankly speculative — turning on the purchase of estates which are subsequently broken up and resold at occasionally enormous profits. Others involve the acquisition of large tracts of territory — apparently with a view to developing their tourist and sporting potential. One of the biggest such investors is the Enessey Company Limited of Lausanne, Switzerland, whose properties include the 61,000 acre Mar Lodge Estate in Aberdeenshire, the 15,000 acre Tulchan Estate in Moray and the 62,500 acre North Harris Estate in the Western Isles. But the Enessey Company's activities have been assiduously emulated by a whole host of individual businessmen and financiers — among them men like the Dutch cattle dealer, Johannes Hellinga, who owns the Kindeace Estate in Easter Ross and the Waternish Estate in Skye; and the Dubai-based Egyptian petrodollar millionaire, Mohammed Al Fayed, one of whose companies, Bocardo Societé Anonyme of Lichenstein, has bought 3,463 acres of farmland in the north-east and the Highlands at a cost of £1,417,316.

Occurrences of this kind naturally push up land prices and make it increasingly difficult for young, working farmers to obtain land of their own; while such is the secrecy surrounding many land transfers, and so complex are the ownership structures of the companies involved, that some Highland communities are completely ignorant as to the true identity of their landlords. That is the unavoidable result of Scotland's lack of a land register; just as the entire phenomenon of external land ownership is the inevitable consequence of this country's uniquely free land market — combined with the obvious attractions of land prices which are, by continental standards, extremely low.

The state of affairs which Carty and Ferguson describe could not occur elsewhere in Western Europe — for the simple reason that other European countries possess legislation designed to prevent such a situation ever arising. That legislation exists, Carty and Ferguson conclude, because European governments of widely-varying political persuasions have long been agreed on their duty to protect farmers, and the rural population generally, from commercial and speculative pressures of the type which are so evident in Scotland. The British Government is the exception — exercising no controls over land purchase and, almost unbelievably, making only a token effort to ascertain a buyer's identity.

Land deals involving foreigners are consequently not confined to the Highlands and are, indeed, particularly prevalent in southern England — a fact which, to cynics at least, explains why they have been the subject of an official investigation by the clumsily entitled Committee of Inquiry into the Acquisition and Occupancy of Agricultural Land (Northfield Committee). Allan Campbell McLean characteristically described this particular exercise as "an excellent example of Labour governments' unerring instinct for setting up inquiries composed of people who will ensure that the *status quo* remains totally unchanged". The committee's composition certainly indicated that its members had not been selected by a Minister hell-bent on reform; while these same members' performance at their solitary sitting in northern Scotland in March 1978 reinforced the opinion that, as far as Highland land policy was concerned, they were actually lagging well behind other officially-sponsored organisations, notably the Highlands and Islands Development Board.

It was symbolically appropriate that the HIDB's present chairman should have expressed mounting concern about the landownership issue while on a visit to Raasay — the Hebridean island which has become a monument to proprietorial neglect and indifference. Standing outside the once magnificent Raasay House, now empty, abandoned and vandalised, Professor Kenneth Alexander said simply: "This is a tragedy." Criticising the way in which Raasay's considerable economic potential had remained unexploited while the island's population had inexorably wasted away, he added: "I really have to say, quite frankly, that this is associated with the ownership of these assets." With a caution entirely typical of the way the HIDB has always been conducted, Professor Alexander immediately qualified his comments by pointing out: "This is a particular anti-landlord remark, not a general anti-landlord remark." Even "particular anti-landlord remarks", however, had never been heard to emanate from the

E

Professor's predecessors. And at that moment in September 1976, the impression was created that the HIDB were at last considering decisive action on the land reform front.

Such action, it is arguable, should have been taken when the board was inaugurated ten years earlier. That, at least, was what MPs seemed to have in mind when they passed the Highlands and Islands Development (Scotland) Act — the measure which brought the HIDB into existence. The Labour government of the day, in the person of Scottish Secretary Willie Ross, then stated categorically: "Land is the basic natural resource of the Highlands and any plan for economic and social development would be meaningless if proper use of land were not a part of it." Noting that the Hill Lands (North of Scotland) Commission had identified "the existing rights of possession and occupation" as one of the major limitations on land development in the Highlands, Ross concluded by remarking that the removal of such constraints was "the purpose of the powers in relation to land which the board will have".

Statements like these were responsible for the occasionally hysterical outcry with which the founding of the HIDB was greeted by the Highlands' landed establishment. In the event, however, the possessors of broad acres were left utterly unmolested by the denizens of the Board's Inverness headquarters. And, while the suspicion remains that this was largely because the original Board lacked the will to embark upon far-reaching agrarian reform, it now appears that a subsidiary reason for their failure to implement the Secretary of State's intentions was their lack of the necessary powers. That, at any rate, is the present Board's explanation of the fact that, 13 years after Willie Ross pronounced their death-knell, Highland landlords continue to prosper exceedingly while the problems of the rural Highlands remain depressingly unsolved.

The basic procedural difficulty confronting the Board is that its land acquisition powers are similar to those possessed by local authorities. These powers are perfectly adequate for obtaining land needed for specific purposes — such as the building of a school, a housing estate or a hospital. But they are quite inappropriate, as is remarked in the HIDB's annual report for 1976, "for the acquisition of relatively large tracts of land over most of which the main use will be agriculture or forestry". Hence the Board's view, contained in the same annual report,

that "there is a need for it to be able to act . . . where there
are obvious examples of underuse or mismanagement of land
which are hindering the development of rural communities or
even endangering their future existence". And hence the HIDB's
decision to request an extension of its powers to acquire and
control land.

Board members have been at pains to play down the
significance of this request by stressing repeatedly that the sought-
for powers would constitute no more than a rarely employed
ultimate sanction for use against unusually recalcitrant landlords.
If granted, however, those powers would undoubtedly make
possible a fairly formidable assault against the bastions of landed
power in the Highlands. That is why anyone familiar with the
long and largely ineffective campaign to ensure the better use
of the Highlands' natural resources must suspect that Parliament
is most unlikely to accede to the HIDB's demands.

This paper thus returns to its starting point. For while
Highland problems have ranked high on the Westminster agenda
only when, as happened in the 1880s, Highlanders have promoted
their interests by decidedly violent means, that may not
necessarily be true of a Scottish Assembly. There is justifiable
apprehension in northern Scotland that many members of any
future Scottish legislation will be unable to see beyond the
undeniably urgent needs of the central belt. But there is also
evidence, as already noted, that many Lowland Scots care deeply,
if not always knowledgeably, for the Highlands. And there is
no reason why that feeling should not manifest itself in support
for a Highland land reform programme.

The case for such a programme is usually presented in purely
material terms. Its biggest immediate impact, however, might
well be psychological. The Highlands and Islands today, for all
their continuing difficulties, are much better placed economically
than was the case ten or twenty years ago. There is a new air
of confidence in the region — evident in young Highlanders'
increasing unwillingness to migrate southwards; evident, too, in
the cultural and linguistic revival which is most apparent in the
Western Isles but which is increasingly discernible in other
districts also. But over this awakening there still broods the
Highlands' landlord class — rightly associated with two centuries
of exploitation, misery, depopulation and decay. That class
deserves to be removed on many counts; but not least because

the destruction of Highland landlordism would, more than any other single development, demonstrate that a new and better era had at last begun in northern Scotland. There are few more appropriate tasks for a restored Scottish Parliament to undertake.

REFERENCES

1. *Who Owns Scotland?*, John McEwen, Edinburgh University Students Publication Board, 1977.

2. *Agrarian Change in the Scottish Highlands,* George Houston and John Bryden. Martin Robertson in association with Highlands and Islands Development Board, 1976.

3. *Power and Manoeuvrability: The International Implications of an Independent Scotland,* Tony Carty and Alexander McCall Smith, Q Press, Edinburgh, 1978.

6

TEN YEARS AFTER —
THE REVOLUTIONARY LEFT IN SCOTLAND

NEIL WILLIAMSON
Freelance Journalist

The revolutionary left celebrates its tenth birthday this year. Of course revolutionary politics go back slightly longer than a decade — as far back as the formation of the Communist Party, or to the nineteenth-century Chartists, perhaps even to the seventeenth-century Levellers — but it was in 1968 that the organisation and politics of today's far left emerged in a recognisable form.

The influences on the left in that first year were inter-national. The student riots and general strike in France, the Tet offensive in Vietnam and the Soviet invasion of Czechoslovakia were the events which shaped a new generation of socialists, and that tradition remains to this day. Any undue concern for home-grown life in Scotland has always seemed drab and parochial in comparison. Certainly many on the left have firmly resisted the label of "Scottish" and there is still no such animal as the "Scottish left", only a series of groups which are, to some extent or other, the functioning branches of organisations based mainly south of the border.

The largest component of this "revolutionary left in Scot-land" is the Socialist Workers Party (SWP) which has around 500 members, with offices and half a dozen full-time workers in Glasgow. The International Marxist Group (IMG) has about 80 members, and its full-time worker can be found in offices sited across the landing from those of the SWP in Queen Street, Glasgow, a fact of unceasing confusion for the postman and lift attendant.

These are the two largest organisations of the left, but there are a host of smaller or less active groupings, each of which has fewer than fifty members in Scotland. There is the Workers Revolutionary Party (WRP) whose members have the exhausting task of selling their quota of the party's daily newspaper *The Newsline,* a task made even more arduous by the paper's concentration, often to the length of four or five pages, on the details of the assassination of Trotsky. Supporters of the newspaper *Workers Action* who were formerly organised as the International Communist League (ICL) are restricted to the east coast of Scotland, as are the handful of members of the Revolutionary Communist Group (RCG).

All of these organisations claim to be in some form or other Trotskyist, and it is often difficult to distinguish exact differences between them. At least one of the organisations concerned, the IMG, has argued that the differences are purely "tactical" and that enough agreement exists for serious discussions to be held on unification, but this view is not shared by the others.

Apart from the Trotskyist left, there are a few members of the Workers Party of Scotland, a Maoist organisation led by Spanish Civil War veteran Tom Murray. After a well-publicised trial in 1972, the party's chairman and treasurer were sentenced to over 20 years imprisonment for armed robbery allegedly to raise funds for the party. The other non-Trotskyist organisation is the Socialist Party of Great Britain, one of the original pre-First World War sects, whose members can be seen at the foot of the Mound in Edinburgh, or in Royal Exchange Square in Glasgow any weekend explaining to an assembled crowd the merits of the coming socialist millenium.

Lastly, there are supporters of the *Militant* newspaper who number between 90 and 100. All of them are members of the Labour Party, but mainly of its youth section, the Labour Party Young Socialists, which the Militant group controls both in Scotland and in Britain as a whole.

Altogether the far left groups have a membership of between 700 and 800. There are another 100 in the Militant groupings, but their committment to the Labour Party usually excludes them from the designation "revolutionary left".

Could this 800 strong contingent not be larger, ten years on from the heady days of 1968? Certainly those involved in politics in 1974 at the time of the fall of the Tory government had every expectation that they would celebrate the tenth anniversary of May 1968 or the Tet offensive with considerably larger forces. The universally shared assumption of revolutionaries after Wilson's election victory was that the working-class militancy seen under the Heath regime would continue, leading to inevitable confrontation with the Labour government. The first months of the new Government only encouraged this view.

The victory of the miners produced an impetus to wage struggles which was especially strong in Scotland. One group of workers after another — organised purely on a Scottish basis — came out on strike. Prominent among them were lorry drivers and dustmen. But it was the strike of teachers which provided the greatest hopes for the left. From October to Christmas 1974 around 15,000 teachers were involved in unofficial actions across the Central belt of Scotland. In the absence of official union machinery, action committees were set up and at least in Lothian, Fife and the Borders young left-wing teachers were thrust into leading positions. Demands such as accountable and elected strike committees, regular strike bulletins and mass demonstrations were lifted from left-wing text books and put into practice in a real trade union struggle. Eventually of course the union leadership re-established control, but the experience tended to confirm the revolutionaries' belief that any social contract would be a fragile one and eventually doomed, and that rising unemployment would be inevitably answered by resistence and factory occupations. There seemed no immediate limits to the trade union militancy of the working population.

There was another factor which encouraged the optimism of the revolutionary left as they surveyed their prospects: the growing problems for their main rival in the trade union movement, the Communist Party (CP). The CP has around 6,000 members in Scotland, one fifth of its all British total. Some of its trade union leaders like Mick McGahey of the National Union of Miners, Jim Airlie and Sammy Barr from Clydeside shipbuilding and Irene Swan from Edinburgh are among the party's best known and respected leaders. In Scotland the party still retains localised electoral support in Clydebank and in Fife and in the 1977 District Elections managed to return two councillors. Their base inside the Scottish Trades Union Congress (STUC) seems as secure as ever, and the role of General Council members who are in the party, like Bill Niven, Hugh D'Arcy, and of course the STUC's General Secretary Jimmy Milne, is a long and successful one.

Yet the picture for the CP is far from happy. Its membership is falling, with its youth organisation, the Young Communist League, down to a couple of hundred members reflecting the rising age of party members. The last years have seen a steady haemorrhage of leading party trade unionists, such as Jimmy Reid of Upper Clyde Shipbuilders fame and Davy Bolton, a former vice-chairman of the Scottish miners. These are not temporary changes, for the very social basis of past CP support is being undermined. The Vale of Leven and parts of West Fife contained areas known as "Little Moscows" where entire communities gave their support to the party's activities and its electoral attempts. But post-war change, especially in the late 1950s and 1960s destroyed these "closed" collectives, the population was rehoused, and the old workforce dispersed. The consequences for the CP are eloquently demonstrated by the fall in support in West Fife, once the seat of Willie Gallagher, Communist MP.

PERCENTAGE OF VOTES CAST FOR COMMUNIST CANDIDATES IN WEST FIFE IN GENERAL ELECTIONS 1945-1974

1945	42.1	1964	7.4
1950	21.6	1966	3.6
1951	10.5	1970	1.7
1955	12.6	F) 1974	4.4
1959	8.4	O) 1974	2.4

Such a clear and sustained drop in votes is not just an electoral phenomenon, but expresses a genuine loss of community identification with the CP in this previously mining area.

To compound its problems the party had internal worries. In Glasgow in 1977 opponents of the leadership captured a majority of the delegates to the annual conference. Their leader John Foster, a labour historian from Strathclyde University, argued for opposition to the "reformism" and "revisionism" of the policy document produced by the leadership, *The British Road to Socialism*.

These weaknesses of the CP, its "vulnerable left flank" as the far left saw it, were not unique to Scotland, but they seemed to give added confidence to those hoping to replace the CP as the "natural home" for militant workers on the factory floor. Faced with such promising opportunities, there were in essence three distinct projects mapped out by revolutionaries in Scotland, all of which, it must be remembered, assumed a developing crisis of government and the economy.

The first position, that of the SWP, argued that it would be possible for revolutionaries to by-pass traditional Labour reformism in this period. To that end "Rank and File" groups were organised in the unions in opposition to the "Broad Left" caucuses traditionally supported by the CP and the Labour left. By far the most successful of these "Rank and File" groupings was in teaching where, capitalising on the leading role of its members in the 1974 strike, "Rank and File Teachers" emerged as the main left-wing opposition to the John Pollock leadership of the Educational Institute of Scotland, the largest teachers' union.

This went hand in hand with the "Right to Work Campaign", but the route marches of unemployed and occupation of dole offices, so much a feature of the work of the SWP down south, never really happened in Scotland. The tactic was obviously modelled on the National Unemployed Workers Movement which claimed 100,000 members at its height in 1933 and one of the leaders of Clydeside unemployed between the wars, Harry McShane, was a frequent speaker at "Right to Work" rallies.

Opposed to this strategy was the IMG who saw it as "syndicalist". They prophesied that the coming battles would provoke divisions inside the leadership of the Labour movement nationally. This, it was argued, would mean the emergence of "left currents" from the unions and the Labour Party lead by opportunist, but demogogic, left social democrats. The "Thesis on Britain" passed by the IMG Conference in 1976 spells this out clearly in the light of the supposedly growing opposition to the Government:

> Under those conditions, where every objective development creates the need for a generalised political response and leadership of the working class, but at the same time the overwhelming majority of even the militant workers, give their political allegiance to the Labour Party, such a leadership and political perspective cannot be created in the immediate future — the coming 12-18 months — outside of the Labour Party, if it is to be credible and acceptable to larger sections of the working class.[1]

This was not to say that the IMG put any great trust in the Labour left. Their argument was that any opposition to the Wilson government would force the Labour left, regardless of their timidity, into action if only to protect their own political base. The parliamentary voting against the cuts in 1976 and the unveiling of Tony Benn's "Alternative Strategy" of generalised import controls, and direction of investment into industry, only encouraged them in this view.

The third scenario for the coming confrontation was more radical in its conclusions. The coming confrontation would not primarily be reflected inside Labourism and its organisations, but in the outright rejection of them. A dramatic growth of nationalist and pro-independence current would be the inevitable corollary, and the essential task of Scottish socialists would therefore be to "straddle" both socialism and this "new" Scottish nationalism, in rejecting Westminster Labourist dominance. The 1,000 people who joined the Scottish Labour Party at its formation in January 1976 essentially shared this perspective, although the majority were far from being revolutionaries.

It is now obvious just how wrong all three projections were. There was no paralysing social conflict. Instead, limited and isolated struggles like Grunwick and the firemen's strike ended in defeat, leaving a passive acceptance of unemployment (at record post-war levels in Scotland) and falling living standards, an acceptance incredible to a left poised for action. Despite their differences in approach, all had expected the opposite to happen, and the price they paid was two years of falling membership, declining paper sales and considerable political confusion.

There is no space to examine the particular twists of the IMG in this period in Scotland. They saw the decision by Jim Sillars, MP, to leave the Labour Party and form the Scottish Labour Party as the first example of left-wing social democratic resistance to the Government and consequently decided to join en masse. Only nine months after joining, in November 1976, the entire left wing of the SLP was expelled at the party's first conference in Stirling, and a short-lived organisation — the Scottish Socialist League — was set up, comprising in bulk the former members of the IMG, with a number of other expellees from the Sillars' SLP. It formally "fused" with the IMG at a conference in the Spring of 1977. Set beside the expectations of the IMG at the onset of its "orientation" to the SLP a year earlier, this tactic, like those of all the rest of the revolutionary left, must be judged something of a failure, for it did not lead to large numerical gains or to any dramatic increase in the IMG's implantation inside the labour movement.

This is not to suggest that these have been years of total darkness for the revolutionaries. Each year a small but well-organised opposition to the STUC General Council has been mounted, often led by delegates from Trades Councils like Stirling and latterly Edinburgh, where the CP recently suffered a real bloody nose. In April 1978 Des Loughney, an SWP member and engineering worker from the Parsons Peebles plant in Edinburgh, succeeded in beating the CP's candidate, Brian Fallon, to become Trades Council Secretary, a full-time job made vacant by the elevation of the previous incumbent to a post with the STUC. The revolutionary "capture" of Scotland's second largest Trades Council was an important blow against the CP-Labour left in the East of Scotland, made all the more impressive by the rare degree of revolutionary unity between the IMG, SWP, RCG and WRP whose combined vote made it possible.

There are of course other, longer established footholds for the left. The Glasgow SWP's shop stewards in important plants like Chrysler, Yarrows and the District Council's Electrical Workshop are an impressive example of this. No other organisation (or significantly, any other SWP branch) can claim a similar strength. But these footholds are precisely that; no more than a sprinkling of members in a very limited part of the Scottish Labour movement, and entire sections of the Scottish workforce, such as the miners, remain alien territory.

Even more disappointing for the far left has been its failure to capitalise on the problems of the CP. Despite the fact that the Broad Left — a caucus of CP and Labour Lefts — has not met for over two years in the West of Scotland, the "Rank and File" has been unable to make any impact outside the white collar unions like the EIS and NALGO, the local government workers' union, and the project of replacing the old network of militant shop stewards across industry with a new "revolutionary" one, is still as distant as ever.

It would be tempting to ascribe the impasse of the far left to some error of judgment, as many on the left still do. But behind the mistaken prognosis of what would happen under the Wilson government, was a fundamental confusion, hesitation and ambiguity over some of the most decisive questions in politics, albeit what the left would call "bourgeois politics" — in particular a failure to understand the tenacity of reformism and Labourism and a myopic prejudice towards the dynamics of the "national question" north of the border.

To take the Labour Party first; nowhere did the party appear more vulnerable to a political challenge from the left than in Scotland. Dundee, Lanarkshire and Glasgow local parties were notorious for their inefficient corruption, with Mrs Catherine Cantley, a Gorbals Labour Councillor, forced to resign in April 1977, after allegations of favouritism in house allocation, epitomising a generation of local government complacency by Labour politicians, especially in the inner cities where their branches were in decay. According to a report prepared for Labour's National Executive Committee in 1975, the average Labour constituency party in Scotland has about 350 members although affiliation fees to the party are based on the assumption that each constituency party has at least 1,000 members.

Yet the Labour Party clearly retains considerable and surprising political reserves. Many members of left-wing groups see it at first hand through their membership of white collar unions like EIS (and to a lesser extent NALGO and the civil servants' union, the CPSA) where Labour Party members like EIS Secretary John Pollock have steered formerly "non-political" professional staff associations into the STUC and the broad labour movement. Instead of "labourism" being a dying and atrophied ideology as the left had projected, it proved itself capable of extending and reproducing itself among newly radicalising sections of the working population.

Just as impressive at another level was the continued intellectual vitality of the party. The publication of *The Red Paper on Scotland* in 1975 was a landmark. For the book was an attempt by socialists to analyse the changes seen in Scotland in recent years.[2] Edited by Gordon Brown, now prospective parliamentary Labour candidate for Edinburgh South and a member of the Scottish Executive of the party, the bulk of its 29 contributors were firmly inside the CP or left Labour camp, and despite the absence of a single article either by, or about, the half of Scotland's population who are female, its tone was radical and original. Nowhere could the revolutionary left point to a similar work of their own.

Needless to say, there were real and important limits to this left reformism. *The Red Paper* remained a literary exercise and any notions that the "leftism" of its themes could be translated into the campaign vigour of the *Tribune* groups of the early 1950s or of the CERES current inside the Socialist Party in France today, were still-born. Labour left-wing contributors like Gordon Brown and Robin Cook MP have been politically impotent in face of what must be the most right-wing government since the war. The dynamism of the Labour Party in Scotland, including of course its recent electoral successes against the SNP, have all been achieved under the firm direction of the right wing of the party. It is interesting to note in passing one demonstration of this right-wing dominance, in the choice of parliamentary candidates. With the success of Donald Dewar as Labour candidate in Garscadden and of George Robertson in Hamilton and the nomination to a supposedly safe seat of Dick Douglas, ex-MP for East Stirling, all of the key figures on the Labour right in Scotland are back on the Parliamentary trail. If the last years have been disappointing for the revolutionaries, they have been a tragedy for the Labour left.

But the hidden strengths of (right-wing) Labourism are not the only problems of "strategy" with which the revolutionaries have been struggling. Just as important has been the emergence of a nationalist movement and of demands for greater self-government which, quite simply, have baffled revolutionaries trained to react to the most direct and unmediated questions of class politics. The phenomenon of SNP bourgeois radicalism is outwith any past experience, and all too often the response of groups on the left has been to echo the confusion and conservatism of the official leaders of the labour movement.

Among all the major parties the subject has produced contortions and manoeuvres which are still being played out today: the Tories went from the pro-devolution "Declaration of Perth" ten years ago to today's rigid opposition, while Labour went in exactly the opposite direction. Its vehement opposition to any form of Assembly, although first challenged through the STUC in the late 1960s, was only finally smashed in the late summer of 1975 by a weighty combination of the Scottish trade unions and the London Cabinet of Harold Wilson at a specially held conference in Glasgow.

So the revolutionary left were not alone in their confusions and hesitations over the so called "national question", but on occasions they committed the ultimate in stupidities when faced with a novel political form — they just ignored it. Typical of this was the election campaign of Peter Porteous of the SWP in the 1978 Garscadden by-election where the entire issue of devolution, the Assembly and self determination did not even rate a mention in one of his leaflets. Bizarre though it may seem for a revolutionary group, supposedly radical and adventurous in its thinking, the break up of Britain's two-party system, the ten year political fight inside the Scottish labour movement and even the latest 40% "sabotaging clause" built into the referendum did not merit a line.

The SWP had, however, made previous attempts to formulate an analysis of contemporary change in Scotland in a pamphlet *Nationalism or Socialism — the SNP and the SLP exposed,* written in 1977 by one of their Edinburgh teacher members, Allan Armstrong. In it he argued that the decisive factor behind the rise of the SNP had been North Sea oil, because this changed the previous hostility of certain Scottish capitalists towards the SNP and, in his phrase, they gained "effective class backing". The clear implication of the argument was that nationalism was some sort of "capitalist plot" designed to carve up the oil money. And he therefore concluded: "Any attempt by an independent Scotland to change the priorities of international capitalism by means of a Scottish Parliament would be a thousand times more futile than King Canute's attempt to hold back the sea . . . The Scottish Assembly and greater Scottish control over oil revenues merely represent a change between capitalists over the heads of the workers."[3]

This intransigence towards any elected Assembly was also shared by the *Workers Action* group, although they gave their argument an extra twist by explaining that they were firmly in favour of a referendum to allow a democratic decision, but just as firmly in favour of a no vote against an Assembly. Ironically this supposed deduction from Leninist orthodoxy — for "self-determination" but against "separation" — found immediate convergence with the views of Robin Cook, MP, in whose constituency many of them worked. But it remains to be seen whether the self-proclaimed Trotskyists of *Workers Action* will end up in alliance with left Labourites to defend the Union.

In the early 1970s the IMG was almost as hostile to any form of self-government. In a pamphlet published in 1972, *Scotland, Labour and Workers' Power* they argued in similar terms regarding the class of the SNP (i.e. oil-hungry capitalists) and concluded with the slogan "The Assembly provides no solution — fight for a "Workers' Assembly". The exact nature of this strange "Workers' Assembly" remained vague, to say the least. The *Militant* current also confirmed the left's distaste for constitutional innovation north of the border, and in the years before the Wilson government consistently argued that the whole issue was irrelevant.

Some organisations were more sensitive to the changing political world around them, however, and by 1977 the IMG published *Socialists and the New Rise of Scottish Nationalism* which marked a firm change from its previous position. It argued that the essential nature of Scottish nationalism was middle-class radicalism, created by and given self-confidence by the social transformation of Scotland in the 1960s. It would therefore be naive and "ultra-left" for the revolutionary left to turn their backs on this demand for the extension of bourgeois democracy, the IMG argued, and they should actively fight for an elected Assembly for Scotland. In the same year the *Militant* current also re-thought their previous position. A long article by one of their leading members Pat Craven, appeared in their paper in February 1977, arguing that the Government's Devolution Bill had to be supported, and any limitations on the Assembly opposed, using arguments very similar to those of the IMG.

But none of this changes the fact that inside the far left groups, any appreciation of the growing autonomy of Scottish political life exists only among a minority. The attempt of the IMG to produce a journal, *Scottish Socialist,* which would relate the wider social, economic and cultural aspects of Scottish change to a socialist perspective, lasted only five issues. It was started by expelled members of the SLP in November 1976 and its last issue appeared in May/June 1977 just before the fusion of the remaining SLP expellees (called the "Scottish Socialist League") with the IMG. There have been no other attempts to relate to the increasing distinctiveness of politics in Scotland in a socialist way — no other journals, or political forums. The fate of publishing ventures from outside the far left in Scotland like the nationalist *Q* or *Seven Days* edited by Labour Party member, Brian Wilson, has only increased this conservatism among the revolutionaries.

This has left the revolutionaries passively watching the dramatic advance of the SNP among young people in central Scotland. Although studies of the social base of nationalist support are incomplete, it is generally agreed that the SNP has captured much of its solid support from young people, from whom the far left should be able to draw recruits. In England the Anti Nazi League (ANL) an anti-racist coalition spearheaded by the SWP, but with wide sections of the left participating, has been capable of reaching out to very large numbers of working-class youth, producing the largest far left demonstration for a decade with ANL Carnival in London in April 1978 attended by 80,000. So far, the left in Scotland has had no similar experiences in large-scale work among youth, and whether such political campaigning would involve approaches to SNP-influenced young people over questions like racism, democratic rights or even "international questions" like South Africa or Chile has not even been considered.

Outside the left-wing groups there were small but coherent forces who likewise expected a social crisis under Harold Wilson, but unlike the far left, actually expected it to take the form of nationalist turmoil. By far the most eccentric of these forces was the grandly named Scottish Workers Republican Party, formed in February 1974 with never more than a dozen members. It always favoured independence for Scotland, claiming to be part of the Home Rule tradition of socialism in Scotland stretching back to John MacLean, the Clydeside revolutionary of the First World War period. Like the IMG it decided to "enter" the SLP in 1976, but instead of being expelled, its political direction was to take it closer and yet closer to the leadership of Jim Sillars. Today the remnants of the SWRP, still inside the SLP, are famous mainly for their preference for the use of old Scots in their paper, *Scottish Worker*. Their rabid dislike of the "English" left and their couthie parochialism has made them into a caricature of the "small town democrat" so typical of the SNP in the 1950s, and they now produce a journal called *Crann-tara* which includes contributors from both the SLP and the SNP.

The other group which sought the mantle of John Mac-lean was the Maoist "Workers Party of Scotland", but their tiny size plus the confusion produced by the trial and conviction of their leading member Matt Lygate in 1972 has meant that an air of timelessness surrounds them and the journal *Scottish Van-*

guard where sturdy proletarians do battle with top-hatted capitalists. The publication, the party and its bookshop in Glasgow are unlikely to survive the retiral of Tom Murray, the aging and distinguished Stalinist who has led the organisation since its formation over ten years ago.

Back in the mainstream of the left, on the two decisive questions of political strategy — the hold of Labourism and the dynamic of the national movement — the left has had to lick its theoretical wounds. But the confusions and ambiguities seem to be only part of a much wider political problem: nowhere has the left managed to produce anything resembling an adequate theory or analysis of representative democracy, a form of political rule whose resilience has so confounded all their certainties of a few years ago. On other aspects of society the revolutionary left may yet prove to be more prescient. For example, their argument that Keynesian economics, (and the post-war boom they heralded) were only temporary palliatives for a fundamentally crisis-ridden economic structure, or their insistence on the "repressive nature" of the modern Atlantic state, many find vivid living proof in the not so distant future. This said, their inability to cope with the parliamentary democracy around them, is still an important, perhaps even decisive, failing

Part of the problem is that groups on the left often construct a notion of what the class struggle *should* look like, rather than examining the actual course of political conflicts and events. For instance, the growing women's liberation movement and the questions of sexuality and social relations associated with it are often denounced as "petty bourgeois". Nuclear power, and the international campaign against its use, have been largely ignored, and the growth of novel and complex forms of political expression such as support for measures of self-government tend to be seen as a distraction. This often goes hand in hand with an almost infantile arrogance, which the SWP summed up — in one of its own bulletins — as "a growth of triumphalism and organisational sectarianism, a contempt among sections of the (SWP) cadre for the non-SWP left".[4]

One of the most interesting attempts to break out of this impasse has been the development of "Socialist Unity" in Britain as a whole. It is sponsored by the IMG, with the support of small grouplets hardly present north of the border such as the

F

"International Socialist Alliance" based on ex-members of the SWP, and the "Big Flame" group, a strongly syndicalist organisation from Liverpool. In the English Council elections this May, Socialist Unity stood 24 candidates as a test run for fielding candidates in the General Election. Most results were naturally pretty modest, but three of their candidates polled over 10% and one of them, an IMG teacher Hilda Kean, received 21% in Spittalfields in London. In most areas where they stood, they defeated both the National Front and the Communist Party on a political platform that explicitly stated that electoralism and parliamentarianism were reformist illusions.

It is indeed striking that the revolutionary left in Scotland has not managed to mount any similar forays into the electoral arena where a much broader and more popular style of work is required than is the norm for left groups.

Of course there have been some on the left anxious to go beyond the limitations of the groups, to take up what could loosely be called political "culture" to deal with the concerns of the working population from a socialist viewpoint, without the (as they see it) "theology" of the far left's search for Leninist orthodoxy. The brief life of the magazine *Calgacus* with its three issues from Winter 1975 to Spring 1976 was an interesting example of this mood. Its editorial board drew together four of the best known non Labour Party, but non groupuscle names in Scotland — Hamish Henderson, Director of the School of Scottish Studies at Edinburgh University and later to join the SLP; John McGrath, playwright and founder of the 7.84 Theatre Group fresh from the huge success of their play "The Cheviot, Stag and Black, Black Oil"; Sorley Maclean, who remains Scotland's finest Gaelic poet, and Tom Nairn, an editor of *New Left Review* and a frequent and influential writer on the evolution and likely direction of the true Scottish "national soul". To this array of talent was added Harry McShane, contemporary of the great John Maclean and still keen despite his advancing years to add his support to any good revolutionary cause. Others on the board were a Welsh radical, Ned Thomas and an Irish Trotskyist, Brian Trench, with the entire venture edited by Ray Burnett living in the far outpost of Dornie in Ross-shire. Although, in the best traditions of impressive editorial boards, it never actually met, the composition of *Calgacus* demonstrated, as the *Red Papers* did a few years earlier, that among some sections of the left, at least the will, if not the means, existed to examine the specifics of Scottish life.

Its very first editorial argued the need to "accept and assimilate the separate development of Scottish society into socialist activity". This had nothing to do with the nationalist ramblings of sects like the SWRP or the WPS. In aspiration at least, it directed its attention to the real world and the real labour movement living in it. "Of necessity", the first editorial continued, the "industrial shop floor remains the arena where such potential (for socialism) is best demonstrated. But it is not the only one. There is also that large amorphous area of life vaguely referred to as the "cultural".[5]

This important idea of fusing labour movement activity with wider cultural and social changes in society never really got off the ground. The first edition started with "Europe's forgotten minorities" dealing with Brittany, continued with five articles on Ireland, some material on Wales and a straight advertisement for the SNP by one of its prospective parliamentary candidates. Scotland was seen as part of some cultural chain of Celtic nations, and later issues developed this theme with exhaustive inquiries into the contribution to Scottish culture of the old Scots language. Translated to a country dominated by the Strathclyde conurbation with its very different traditions of popular culture and life, *Calgacus* became almost an object lesson in irrelevance. The alliance between the folk revivalists of the Edinburgh literari and the Celtic populists of Wester Ross proved to be politically and, more importantly, financially unstable, and Scotland's most adventurous socialist journal was swamped by bankruptcy.

This sensitivity of *Calgacus* to the question of "culture", no matter how ineffective the journal was in dealing with it, came from a remarkable shift in Edinburgh University in the early 1970s and in particular from the development of the Edinburgh University Student Publications Board. "Pubs Board" was the publisher of *The Red Paper,* but was and is truly catholic in its tastes. It was the strange combination of a Maoist student, Chic Maisels, and that previously noted expert on Scottish oral culture, Hamish Henderson, who attempted to insert one of European Marxism's most illustrious thinkers on precisely the subject of "culture" into the minds of the Scottish left. Under the editorship of Maisels *The New Edinburgh Review* was transformed from a lethargic and pretentious student journal into a vehicle for translating and discussing the writings of Antonio Gramsci, the Italian Marxist who died in one of Mussolini's prison and was (posthumously) author of the resulting "Prison Notebooks".[6]

Crudely put, the general theme of "Gramsci-ism" is that the bourgeoise of the West rule by "consent" whereas the bourgeoise of the East (including pre-1917 Russia) ruled essentially by "coercion". Therefore it follows that great attention must be paid to the nuances of culture and ideology which form the bonds tying the masses to capitalism, including of course nationalism, regionalism and other forms of "non working-class" ideas. Naturally, such a university-based project as Maisels and Henderson embarked on through NER could only be limited, and often the political editing and introductions left much to be desired. Even so, there must have been few who thought that these Gramscian plants produced around 1973 would find the Scottish left such a stony soil.

If the organised left groups were either lethargic about or even openly hostile to taking up the wide array of problems of everyday life — sexual, cultural, social — other forces were "spontaneously" to emerge which would. Above all, the women's movement in Scotland has emerged in the last two years, spanning issues as wide as finance and independence (for women, that is), equal pay and abortion. It is this latter issue above all which threatens to become a major issue in political life in Scotland, with the Catholic Church and the Society for the Protection of the Unborn Child (SPUC) making themselves felt in their anti-abortion intervention into the Garscadden by-election. The revolutionary left were active in challenging them — the IMG working through the National Abortion Campaign, the SWP women through their journal *Women's Voice* — but it will be the women's liberation movement which will play a decisive part in deciding how that challenge is met. In the specifically Scottish context, a journal, *Scottish Women's Liberation Journal,* has now run to four issues, all of which have sold out. It is doubtful today if any new equivalent of *The Red Paper* were to be devised, that women's rights would be so easily ignored.

Other activist movements are growing thick and fast. The anti-nuclear movement has clearly only just started with its successful rally against the proposed Torness nuclear power station. There is also the Conference of Socialist Economists, originally a small group of academics (organised on a UK basis) and now a rapidly growing forum for debate inside the revolutionary left.

These developments may be encouraging for the revolutionaries, but they are overshadowed by the failures and difficulties seen earlier. Although the Labour left and the "centrists" in between cannot take much comfort either, ten years after 1968 it is the revolutionaries who must feel the most frustrated by their lack of growth and development. Ironically all the signs are present that this stagnation is changing: there has been the recent numerical growth of the SWP to around 5,000 members nationally, the political successes of Socialist Unity, but above all, the dramatic scale of the Anti-Nazi League whose Carnival generated an excitement and *élan* not seen since precisely ten years ago, since the days of the campaign against US involvement in Vietnam. All the better reason perhaps to look soberly and calmly at some of the lessons of the last few years, before they are lost in yet another lurch forward into political space.

REFERENCES

1. International. Spring, 1976.

2. *The Red Paper on Scotland.* Edited Gordon Brown, E.U.S.P.B. 1975.

3. *Nationalism or Socialism — the SNP and the SLP exposed.* Allan Armstrong. He has since modified his position. See *Some Criticisms of the Left's Analysis.*

4. Members' Bulletin. January 1978.

5. *Calgacus.* Volume I.

6. *Antonio Gramsci. Letters from Prison. Political History and Conference Papers.* Collected edition of three special issues of New Edinburgh Review. E.U.S.P.B. 1975.

7

LOCAL HEALTH COUNCILS: THE CONSUMERS' VOICE*

DOROTHY BOCHEL and MORAG MACLARAN

Department of Social Administration, University of Dundee

The voice of the consumer in the health service was given statutory recognition for the first time by the invention of local health councils whose sole function is to represent the interests of the public in the health service. Health councils were set up in Scotland in 1975 (they appeared a little earlier as community health councils in England and Wales), following the reorganisation of the health service. They have no executive power; they can offer advice. There are forty-eight such bodies with memberships varying from twelve to thirty-one, and representing populations ranging from 6,690 to 476,635.

The bodies charged with receiving and taking account of the health councils' advice are the fifteen health boards. Each health board is responsible to the Secretary of State for the planning and management of all health services in its area. The boards took over in 1974 the functions of outgoing regional hospital boards, hospital boards of management, executive councils and local authority health committees. A single body and one-tier system thus replaced a tripartite and partly two-tier system. For purely administrative purposes some boards have constituted "management districts" run by district executive groups, composed of four senior officers, and responsible to an area executive group at board level.

The number of health councils in a board area varies considerably. The Orkney, Shetland and Borders health boards have only one council each, whereas there are eight in the Highland board's area. Decisions as to number and geographical boundaries were made by health boards using a variety of criteria and

*This paper is based on data acquired in the course of research into the establishment and the first two years' operation of the local health council system, for which financial support was received from the Scottish Office.

bearing in mind the administrative structure they had already adopted. Where management districts had been established, the precept usually followed was that there should be at least one local health council to each district. Since local authority district boundaries were taken into consideration when management districts were set up, there is usually some clear relationship between local health council and local authority boundaries.

Until reorganisation, the system had included a substantial number of lay participants. Health councils were in part an attempt to compensate for the reduction of lay involvement in health service management at a time when a movement towards participation was much in vogue. Health councils could also be regarded as a gesture towards those concerned that centralisation would increase the gap between the governors and the governed. The rationale for national health service reorganisation was managerial efficiency, and the health councils have been cited as one of the "imaginative participative mechanisms"[1] which might help to redeem the bureaucratic nature of the health service.

Local health councils were born into a largely unfavourable environment. In recent years participation and consumerism have made great strides elsewhere in Britain, but in Scotland there has been little demand for participation; and while one person in 92 of the population in Britain is a member of the Consumers Association, in Scotland only one in 131 is a member. The Scottish consumer tends to be characterised by acquiescence, stoicism and, especially where the health service is involved, by gratitude. Dissatisfactions rarely get beyond the stage of grumbling. The chairman of the Scottish Consumer Council, Joan Macintosh, has stated that

> Scottish consumers are less inclined than English consumers to exert themselves, either individually or in groups, against rising prices, monopoly exploitation or infringment of their legal rights.

One health council participant attributed this torpor to a peculiar "Scottish conservatism", and an activist on behalf of patients believes that "backwardness in claiming our rights" is due to a deeply rooted "fear of standing out from the crowd". The historian, T. C. Smout, recently described Scots as "suspicious of one another, conservative and inflexible".[2]

Smout indicts the education system: ". . . the Scottish working class and middle class alike has been exposed for a century
to a miserable education system . . . which believes that
teaching consists of trying to smash facts into children."[3]
Another oft condemned influence on Scottish life is the restric-
tive legacy of Calvinism. Also, the established church in Scotland
maintains an influence, especially in public life, not matched by
its counterpart in England. Its ministers still tend to be accorded
the status of "community leaders", and whilst many of them
individually are innovative and decidedly not conservative in the
peculiar Scottish manner, it would seem unlikely that this
hierarchical set-up could encourage greater lay participation.

With these peculiar Scottish disadvantages, the Scottish
health service consumer is in an even weaker position than
patients elsewhere. The lowly status of patients has been well-
documented and Margaret Stacey thus explains the dilemma:

> There is first of all the difference in knowledge and skill
> between the doctor and the patient: the "competence gap".
> There is the fact that in general terms most patients are far
> less highly educated than doctors and do not readily treat them
> as social equals. The nature of illness itself is relevant. When
> ill, patients are not in a good position to argue; when well,
> they seem not to care.[4]

The public consistently records high levels of satisfaction
with the health service. A recent poll showed 45% of those
questioned to be "very satisfied" with the NHS and 39% were
"fairly satisfied".[5] Ann Cartwright, discussing patients' satisfaction with general practitioner services, judges that ". . . behind
the satisfaction of most patients there lies an uncritical acceptance and lack of discrimination which is conducive to stagnation
and apathy".[6] The belief that the British health service is the
best in the world tends to militate against any activity which
might rock the boat. Within health service circles there is much
stress on consensus and a naive faith in the possibility of a "best
possible health service for the public". The existence of competing interests, professional or public, receives little recognition
and, in a service where political decisions on allocation of
resources have to be made, much play is made of the need
to keep politics out of the health service.

The health service tends to be reluctant to give information
about its policies even where decision-making is overt. While

health boards meet in public, decisions are made in private in committee. This makes it easy to dismiss critics as uninformed. Whilst other professionals — teachers, for example — are regarded as fair game for public criticism and it is the "done thing" to have views on how the education system should be run, the health service professionals are relatively little criticised and expert opinion tends to weigh heavily. When criticisms of health service provision are made, there is a tendency to make a special point of exonerating the staff; for example, "Despite heroic efforts by the staff it is still a depressing hospital", or, "Staff doing their best in very poor buildings".[7] Former patients write letters to local newspapers expressing gratitude for the care received whilst in hospital. We cannot recall coming across a letter of thanks for a wonderful education received. Joan Macintosh judges that health councils will have an uphill battle "if Scottish laymen are ever to show the courage to stand up to the professionals".

The problems involved in getting a consumer body specially concerned with health services off the ground in such an environment were compounded by the fact that severe reservations existed within the health service itself about the introduction of such an innovation. Coming so soon after the upheavals of reorganisation, the prospect of an additional and particularly a new type of input which might further disturb the balance of power was viewed with some anxiety by many in the health service. Scepticism existed about the ability of such bodies to represent the interests of the public (which some saw as a responsibility of health board members). The disappointing performance of consultative councils in the nationalised industries was quoted as evidence that such a system could not work.

It was anticipated that local health councils would be "a pain in the neck", "a thorn in the flesh"; that they might be "too political" or provide a forum for grumbling and complaints. A frequently quoted administrative reason for not welcoming them was that health boards were already feeling the burden of having to consult "a myriad of advisers". An obligation to consult local health councils in addition to bodies such as professional advisory committees, local authorities and trade unions was seen as compounding existing difficulties.

Concern about a possible erosion of power of board members and of officers was implicit in the fear that local health councils might trespass on the management role, and in the contention that they were being given too large or too vague a remit, or would fail to stay within it.

An important source of doubt emanates from a strongly-held view that the professionals know best about policy, and that, because of the complexity and technical content of planning and decision-making, local health councils composed of "lay people" and lacking "professional" advice could have little or no contribution to make. Some wondered why highly-paid officials were employed, only to have less knowledgeable persons monitor and question their work. In particular, planning and the assessment of the general quality and adequacy of services, which the Scottish Office had suggested might figure among the interests of health councils,[8] were seen as professional and management preserves. The importance with which the medical profession a two- to a one-tier management system, the proposed health service is illustrated by the statement in the report of a working-party of doctors set up by the Secretary of State to consider the organisation of medical work in a reorganised service:

> It is the profession that has the fullest knowledge about the present medical work of the health service, about current trends and about future possibilities. This information, and guidance on its interpretation, should, in our view, be the foundation on which policy and management decisions are made.[9]

Mr William Ross anticipated professional reservations when he observed in the course of the passage of the Bill that "the medical profession hold up their hands in horror when they hear about public participation".[10]

Not everyone, of course, was against the idea. To some who had strongly opposed the change upon reorganisation from a two- to a one-tier management system the proposed health councils represented some compensation for what they had valued in a lower tier; they were "necessary to take the place of old boards of management" since "reorganisation means the consumer is unrepresented". Lay participation in management such as had existed under the old system had not itself come under much criticism — it had had to be sacrificed to other goals. It was a form of participation the parameters of which were known and accepted by both laymen and professionals.

Dilys Hill has pointed out that in health service bodies "the dominant set of conventions come from the traditions of the medical profession and the full-time administrators", and

> the lay members must work within a framework of accepted rules and procedures which they can do little to change . . . The members of the stage army are drawn into an efficient and self-perpetuating system which induces strong loyalties.[11]

But to the more perspicacious the new form of participation conjured up the prospect of the involvement of a different sort of lay person, and in a different relationship with those operating the service. They foresaw a possibility that bodies of this kind could turn out to be "irresponsible", "merely anti-health board", or "only strident and destructive critics".

At best, local health councils were considered as potentially useful in pointing out gaps or specific problems about waiting or transport, as assisting with health education projects or explaining constraints to the public. It was not envisaged that they should be involved in decision-making concerning, for example, the definition of objectives or the allocation of resources. These were seen as management activities. Health board administrators, as was consistent with the conventional British image of the good public servant, whilst largely sceptical of the advantages to be gained, took the pragmatic attitude that "if Parliament has decided we are going to have local health councils, we must co-operate as best we can"; or, slightly more constructively, that now councils were to come they would try to "make them work".

Outwith the health service, voluntary organisations welcomed local health councils as an additional channel for involvement and influence in public life as well as an opportunity to further their objectives. The trade unions, though regarding health councils as a poor substitute for a health service run by elected bodies, were smarting under what they considered to be unfair treatment in the apportionment of health board seats. They were therefore keen to gain influence in the health council system and requested (and were granted, as unions south of the border were not), a specific allocation of seats on the local health councils. Others, particularly in the Labour movement, to whom reorganisation represented an erosion of "democracy", were interested to ensure that health councils, as the only readily available compensatory element, were as effective as possible.

Since the legislation contained only very basic provisions relating to the health council system, much was seen to hang on subsequent ministerial prescription and guidance. Those interests external to the health service expressed views about the essential requirements to ensure that local health councils could operate effectively. The independence of health councils from health boards, and their provision with adequate powers and resources, were regarded as of particular importance.

When, therefore, the Scottish Office had to make firm decisions about the health council system, it was aware on the one hand of the "lobby" interested in ensuring that health councils were in a position to be effective as consumer bodies, and on the other of the anxieties and lack of conviction of many in the health service. Klein has drawn attention to the importance of organisational factors or bureaucratic politics in policy-making. It may be that the civil servants in this situation were "reluctant to risk a confrontation" with the health service interests, not necessarily because they agreed with them about health councils but because they put high value on maintaining good relations with them since they depend upon them for the day-to-day running of the health service and "as a form of investment for the future".[12] At any rate they managed to put together a set of prescriptions which on the face of it took care of the immediate anxieties of the non-health-service interests whilst leaving to the health boards considerable latitude to "contain" the health councils once they began to operate.

Fears about insufficient independence stemmed from a desire that health councils should have every opportunity of being "consumer" rather than "service" oriented. Members on both sides in Parliament had expressed anxieties on this score: there was a danger that councils would be "inseminated, gestated, produced and weaned"[13] by the health boards; "sometimes consultative bodies turn out to be the creatures of the executive bodies they are supposed to advise".[14] Such anxieties were met by allowing health boards relatively little control over the personnel to be appointed to health councils even though they theoretically appointed two-thirds of them.[15]

It was further decided that the post of secretary to local health councils should be open and not, as might have been the case, confined to health service employees. Although employees of the health boards for salary and other purposes, secretaries are regarded as in the service of the local health council and accountable to it.[16] Secretaries have come from a very wide variety of backgrounds, about a quarter of which might be labelled "health service". Some difference of opinion exists about the advantage or otherwise of a council having a secretary with a health service background. Did "knowing the ropes" — and in some instances the people — compensate for the possible disadvantage of having been "socialised" into the values and perceptions of the service providers?

When local health councils were under discussion, the ideal office for them was envisaged as a shop front in the High Street. Few achieved this, and most councils are located within health service premises, while half a dozen of the smaller councils operate from the secretary's home. These arrangments do not assist in making the councils accessible to the public and most have expressed disappointment about the extent to which they have been "used" by the public.

Lack of information about proposals and plans is often cited as a major obstacle to meaningful public participation in policy-making. Some attempt to preclude this was made in the regulations relating to health councils. These made it the duty of a health board

> to provide each Council in its area with such information
> about the planning and operation of the health service in the
> area . . . as the Council may reasonably require in order to
> carry out its functions.[17]

Such a regulation is clearly open to interpretation, and health councils have enjoyed differential success with their boards over requests for information. One of the larger boards told the Scottish Office at the outset that it foresaw difficulty in fulfilling even "reasonable requirements" for information. A ministerial decision in England and Wales to give community health councils the right to non-voting "observer" membership of their Area Health Authorities (the lower of two tiers) considerably strengthened their powers of access to information. No similar right exists in Scotland.

In view of the more parsimonious resources afforded to community councils, it might well be construed that the Government responded handsomely to fears that health councils would lack effectiveness on account of inadequate resources. Most health councils appear satisfied with their annual budgets which range from about £3,000 to £12,500. This enables them to employ a secretary, either full- or part-time, and most also to have secretarial help. The rest has to cover postage and telephone costs, members' expenses, publicity and other activities.

The satisfaction of health councils may be a realistic assessment of the balance of power rather than of the real cost of performing their function; but it may also reflect their perception of their task and of its relative value in the national health service. In our opinion health councils were given minimal resources for their work. They are as a David to the health board Goliath, and largely lack compensatory skills such as were possessed by the former. Certainly they do not approach being the "counter bureaucracies" considered necessary by Klein if the consumer's position in the national health service is to be strengthened.[18]

Although it went through the motions of ensuring that local health councils would be equipped with the necessary rights and resources, the Scottish Office provided minimal guidance about what the new bodies were really supposed to do and how they should go about it. It was

> for each local health council to decide how best to fulfil its statutory role of representing the interests of the public in the health service in the district for which it is set up. In general it will review the operation of the health services and make recommendations for improvements and will otherwise advise the Health Board on any matters relating to the operation of the health service . . . It will consider questions at the request of the Health Board, the Secretary of State, or on its own initiative.[19]

Whilst this might appear satisfactory on paper, in practice most new health councils were at something of a loss. One member observed:

> If local health councils are expected to become effective, the Home and Health Department would require to clarify the remit not only to the councils but to the health boards, district administrators, hospitals, doctors and all concerned. So far we seem to be operating in a cotton-wool limbo, left to find our own way and level.

One health board official observed that they seemed "mixed up about what to do". The Scottish Office failed to provide examples of what might be construed as "the interests of the public" — a matter not likely to be evident to most lay people in view of what we have described as the prevailing milieu into which councils were born. The relative power, interests and values of the various participants in the health service have been little rehearsed in public. Nor did they indicate whether "representing" entailed ascertaining the views of the public — as was made clear in the case of community councils — or whether they should construe themselves as inherently "representative". No "training" independent of what health boards chose to provide was arranged as was the case when the Children's Hearings system was introduced. Nor did the Scottish Office seem to have been prepared to emulate the arrangement made by the Department of Health and Social Security in England and Wales to provide initial support for councils by appointing independent advisers, part of whose job was "to offer informal advice to individual CHCs". Instead, it resorted to the more timid step of appointing as liaison officer for a period of six months one of its own officials. Even this was resented by health boards.

Beyond that the Scottish Office retreated from the scene, leaning heavily on the principle that "councils should look to district executive groups and, where appropriate, area executive groups for any advice, support and information they require".[20] Health boards readily accepted the emphasis on local health councils' relationships with district executive groups; some appeared to use such distancing from area level as one of the ways of keeping the councils within bounds.

It is our contention that much more vigorous and imaginative steps were necessary on the part of the Scottish Office to compensate adequately for the disadvantages likely to be encountered by statutory consumer bodies in the health service. They not only failed to inject adequate compensation; they additionally tried to head off any possibility of conflict, as also did other "establishment" spokesmen, by repeated references to the need for the relationship between board and council to be one of co-operation and partnership, by reminding local health councils (on the basis of doubtful fact) that they had "placed on them the responsibility to consider and take account of the problems of management", and by urging that criticism be "constructive". Additionally, as had been feared by some in Parliament, councils were expected to act on occasion as a kind of public relations agency for the board by "assisting in interpreting the health board's objectives to the community".[21]

It may be that in the light of their perceptions of the attitudes of many in the service, the taking of such a line was considered essential by the Scottish Office if the local health council system was to get off the ground at all and not to be the cause of an unacceptable level of dissatisfaction on the part of health boards and their employees. At a gathering of local health council office-bearers, a senior official told his audience that the Department was trying to monitor the new system and to advise and guide behind the scenes. They were interested in what local health councils were thinking, but the health boards were "nervous" about councils communicating with the Department on purely local matters which were within the responsibility of the boards. There and elsewhere[22] reference was made by the Department to the desirability of there being a national organisation of local health councils. Delegates were told that without a national organisation "the voice of . . . councils might go by the board in matters of national policy". Whilst making no secret of its desire to see the establishment of such a body, the Scottish Office regarded it as essential that any initiative should stem from the councils themselves. Although a substantial minority of councils were opposed to the move, a national association was inaugurated in September 1977. Despite approving objectives which include engaging in research, the provision of information, and the development and organisation of training, the councils were reluctant to accord the association more than minimal resources. This cautious approach mirrored earlier unwillingness on the part of councils to appoint full-time secretaries. We have no reason to believe that, in either case, this was due to Scottish Office parsimony. In fact their liaison officer chided one council for contemplating less than full-time staff.

Since consumerism was so little developed in Scotland, perhaps more consideration should have been given to the membership of local health councils. As it was, the members of the new bodies were expected to adopt a consumer perspective without necessarily having had a previous interest in it and certainly without any special effort being made to help them develop such an orientation. The National Consumer Council has remarked on the tendency of members of consultative councils in the nationalised industries to "become identified with", and to sympathise too readily with their industries in the light of knowledge of the constraints and of the sometimes unjustified criticisms which they experience, thus being distracted from a single-minded pursuit of their own role.[23] The sources from which local health council members were recruited made such an occurrence more likely than it might otherwise have been, even given the general climate we referred to earlier. Apart from the third of the membership of each council directly appointed by the local authorities, just over one third were appointed on the nomination of voluntary bodies and about one eighth by trade unions; a further eighth were persons chosen by the health board itself because of their "special knowledge of the health service".[24]

The members of this last-mentioned group were drawn overwhelmingly from the pool of one-time members of now defunct boards and executive councils; thus they had experience mainly of the problems of management. They also had know-how about how the health service works, which was potentially useful to local health councils; but a leap of imagination was required to move from a service to a consumer orientation. Nevertheless, the experience of these members seemed to be highly regarded by others on the new councils, and a disproportionate number from this group were appointed chairman or vice-chairman. That there were a considerable number of resignations of members of this group in the first year of the health councils' operation is perhaps indicative of the difficulty found in adjusting to a different role.

A similar shift in orientation may have been required of the voluntary sector nominees. A substantial proportion of these members came from organisations which had long-standing and close associations with the health service in a "helping" capacity, for example Friends of Hospitals and the Women's Royal Voluntary Service. This group may have been used to a perspective not necessarily reconcilable with consumerism. Only two persons came into this group of members through nomination by a consumer body.

The bodies from which members were drawn — which incidentally were very similar to those which suggested names

G

for health board appointments — strongly influenced the age, socio-economic class and sex composition of the membership. In practice, because bodies almost without exception nominated their own members, it was necessary to be a member of some organisation in order to be nominated; and indeed many members were office-bearers in their organisations. There is ample evidence to indicate that members of local authorities are more likely to be male, older and from a higher socio-economic class than the populations they serve; that more males than females join trade unions; that membership of voluntary organisations is a more middle- than working-class activity, and that there is a positive relationship between occupational status and leadership positions in voluntary organisations.[25]

It is not therefore surprising that local health councils, like health boards and many other public bodies, are not "representative" of their populations in a microcosmic or "mirror image" sense. A survey of local health council members in Scotland undertaken by the authors in 1976 found that males outnumbered females by 3 to 2 — a more balanced sex representation than on most public bodies, and attributable to the fact that the voluntary organisation nominees, apart from those of the Church of Scotland, were largely female. There were no members under the age of 25, persons under 35 and over 70 were substantially under-represented (appointment of the latter having been prohibited except in special circumstances); and those between 45 and 69 were very much over-represented. 80% of the membership came within the non-manual category of socio-economic class while only 40% of the population of Scotland is so classified. Within the non-manual group a disproportionate number of members came from professional and managerial categories. And within the under-represented manual category, skilled workers accounted for 15% of the membership, semi-skilled and unskilled for only 3%. In fact, there was only one unskilled manual worker among the respondents in our survey. Whilst manual workers may be under-represented among respondents we know that many non-respondents were not in fact from this group. And whereas only 29% of the population of Scotland are owner-occupiers, 64% of the local health council membership fell into this category.[26] In these respects the membership of Scottish health councils is very similar to that of their English and Welsh counterparts,[27] though in Scotland there is a more marked tendency towards maleness, greater age and higher socio-economic class.

Discrepancies of this nature between councils and the public in their districts are sometimes accepted as inevitable or even desirable. Members needed to be articulate enough to deal with people like him, said one official. But such a lack of "fit" does open councils to the criticism of not being "really representative": "The councils are being peopled with eager-beavers who do not represent the community"; "members . . . are not necessarily truly men-in-the-street citizens"; "the method of selecting members . . . does not in the end produce a representative cross-section". Criticisms of this kind can be invoked to devalue the advice of a council. And devaluation is thought all the more defensible if it appears that a council is not making strenuous efforts — resources or no — to consult "the public".

With little guidance to assist the health councils in working out their role, inevitably a variety of styles and interpretations have developed. Differences in councils' perception of role are apparent when asked by the boards for the public view. This can be illustrated by examination of councils' responses to the question of fluoridation of the public water supply. Health boards consulted health councils in the course of deciding whether to provide the funds should the water authorities (the regional councils) agree to fluoridation which was being pushed by the central government. As one health council said, this was an "explosive issue" since it appeared that more members of the public were willing to express views on this subject than on most health-related topics. In one way however, it was an issue only peripheral to the concerns of the health councils since the boards, like the councils, could only make recommendations; the final say rested with the regional councils.

Health councils were inundated with "anti" literature from the Scottish Pure Water Association, and "pro" literature from the dental interests. Debates were held in some areas with speakers from both sides. In one area, the health board specifically asked the health councils to ascertain public opinion, but elsewhere any decision to seek out the views of the public was left to the councils. Four or five councils sought the views of the public through the local press, one contacted voluntary bodies, and two held public meetings; the public meetings were

poorly attended and judged by the councils to be unrepresenta-
tive; one of the two councils involved in this exercise voted
contrary to the vote of the public meeting.

Most councils, however, studied the evidence for and
against and took a vote, slightly more councils coming down
in favour of fluoridation than against. Some felt disquiet at
voting on their own account. One council regretted that the
timing of the consultation had prevented any testing of public
opinion; and a number of council members personally in favour
of fluoridation voted against in view of what they judged as
public opposition to fluoridation. There was also some concern
expressed over the local authority representatives voting by
party line. In debates which resulted in a "pro" vote there was
some element of the councils' regarding themselves as guardians
of the public interest. Rather like MPs who take a liberal line
on issues like capital punishment, some health councillors
supported a leadership role while recognising that they were
"in advance" of public opinion.

For the health councils, it had been a disruptive and
perhaps instructive exercise. Not only did they have to give some
consideration to the way in which they saw their own role in
representing the interests of the public, but some indications of
boards' perceptions of the role of health councils became
apparent. One council chairman had judged the fluoridation
question as "custom-built as an issue upon which the local health
councils were ideally designed to advise area boards"; when the
board voted in the opposite way he was convinced "that the
views of the local health councils are not significant in the
workings of the health service in this area" and resigned, taking
along with him the vice-chairman and two members. One
health board did not wait for the advice of its health councils
before taking its decision, and in another area the health board
asked the councils which had voted against to inform the board
of the steps they had taken "to canvass opinion in this district"
while those councils which had agreed with the board were not
requested to supply this information.

As well as roles implying "leadership" or reflection of public
opinion, health councils have been cast in the roles of helper,
critic and apologist for the health boards. The roles of "helper"
and "critic" to some extent overlap, but criticism is not always
construed as helpful by officials who at times judge that it is

based on a less than full appreciation of the factors involved. It is not always possible to make criticism "constructive" and very easy to label it "unconstructive". The identification of "gaps" or deficiencies in service is widely agreed to be a legitimate function of local health councils. One council drew attention to the lack of a clinic facility which "had escaped the notice of those providing the service". Another identified a gap in provision in the shape of

> support for [mentally handicapped] children under school-age and for their parents who tend to become isolated in the early and formative years after the hospital had completed its care and before the Education Service is able to cater for them.[28]

This council has used its initiative "despite a rather discouraging reply" from the district executive group of the health board, to set up a working party composed of people within and without the health service to investigate the possibility for setting up a Centre for such children and thier parents. It is, however, a frequent contention in health board circles that health councils "never come up with anything not already known by health board people".

One unequivocal example of a "helping" role was urged upon councils when health education began to be pushed. The Government's consultative document "Prevention and health — everybody's business" stated that ". . . local health councils have a special responsibility for developing the preventive aspects of their work".[29] The Scottish Health Education Unit and the Scottish Council for Health Education co-sponsored regional conferences designed for the health councils during 1977; these were entitled "Health Councils — A Role in Health Education". Health council delegates were told, "If local health councils . . . perceive and understand the message of prevention and health, the contribution they can make to the health of the community will be immense".[30] Some health boards welcomed the idea that there was a role for health councils in health education "at the right cost". One official thought that involvement in health education "would give them something to do since they're here". Cynics might say that health education was regarded as a relatively harmless channel for the health councils' enthusiasm and energies.

Many health councils willingly accepted this role, believing that this was "a field in which local health councils can hope to have some influence". [31] Not all endorsed this view, and indeed some which did accept the emphasis on health education have been unable to find the mechanics necessary for putting this role into practice.

One of the earliest approaches to health councils came from the pressure group Action on Smoking and Health (ASH). About a dozen health councils subsequently banned smoking at their own meetings, several approached the local authorities in an attempt to restrict smoking on buses and in public places with little success, and one council asked the Red Cross to stop selling cigarettes in hospitals. One or two councils were worried about infringement of the smokers' liberty. Aberdeen local health council was particularly active on this issue and set up a working party "to deal with Aberdeen's easy-going attitude towards smoking in public places".[32] By letter and personal approaches the working party persuaded about a dozen restaurants to offer non-smoking tables and others agreed to display a wall sign requesting customers not to smoke. The council distributed an ASH notice for display in tobacconists' shops pointing out the legal age requirement relating to the sale of cigarettes. The council is at present co-operating with other bodies (such as the health education department, community councils and the Medical Sociology Unit) in setting up a self-help group for smoking withdrawal problems.

Health councils have also considered the problem of alcoholism and several have assisted in getting local councils on alcoholism off the ground. A number are currently engaged in distributing Kidney Donor Cards. One council enlisted the aid of some 80 local employers and the community councils and have now distributed 17,000 cards. The secretary of this council found that in this exercise they were tapping "a terrific fund of public goodwill" which supports any efforts directed towards health matters. Currently, some councils are supporting the new "Fit for Life" campaign by distributing leaflets or actively participating.

The ideals behind the specific activities councils have taken up in the interests of health education are lofty indeed. The Perth and Kinross council supported "encouragement of preventive measures and the development of a fully responsible attitude to health on the part of the individual".[33] Obviously, this is a long-term goal and it is understandable if frustration sets in. A council which found suggestions on its role in health education "too airy fairy" found its three positive suggestions — for a "Stop Smoking" clinic, a clinic for alcoholics, and a display of health education literature in a new ante-natal clinic — immediately turned down by the board's health education officer. The councils' efforts in this area are not always welcomed and we were told by several senior health board officials that health education was a matter for the professionals.

Closely related to the "helping" role is the role of board's apologist which appears in the official guidance as "assisting in interpreting the Health Board's objectives to the community".

> Local health councils may well find themselves in the role of explaining to the community why a particular proposal for improving the health service . . . cannot be implemented immediately.[34]

When the health board have got advice and taken a decision, it is "up to the local health council to convey this to the populace" said one health board chairman. Although to our knowledge health councils have not all specifically rejected such a role, they have not espoused it either. Even where they have agreed with the board on an issue, they have been wary of giving the appearance of being "the board's mouthpiece".

There have been differences of opinion about the "level" at which local health councils should represent the interests of the public in the health service. Some consider that local health councils "need to know the minutiae; the health board needs to look at bigger things". Others consider that the councils have been too concerned with the "day-to-day running" of the service and with "trivial matters". "Local health councils should not be talking about the drains." Perhaps one factor militating against their looking at larger issues which have wider implications than for their own district, is that there is no provison for a consumer voice at area level, whereas professional advisory bodies to the board exist at both district and area level, the latter appearing to be regarded by the health board as the more important.

Visits to hospitals and other establishments have been a feature of the activity of most councils. This may have been a means of getting to know the facilities; it is also reminiscent of the practice of boards of management and an activity which it was easy for health boards to suggest and arrange when health councils came into being. Perhaps partly as a result of this, but also because the quality of physical facilities is more easily assessed than parts of the service that are even more labour intensive, such as community nursing, local health councils were initially much concerned with hospital aspects of the service. There has been little, but perhaps growing interest in the general practitioner service, but like the health boards themselves, health councils are in a weak position *vis-à-vis* general practitioners because of their status as "independent contractors".

It was envisaged that health councils would become activated in the face of proposed changes of use or closure of health service facilities. Some councils got off to an active start as a result of having an issue such as this to deal with, and were indeed "envied" by others which found it more difficult to discover a role. In one or two cases councils which have agreed to the withdrawal of a facility have been out of line with organised public opinion and have found themselves "taking the stick" along with the board.

Where councils have disagreed with board proposals and some modification in plans has resulted it is, of course, unwise to attribute this to health council pressure. As Pickvance has pointed out it is insufficient to assume that "an antecedent event causes a subsequent event" and in particular that action or advice by advisers or external bodies is the cause of a particular decision on the part of the authorities.[35] Nevertheless, one health council was satisfied that its mobilisation of public opinion had resulted in the retention of a limited obstetric service in an outlying cottage hospital, when it was feared that this service would have been withdrawn completely. Certainly, the board's working party had agreed

> that there were no valid paediatric or obstetric reasons for the continuation of the general practitioner obstetric unit . . . the only arguments in favour of the retention of the general practitioner obstetric unit were those based on social grounds.

The contention by health boards that removal of a facility as a result of centralisation will lead to the provision of a "better service" if at a greater distance and at greater inconvenience

to patients is a recurrent theme. The onus is on health councils
to argue on social grounds and to point out that what may
appear to be a saving to the health service is merely a shift of
costs in the form of travelling expenses on to patients, relatives
and staff. A difference in values becames apparent on issues such
as these between the providers of the service and the consumers.
Some health councils have already recognised this divergence and
we would contend that the possibility of denial of dominant
belief in consensus in the health service is at least a basis for
the growth of consumerism.

REFERENCES

1. Hunter, D., "The Reorganised Health Service", in Clarke, M. G.
   and Drucker, H. M. (eds.), *Yearbook of Scottish Government 1976-77*.
   Edinburgh 1976.
2. Smout, T. C., "The Scottish Identity" in Underwood, R. (ed.) *The
   Future of Scotland*. Croom Helm, London 1977.
3. Ibid.
4. Stacey, M. Paper given to conference "Representing the Patient",
   York 1976.
5. Political Social Economic Review, No. 12, December 1977.
6. Cartwright, A., *Patients and their Doctors*. Routledge & Kegan Paul,
   London 1967.
7. Annual Report of Renfrew District Local Health Council, 1976.
8. Scottish Home and Health Department, *The Constitution and Functions of Local Health Councils:* A Discussion Paper. July 1973.
9. Scottish Home and Health Department, *Doctors in an Integrated
   Health Service*. HMSO 1971.
10. Scottish Grand Committee, National Health Service (Scotland) Bill
    H.L. Consideration of Principle, 2 May 1972, col. 19.
11. Hill, D. M., *Participating in Local Affairs*. Penguin Books 1970.
12. Klein, R., "Policy Problems and Policy Perceptions in the National
    Health Service" in *Policy and Politics*, vol. 2, No. 3, March 1974.
13. Scottish Grand Committee, National Health Service (Scotland) Bill
    H.L. Consideration of Principle, 4 May 1972.
14. Parliamentary Debates Lords, Vol. 327, col. 1083.
15. NHS Circular No. 1974(GEN)38, Local Health Councils: Memo-
    randum of Guidance.
16. NHS Circular No. 1974(GEN)90.
17. S.I. 1974 No. 2177 (S.300), The National Health Service (Local Health
    Councils) (Scotland) Regulations 1974.
18. Klein, R., "Health Services: The Case for a Counter Bureaucracy"
    in Hatch, S. (ed.), *Towards Participation in Local Services*. Fabian
    Society, 1973.
19. NHS Circular No. 1974(GEN)90.

20. SHHD letter to Chairmen of Local Health Councils, July 1975.
21. e.g. NHS Circular No. 1974(GEN)90; Scottish Council of Social Service, *Local Health Councils:* An Account of a Conference, 1973; and "The Health Service and the Community" in *The Hospital and Health Services Review,* vol. 71, No. 9.
22. e.g. Scottish Home and Health Department, *The Constitution and Functions of Local Health Councils:* A Discussion Paper, July 1973; NHS Circular No. 1974(GEN)90; and Scottish Home and Health Department, *The National Health Service and the Community in Scotland,* 1974.
23. National Consumer Council, *Consumers and the nationalised industries.* HMSO, 1976.
24. NHS Circular No. 1974(GEN)38, Local Health Councils: Memorandum of Guidance.
25. e.g. Royal Commission on Local Government in Scotland, 1966-69. Appendices, pp. 104-105; Royal Commission on Local Government in England, 1966-69, Vol. III, Appendix 7; Wirz, H., "Social Balance and new Town Organisations" in *Policy and Politics,* Vol. 2, No. 2.
26. Most of the data employed here comes from a survey of all local health council members carried out by the authors in 1976. The overall response rate was 66.4%.
27. Klein, R. and Lewis J., *The Politics of Consumer Representation.* Centre for Studies in Social Policy, 1976, Chapter 2.
28. Annual Report 1967/77 of the Western District (Greater Glasgow) Local Health Council.
29. *Prevention and health — everybody's business,* DHSS. HMSO 1976.
30. Report of the second regional conference on "Health Councils — a Role in Health Education". Scottish Health Education Unit, July 1977.
31. Second Annual Report of West Fife Local Health Council, 1977.
32. Second Annual Report of Aberdeen Local Health Council, 1977.
33. Second Annual Report of Perth and Kinross Local Health Council, 1977.
34. NHS Circular No. 1974(GEN)90.
35. Pickvance, C. G., "On the Study of Urban Social Movements", in *Sociological Review,* Vol. 23, 1975.

8

SCOTTISH CRIMINAL POLICY —
THE CASE FOR REFORM

JOHN WATERHOUSE

Lecturer in Social Work and Social Administration,
University of Edinburgh

On 5 April 1976, *The Scotsman* carried the banner headline "Work Orders for Scots Offenders" across its front page. The paper was reporting the announcement made the previous Saturday by the Solicitor General for Scotland at a meeting of the Howard League for Penal Reform that the Government was to introduce, on an experimental basis, a scheme by which offenders who might otherwise be sent to prison could be required to perform a period of service to the community. In the two years which have passed since this initial announcement was made, the scheme has moved from concept to reality, and in four Scottish regions, Lothian, Strathclyde, Grampian and Tayside, selected courts are now able to order such a disposal. Implementation of the scheme depended both on the acceptance of the central government initiative by the four regional authorities who were asked to make the administrative arrangements, and the co-operation of the judiciary in making the orders. The four authorities were encouraged by the provision of financial backing from central government made possible because the scheme was designated "experimental", and a total of £100,000 was allocated to cover an initial two year period. Judges too were consulted and found to be favourably disposed towards the new measures. A legislative base for community service has recently been enacted through the Community Service by Offenders (Scotland) Bill introduced into the House of Commons in April 1978. When the Bill becomes law, the option of community service should gradually become available to courts throughout Scotland. The Bill also provides for the costs of introducing community service on a national basis to be met through grants from the Treasury. This action indicates that the Government no longer sees community services as an experiment, and the new disposal is likely to become a permanent weapon in the judicial armoury of sentences available to Scottish Courts.

As a disposal, community service by offenders is not new, The measure was first introduced in England and Wales in 1972 and its implementation south of the border has already been the subject of two evaluations by the Home Office Research Unit.[1] In carrying out community service, offenders are required to work for a period of between forty and two-hundred and forty hours in any one year, usually in their spare time. Tasks have ranged from house decoration and rehabilitation to providing services for the elderly and the handicapped. Frequently, offenders work alongside non-offenders, and a review of an offender's suitability for community service includes an assessment of the kind of contribution he may be able to make. Commentators have noted that community service schemes have the potential of reducing the stigma of many sentences, and as a disposal, community services appeals to a wide spectrum of opinion. The liberal is attracted by the prospect of reform, the conservative by the expectation that the offender will make reparation.[2]

It is perhaps for this reason that the Government has now chosen to introduce community service in Scotland. Its introduction is the first significant innovation in Scottish criminal policy in the last decade and marks a cautious step in the direction of change. This chapter outlines the need for change and suggests some possible explanations for the lack of positive initiatives in recent years. Its thesis, which some may regard as partisan, is that there is a pressing need for reform in the fields of criminal justice and the treatment of offenders in Scotland.

The Legislative Background

It is not always realised that although the Act of Union in 1707 created one legislative assembly for Scotland and England at Westminster, Scotland has maintained a separate legal system with its own history and traditions, and separate provision for the administration of criminal justice. In those fields where these traditions and provisions are well established (and criminal justice is one such) it is usually necessary to introduce separate legislation for Scotland into the Westminster Parliament. This procedure has drawbacks, the most serious being the problem of finding adequate time in Parliament to debate Scottish affairs, but it has also enabled Scottish policy makers to exercise some autonomy in the framing of legislation. In the criminal justice field, however, legislation has been more conspicuous by its absence than by anything else.

In recent years, the only pieces of Scottish legislation of any significance have been the 1949 Criminal Justice (Scotland) Act which introduced the present legislative framework for probation, and the 1963 Criminal Justice (Scotland) Act which established fines' supervision and the present framework for Young Offenders' Institutions and statutory after-care. In addition, Scotland accepted either in whole or in part two United Kingdom Acts, the 1967 Criminal Justice Act and the 1974 Rehabilitation of Offenders Act. From the former, Scotland adopted only the system of parole which allows for a proportion of offenders with sentences of 18 months or longer to be released from prison under supervision on completion of one third of their sentences. The latter has little direct effect on those sentenced to imprisonment, but allows for setting aside of criminal convictions for some of those who have subsequently "gone straight". The official guide to the Act published by the Home Office states unequivocally that the Act "does not help persistent offenders who have ever been sentenced to more than $2\frac{1}{2}$ years in prison". Whilst English legislation and services cannot be regarded as wholly exemplary, the fact remains that the English, legislating through the same Parliament, and ironically perhaps depending on occasion on the votes of Scottish Members of Parliament for a parliamentary majority, have pushed through a number of legislative and administrative reforms including the Criminal Justice Act of 1972. Although limited in scope, this Act widened the range of options available to the police and courts for dealing with the adult offender. The measure makes possible the decriminalisation of drunkenness offences, the wider use of hostels, the introduction of day training centres for the inadequate recidivist and the implementation of community service, the measure which six years later is now being introduced in Scotland.

Scotland's Criminal Policy Hiatus

What has been the impact of the legislative neglect in the

field of criminal justice and the treatment of offenders during the post-war period, and how can it best be understood?

In 1975, the latest year for which figures are available, a daily average of 4,951 persons were held in Scottish prisons. With the exception of Finland, where motorists driving under the influence of alcohol receive a mandatory prison sentence, the figure taken as a proportion of the national population is the highest in Western Europe. A breakdown of prison receptions in 1975 provides some indication of why this is the case. The majority (over 65%) were not sentenced to imprisonment but held on remand or in default of the payment of fines.[3] Of particular concern is the figure not yet made available in published Government statistics but revealed through the probing of a parliamentary question[4] which showed that more than 250 of those held on remand in adult penal establishments in 1976 were juveniles under the age of 16. Of the men over 21 held in default of the payment of fines, 33% were given no time to pay and over 40% served the full period of imprisonment in lieu, demonstrating that in many cases imprisonment did not have the desired effect of making them pay up. What seems clear is that fines are being used as disguised prison sentences and imposed in the full knowledge that the offender will be unable to pay and will therefore go to prison. The way in which an offender's means are presently assessed is inadequate and it is not unknown, for example, for a judge or magistrate to fine someone whose sole income is a subsistence payment from the Department of Health and Social Security. Another disturbing aspect of the high prison population in Scotland is the large proportion of offenders under the age of 21 held in custody (more than 25% of the sentenced prison population).[5] Although it is true that the incidence of criminal behaviour in this age group is high, the numbers committed to prisons and Young Offenders' Institutions compare very unfavourably with the figures for England and Wales[6] and illustrate the lack of alternatives to imprisonment for offenders in this age group.

These are some of the worst manifestations of the cumulative neglect that has characterised criminal policy and practice in Scotland. In summary, a close study of the prison statistics for Scotland indicates that the bulk of receptions into prison consists of persons on remand, persons committed to prison for failing to pay fines, young offenders and persons sentenced to short terms of imprisonment for comparatively minor offences. Many of these present problems are social rather than criminal yet they continue to be processed through a system which has the primary objectives of security and order, and which may have the effect of reinforcing rather than reducing criminal behaviour. The Prisons Division of the Scottish Home and Health Department in a rare moment of insight has acknowledged as much. Their report of 1971 referring to the question of short term prisoners contained the following admission: "For all of these, comprising altogether more than 40% of the whole penal population . . . there is no practical possibility of planning or carrying through meaningful individual or group treatment programmes, even if the facilities were available. The prison service's role in relation to this section, proportionately very much larger than, say, in England and Wales, is primarily therefore one of containment and physical care."[7]

One practical outcome of the large number of persons passing through Scotland's prisons is that the conditions in which they are held are very poor. Many prisons are overcrowded with two or three prisoners confined in cells which were intended for one person, and sanitary arrangements in the older prisons are primitive and degrading. The work which prisoners are required to undertake often has little relevance to work opportunities which may be available outside prison (some prisoners are still sewing mail bags by hand) and prisoners, especially those on remand, spend long periods locked up in their cells. The introduction of the more liberal Special Unit at Barlinnie Prison for long-term prisoners who present particular disciplinary problems is a welcome step but caters for only a tiny proportion of the total prison population. Its creation and management has provoked heated public and political debate, because the principles on which it is run are in conflict with the attitudes of the general public and many administrators and discipline staff working within the prison system.[8]

In general terms, reforms within the Scottish penal system have been of a conservative nature. Despite calls for more hostels and half-way houses, a number of new secure establishments have been built, including a women's prison at Cornton Vale. At Dungavel an attempt has been made to organise the prison regime on an industrial model which simulates outside working conditions, but with this exception, planning has been relatively unimaginative. Statistics show, for example, that three times more money was spent in 1975 on paying travelling and removal expenses for prison staff than was spent on the educational and recreational needs of prison inmates.[9] The emphasis to a quite unjustifiable extent is still on security, and little attempt is made to devise training or treatment programmes which might assist an inmate to cope with the demands of the outside world. In common with prison inmates in some other parts of the world, Scottish prisoners have few rights — incoming and outgoing mail is censored, meetings with visiting relatives are strictly supervised, political rights, including the right to vote, and the right to a recognised representative organisation are refused, and access to genuinely independent hearings in matters of prison discipline is problematic. All the evidence suggests that the policy of the Prisons Division of the Scottish Home and Health Department continues to rest on the division's assumptions that the experience of prison both deters and rehabilitates.

Neglect — The Reasons

The shaping of criminal policy is a sensitive political issue. In a situation where the incidence of recorded crime is rising, governments intending to introduce any legislative reform must continually glance over their shoulders for signs of a possible backlash, whilst political parties seeking power may choose to exploit "law and order" issues as a means of gaining the popular vote. Issues are further clouded by the fact that empirical research has not provided much assistance to the policy maker. The results of studies into the effectiveness of different kinds of sentences tend to show that they are neither more nor less effective than each other.[10] This leaves the policy maker in the position of having to balance political expediency with such basic principles as humanity, justice, economy and efficiency and tempts the timid or the sceptic to leave things alone. Besides, it is not always clear which people or what circumstances ultimately influence the direction of criminal policy. There are many actors on the scene, politicians, civil servants, lawyers, academics, pressure groups, the media and everyman in the guise of "public opinion". What is more, those working within the present system are able to exercise considerable discretion in the way they choose to carry out their responsibilities. The use or abuse of this discretion has been an important feature in the administration of Scottish criminal justice.

The Question of Discretion

Scotland has a system of public prosecution, and the Lord Advocate and his agents, the Procurators Fiscal, have the right to exercise discretion in matters of prosecution. The criminal law as it presently stands also allows discretion to sentencers (save in the very small number of serious offences where the sentence is prescribed) to impose a sentence from alternatives which may involve fining, imprisonment, or social work help. Under the Social Work (Scotland) Act of 1968, local authority social work departments have the general responsibility of making rehabilitative resources for offenders available within the community. It can therefore be argued (and this argument has frequently been put forward by central government administrators in the criminal justice field) that the framework for the development of a more progressive policy exists without the need for further legislation, and this argument has been a potent force behind the reluctance to legislate further. To the observer the argument appears suspiciously like "passing the buck". The Home and Health Department can say that its first priority must be to cope with the large numbers committed to prison from Scotland's criminal courts, and that this influx effectively prevents a more progressive approach; sentencers can say that the lack of community-based alternatives to imprisonment means that a greater number of offenders are committed to prison than they would ideally wish; and finally social work departments can say that their resources do not stretch to cover a full range of community-based services for the offender given the scale of provision which they must make for other disadvantaged groups within the community.

The overall picture is a confusing one, with the responsibility for reform effectively dispersed between groups who tend to view each other with suspicion, if not open hostility. The problem is further complicated by the fact that the administrative and advisory functions of central government relating to penal institutions and community-based services for the offender are split between two government departments. Prisons are centrally administered as a division of the Scottish Home and Health Department, whilst the Social Work Services Group, which

H

advises local authorities on the development and provision of social work services, including services for the offender, is a division of the Scottish Education Department. With functions scattered between central government departments, and central and local government, it is clear that no one ultimately accepts administrative responsibility for drawing the threads together. Three factors in particular can be identified as having compounded the problems which have been described. These are the lack of an independent advisory body in the field of criminal policy; the fragile relationship between central and local government, and the problems involved in the joint funding of services; and finally, and most crucially, the lack of any concerted political initiatives to bring about change in Scottish criminal policy.

The Lack of Advice

The reasons which push governments to form committees of enquiry, Royal Commissions and permanent advisory bodies, are several. The establishing of a Royal Commission can be a delaying tactic or a move to take the pressure out of a "hot" political issue. The corridors of power, and access to confidential memos and the machinery of the Civil Service are seductive and an invitation to an outsider to sit on an advisory committee or committee of enquiry accords status and can be a means of co-opting and even silencing previously independent critics. Reports frequently take several years to prepare and may collect dust in libraries and offices without being implemented. With these reservations there is nevertheless an urgent need for governments to seek expert advice. Politicians who take the final decisions cannot hope to master in detail all the policy areas for which they are responsible, and a rather curious tradition of the Civil Service means that many civil servants who carry important advisory and administrative functions, may have little or no specialist knowledge of the fields in which their advice is sought.

In Scotland where the Secretary of State's brief is very wide, the need is particularly acute. Yet in the field of criminal policy and the treatment of offenders, the only body with the remit to take an overall view of criminal policy developments in Scotland, the Scottish Council on Crime, was not re-convened following the change of government in 1974. No reasons for this decision were ever given. Perhaps it had to do with the fact that the first and only report of the Council[11] was a very general one, confining itself to the theme of preventing crime rather than the functioning of the penal system and the treatment of offenders; perhaps it had to do with the fact that the composition of the Council was somewhat eccentric with several of its members having little specialist knowledge of the areas under discussion. In recent years two other government committees have produced reports on aspects of the criminal justice system, the Thomson Committee on Criminal Procedure, whose main report was published in 1975,[12] and the Dunpark Committee on Reparation by Offenders which reported in 1977.[13] Both reports made recommendations which would substantially change aspects of law and criminal procedure in Scotland, but none of the recommendations has yet been translated into appropriate legislation. Another body with a possible role to play in the development of policy for the treatment of offenders in Scotland is the Advisory Council on Social Work. Yet this body has not published any reports, or provided any lead for social workers facing the problems of rehabilitating the offender in the community.

In England and Wales some of the impetus for change, including the introduction of community service, has been created by the existence of a permanent Advisory Council on the Penal System, drawing its membership from acknowledged experts in the fields of law, social policy, criminology, psychology and social work.[14] The present neglect of criminal and penal policy in Scotland underlines the need for a similar body to be constituted in Scotland.

The Relationship between Central and Local Government

The reorganised structure of local government in Scotland, and the further changes which may follow the setting up of a Scottish Assembly in Edinburgh, have been much debated. The creation in 1975 of nine regional authorities carrying responsibility for local economic and strategic planning, and the major public services of education, police, and social work, was intended to provide both a more rational administrative structure and a greater delegation of power from the centre. Whilst the new authorities have undoubtedly gained in power, the extent of this power is circumscribed in a number of ways. Firstly, and most importantly, central government holds the purse strings, providing more than half of the local authority expenditure each year through the rate support grant. Secondly, through the issuing of circulars, the vetting of capital projects, the provision of some financial incentives, the offering of advice and the inspection of services such as education, central government exercises indirect influences on the way that local government carries out its functions. The continued existence of these powers means that the relationship between central and local government in Scotland remains uneasy. Many local politicians and local government employees still feel constrained by the extent of central government influence, whilst central government officials argue that their hands are tied by the increased *de facto* power of the new larger local government regions.

The respective powers of central and local government are of particular importance in the field of criminal policy because the Social Work (Scotland) Act of 1968 abolished the separate Probation and After Care Service which had provided services to offenders in the community, and gave this responsibility to local authority social work departments. Although the Probation and After Care Service was not directly under the control of central government, this transfer of responsibility has lessened the grip which central government once held on this important area of service. Two consequences stand out. First, although central government can influence and constrain local authorities in a number of ways, it cannot direct the way in which their money is spent. Secondly, the separate budgetting systems of central and local government make it virtually impossible for money which is spent on the building and running of penal institutions (a central government responsibility) to be redirected towards the establishing of non-institutional community-based services for the offender, a trend which is apparent in countries with more progressive criminal justice policies and programmes.

Moreover, local government services are seen by the public at large to be financed through the levy of rates, an unpopular local tax. Political expediency militates against an increase in expenditure on services for the offender when other disadvantaged groups, such as the elderly and the handicapped, are more obvious vote catchers. Those responsible for central government expenditure, raised through direct and indirect taxation, are not accountable to public opinion in such a visible way, and it is arguable that because offenders are a stigmatised group whose problems are unlikely to receive much informed understanding or support, it would be more sensible to finance services for them from central government rather than local government sources.

In England and Wales, Probation and After Care has remained a separate specialist service jointly financed by central and local government, but answerable to independent probation committees. This arrangement has undoubtedly enabled more resources to be directed towards the offender, but the retention by the Home Office of important powers of advice and inspection has meant a greater degree of control from the centre. The reasons for integrating the Probation Services with social work departments in Scotland were more connected with ensuring an even spread of resources and trained social work staff across a broad spectrum of social need, than with the provision of better services for the offender. Their integration in 1969, and the reorganisation of local government in 1975 have done little to improve the provision of rehabilitative services for the offender in the community. Indeed, the changes could be said to have contributed to the neglect which is the theme of this chapter. Whether this neglect is wholly the fault of local government, or whether central government has failed to use the powers that it has in a forceful and imaginative way, is an open question. Central government has a highly paid team of advisers with a duty to promote developments in policy and practice in the social work field, yet they have remained remarkably silent on the question of services for the offender. Unless there is better planning and co-operation between central and local government in the development of rehabilitative services, the case for the re-introduction of a separate social work service for the adult and young adult offender, more closely aligned to the centralised court and prison system, will remain a strong one.

The Lack of Political Initiatives

Social change often requires the exercise of influence at the political level. Politicians and political parties introduce legislative and social reforms as a practical expression of their personal and political philosophies, as a response to well-organised lobbying, or through an appreciation of political realities. As ambitious men and women they also know that

careers can be made or lost through association with particular
legislation, or a particular ministry. What is striking about
Scotland, and what may account in large measure for the
reluctance to legislate in the field of criminal justice, is the
absence, until recently, of any concerted political lobby for
reform of the Scottish penal system. It would be nearer the mark
to say that many Scottish MPs have aligned themselves against
rather than for any ideas of reform, striking this posture with
very little knowledge of the facts.

In the absence of political pressure the responsibility for
reform has rested with the Scottish Office. Here the brief for
criminal justice matters is shared by the Lord Advocate and the
Under Secretary at the Home and Health Department. This
latter post, which includes the important job of overseeing the
workings of the prison system, has never carried much political
weight and a succession of Under Secretaries have failed to make
an impact. Annual Prison Department Reports consistently
ignore the evidence of failure which surrounds them and are
confined to a descriptive account of prison routine and procedure,
with little attempt to discuss policy issues or make use of the
evaluative research which is available.[15] In the absence of
political direction or initiatives, the civil servants seem content
to administer the system and are understandably loath to take
steps to introduce change.

The Introduction of Community Service

The introductory paragraphs to this chapter sketched in
the arrangements for introducing Community Service in Scotland as a new disposal available to the Criminal Courts which
marked a cautious step in the direction of change. The
background of neglect from which this new disposal has emerged
has been dealt with in some detail to demonstrate both the need
for initiatives of this kind in Scotland and to provide an analysis
of why so little has been accomplished. How did the initiative to
develop Community Service come about, and what implications
does it hold for the future?

Over the past few years the problems facing the Scottish
penal system have in fact received greater public attention. In
1975 the Howard League for Penal Reform in Scotland,
published a policy review on the prison system.[16] This review
drew attention to some of the more unpalatable facts and

received wide coverage in the press. It was later followed up by a further policy review[17] which documented the decline in the use of probation in Scotland at a time when the prison population was rising. Strong criticism also came from a number of sheriffs who were concerned about the standard of social work services to the courts. The Parole Board for Scotland, who needed assurances of the adequacy of social work supervision and support before releasing prisoners on parole added their voices to this criticism.[18] In 1976, following a joint initiative by the Scottish Association for the Care and Resettlement of Offenders and the Howard League for Penal Reform, an all-party group of Scottish MPs was established to bring pressure to bear at Westminster. Since then a small but committed group of MPs has tabled a wide range of questions about Scottish criminal policy in the House of Commons.

The decision to introduce Community Service in Scotland was probably a response to these pressures. The Government, embarrassed by the evidence of its own inactivity, decided that something should be done. Once the decision was taken, those responsible had to grapple with the problems of implementation resulting from both the lack of suitable legislation and the fact that no ready way existed to provide the local authorities with the necessary money to make community service available on a permanent basis. In the event, use was made of a clause in the Social Work (Scotland) Act which enabled central government to finance experimental projects and this was the major reason for introducing community service in Scotland as an "experiment". To surmount the problem posed by the lack of legislation it was decided to make community service a possible requirement of a Probation Order, a move initially thought to be of doubtful legality and one which could have led to arguments on appeal.

That the Government has now brought forward legislation (the only part of an originally much more extensive Criminal Procedure Bill for Scotland to be saved) indicates concern about these makeshift arrangements. The new Bill shows signs of hasty drafting. It borrows heavily from the legislation passed for England and Wales and compromises on the question of whether community service should be a separate disposal or a condition attached to a Probation Order by making possible both alternatives. With more forward planning this compromise would not have been necessary. Perhaps the most significant aspect of the Bill is that it legislates for the introduction of community service throughout Scotland and includes a clause which provides for the local government expenditure involved to be defrayed from central government funds. A government statement which accompanied the introduction of the Bill indicated that half a million pounds is to be spent on Community Service over a five year period. This move is a welcome acknowledgement of the fact that community-based services for the offender in Scotland need more central government support. Whether the sum allocated is sufficient and whether local authorities will provide adequate resources for community service at the end of the five year period remains to be seen, but at least a start has been made.

The Future of Criminal Policy — Scotland

The introduction of Community Service is a belated attempt to inject some new thinking into meeting the challenge of Scotland's high prison population. As a measure it is hardly radical, having already been tested in England and Wales, and on its own it will do little to reduce the number of people incarcerated in Scottish prisons. In putting the case for reform this chapter has indentified a number of factors which have contributed to the lack of impetus for change. The most important of these have been: —

1. The lack of advisory and executive bodies with the remit to develop and implement an overall strategy for the direction of criminal policy, and the management of the penal system.
2. The effects of placing community-based services in the criminal justice field under local authority control, and the problems involved in the joint financing by central and local government of services and resources for the offender within the community.
3. The absence of political initiatives in the field of criminal justice which have led to the legislative and administrative neglect of an important area of Scottish social policy.

These problems must be tackled if progress is to be made. As immediate steps, aspects of criminal procedure such as bail,

remand, and the collection of fines, some of which have already
been examined by government committees, should receive urgent
legislative attention, and new ways of financing local initiatives
by social work departments and voluntary groups and organisations explored. As a long-term strategy, policy makers must
consider the possibility of redirecting resources from the building
of more penal institutions to the provision of a wider range
of community-based services. There is also a need for a thorough
review, both of the scope of the criminal law and of the
possibility of dealing with some offenders without proceeding to
trial, a step which, with appropriate safeguards, would be
practicable in Scotland, given the system of public prosecution.
It is to be hoped that the government committee recently
established by the Secretary of State to examine "Alternatives
to Prosecution"[19] will have some positive proposals to make in
this regard.

But what of the crucial question of the political will to act?
The recent legislation on community service was only one part
of a proposed Criminal Procedure Bill for Scotland which was
dropped from the parliamentary timetable. No reasons have been
given for this decision. Perhaps it was felt that Scotland had
received more than its fair share of attention as a result of the
Scotland Bill. Perhaps it was felt that criminal policy should
be a matter for the proposed Scottish Assembly. Perhaps the
Government was simply "clearing the decks" for a General Election. Whatever the reasons, this chapter has drawn attention to
the neglect of criminal policy matters in Scotland and to the
pressing need for reform.

REFERENCES

1. *Community Service Orders* HMSO 1975, and *Community Service
   Assessed 1976* HMSO 1977. Both are Home Office Research Unit
   Reports.
2. Harding, J., "The Offender and the Community" *Social Work Today*
   17 October 1974.
3. *Prisons in Scotland, Report for 1975* (Cmnd 6546) HMSO. See
   Appendix 3. Receptions — sex and type of custody.
4. Hansard written answers 3 March 1977. Questions tabled by Mr
   R. Cook.

5. *Prisons in Scotland* (as above).
6. *Social Trends No. 4* HMSO 1973 p. 182.
7. *Prisons in Scotland, Report for 1971* (Cmnd 4998) HMSO.
8. For a consumer's point of view of the Special Unit, see J. Boyle *A Sense of Freedom,* (Canongate Press, 1977).
9. *Prisons in Scotland 1975* (Appendix 17).
10. See for example, Hood and Sparks, *Key Issues in Criminology* (World University Library, 1972).
11. *Crime and the prevention of Crime — A memorandum by the Scottish Council on Crime* HMSO 1975.
12. *Criminal Procedure in Scotland (2nd Report)* (Cmnd 6218) HMSO 1975.
13. *Reparation by the Offender to the Victim in Scotland* (Cmnd 6802) HMSO 1977.
14. The genesis of Community Service for offenders for example is to be found in the Council's report *Non-custodial and semi-custodial Penalties* HMSO 1970.
15. See for example, Appendix D "Research" which forms part of the report "The Young Adult Offender" prepared by the English Advisory Council on the Penal System and published by HMSO in 1974.
16. *"Taken in": Facts and Comment on the state of penal policy in Scotland. Howard League Policy Review No. 1.* April 1975.
17. *Probation in Scotland — A programme for revival. Howard League Policy Review No. 2.* July 1976.
18. *Report of the Parole Board for Scotland 1974* p. 8. "The Parole System and the Social Work Department" HMSO.
19. This committee, under the Chairmanship of Lord Stewart, began its work in October 1977.

9

APPOINTED AND *AD HOC* AGENCIES IN THE FIELD OF THE SCOTTISH OFFICE*

SIR DOUGLAS HADDOW
Formerly Permanent Under Secretary of State for Scotland and currently Chairman, North of Scotland Hydro-Electric Board

The first thing to be said about bodies functioning in fields of concern to central government, not being government departments or elected local authorities, is that they come in an infinite variety. Some are set up under statute, some by Royal Charter, some by Royal Warrant, some by Ministerial Minute of Appointment, some even under the Companies Acts. Some are made up wholly of ministerial appointees, some include nominations from other sources, some have an elected element. Only a minority of members are paid by way of salary or fee, as distinct from expenses and payment for loss of remunerative time. Some are appointed for a specific task and disappear when they have discharged it, while some are standing bodies with continuing functions to perform.

Some have executive functions in their own right, some are executive agents of Ministers, some have no executive functions at all. Some are spending money voted by Parliament, some operate commercially, some have other types of income (e.g. levies or registration fees), some incur no expenditure beyond their own expenses. Some are advisory, either in the sense of advising departments on points arising in the course of day-to-day administration, or in the sense of conducting their own studies and producing formal reports with recommendations on matters of policy.

If I attempted to cover the whole field in this chapter in any detail, the result would I fear be almost as chaotic as the

*An earlier version of this paper was presented to a seminar in the University of Edinburgh in May 1978 organised jointly by the Scottish Government Unit and the Social Science Faculty's Seminars Committee. Sir Douglas writes in his personal capacity.

starting point. What I shall therefore do is to seek to identify the main segments of the field, and look more closely at one or two of the most recent Scottish additions to it that have special features of their own.[1]

The simplest group is that of more or less expert advisory committees, where the object of the exercise is to contribute to the deliberations of Ministers and departments an expert input that may not be available at all, or not on a sufficiently comprehensive basis, among officers of the department. Committees composed predominantly of professional members are the clearest example of this, whether the professionals are doctors, farmers, teachers, or what you will. Especially where the bodies are set up by statute, an important part of the objective has been to reassure professional groups outside that they will have proper opportunities and facilities for making their views known at the appropriate stage in policy development or executive action by Government.

Usually the statute will enjoin the Minister who has responsibility for appointing the members to consult with such organisations representing specific interests as may seem to him appropriate; and where the body is not statutory he will do so anyway. In practice some of the individuals suggested for appointment in the course of such consultations will in fact be appointed, but Ministers usually expect to be given a choice — i.e. there should be more suggestions than there are vacancies. Moreover the Minister may, for reasons of balance, find it necessary to appoint someone who was not included among the original suggestions. Provided consultations are conducted in good faith, I do not myself think there is much wrong with this part of the system.

A variant in this group of bodies is the consultative council or committee, where the declared purpose is to provide a forum for full discussion between departments and outside interests of topics of mutual interest to the participants. Here, nomination of non-official members may be entirely appropriate. Ministerial or official chairmanship may also be useful, a device sometimes adopted for so-called advisory bodies but which has always seemed to me less appropriate in that particular context.

Besides the expert advisory committee, which will usually have a continuing existence, more broadly based groups are set up from time to time to consider topics with considerable ramifications, in the hope that a consensus of views will ultimately emerge as a basis on which administrative or legislative action can then be taken with the minimum of dissension. For major issues such groups are often constituted as Royal Commissions, where the appointments are the responsibility of the Prime Minister as the Sovereign's principal adviser, and the Warrant of Appointment confers powers to compel the attendance of witnesses and the production of information.

The issue that arises here is that such bodies may be set up in circumstances in which the Government itself might have taken a policy decision or initiative. This criticism is more a criticism of lack of political will than of the performance of such Commissions or committees, and gains in validity when it becomes clear that the resulting report is taken as serving no more definitive a purpose than the basis of a further round of consultations with all interests in sight — or, worse, where no further action is taken at all.

The next broad division I take to be that of bodies established with executive power exercised in the name of the Minister and at his expense. In financial terms much the most significant group is that of the health boards, of which there are now 15 in Scotland, spending something like £750 million of Government money this year. Except as regards general practitioner services, where the rights and duties of practitioners are closely governed by statutory regulations, the health boards discharge a fairly wide remit as agents of the Secretary of State, who can for this reason be called to account by Parliament for any of their actions. It is almost invariably his officers who appear before the Public Accounts Committee when health expenditure is under scrutiny. At the same time the boards can themselves sue and be sued and are not entitled to Crown privilege.

Membership of the boards is not closely regulated by the statute, which contents itself with requiring consultation with local authorities and professional organisations, and also with universities for the medical teaching interest. Control by the Secretary of State is exercised partly by general guidance and partly by a system of budgetary approval.

Historically, largely to overcome the initial reluctance of the medical profession to participate in a national health service at all, two separate administrative machines composed of appointed members were created to administer the hospital services and the general practitioner services respectively. Local authorities continued to administer the public health services already established. This tripartite structure has now formally been replaced by a unified system of administration by appointed health boards, and the major question is whether such boards are needed at all.

It is I suppose still the position that administration of the comprehensive health service by local authorities would not be acceptable to the professions. It is not quite so clear that administration by the Government department at its own hand, through decentralised offices as appropriate, would be equally unacceptable. What is clear is that the health boards have developed very extensive bureaucracies while at the same time there are still considerable numbers of staff in the central department concerned with the business of the boards. General policy and major items, such as the hospital building programme, are in fact in the hands of the central department. It is difficult to avoid the conclusion that some simpler system could reduce expense and increase efficiency.

There is also in Scotland a statutory Central Services Agency, a rather curious animal. Its purpose is to discharge such health service functions as are thought to be best handled centrally rather than by health boards. Such functions may either be functions of the Secretary of State "delegated" by him, or functions of health boards referred to the Agency by statutory order and discharged by it on behalf of the boards. The major referred function is that of actually building hospitals, a task calling for highly specialised expertise that could not reasonably or economically be provided by each board as and when required. The Agency is under a Management Committee, appointed by the Secretary of State but partly on the nomination of health boards and partly after consultation with the boards. The need to maintain it alongside the central department is not to my mind self evident.

Nor is Parliament by any means content to trust the Secretary of State and the health boards to get on with their assigned tasks. The statute provides also for the creation of a Scottish Health Service Planning Council, which has the duty of advising the Secretary of State on the exercise of his functions and also of making an annual report to him which he has to lay before Parliament. Not all the members of this Council are appointed by the Secretary of State; each health board appoints a member, and so also do the university medical schools. The object of setting up the Council is partly to enlist all relevant expertise for planning and the formulation of policy, but partly also — and this is at least as important — to reassure the various professions that their interests and their expertise will in fact be given full weight.

At health board level, there is another complete set of advisory bodies, the local health councils, charged with the task of representing the interests of the public in the health services in their localities. Here again the purpose is mainly to provide reassurance that health boards will be properly responsive to local needs and local views. In addition, there is an elaborate professional advisory committee structure at health board level. All parts of the advisory machinery — central and local — could of course be attached to a structure of administration by the central department itself.

Other groups of bodies with executive responsibilities operating almost wholly on Government money include a number of Boards of Governors of specialist education establishments, such as Colleges of Art and of Agriculture, Colleges of Education, and certain technical institutions falling outside the local authority field but short of university status; and also governing bodies of agricultural research institutes. The members are mostly drawn from a variety of nominating bodies, but some — and in a few cases all — are appointed by the Secretary of State at his own hand. Some of them provide expertise not readily available within the appropriate central department, and they give a valuable sense of identity to the individual institutions. They are not festooned with advisory bodies in the way the health boards are.

Then there are two fairly distinct groups of regulatory bodies. On the one hand there are a variety of marketing bodies, e.g. the Milk Marketing Boards, the Herring Industry Board, and the White Fish Authority, where some kind of regulation and development of the industries was thought necessary. In some of these cases there is provision for elected as well as appointed members, and the degree of Ministerial intervention in their affairs is relatively limited. I suppose they carry in some degree the classic monopoly risk, as illustrated by the recent

EEC attack on the Milk Boards, but their operations seem to be generally acceptable.

A second set of regulatory bodies are those concerned with the internal affairs of particular professions. The General Medical Council is the oldest of these, with detailed statutory composition and powers in relation to which Ministers play relatively little part. It was followed in due course by such other bodies as the General Dental Council, the General Nursing Council, the Central Midwives' Board, the General Teaching Council and many others. Election by the professions concerned, together with appointments by the teaching institutions, play the major part in providing the members of this Councils. If there is a criticism, it might be that these bodies — especially those concerned with ancillary workers — could become too inward-looking, perhaps attaching more importance to status and formal qualifications than to the practical skills necessary in the provision of services to the public.

I must not yield to the temptation of going into the vast field of tribunals and analogous bodies in the social field, including such diverse growths as the Rent Tribunals and the Children's Panels, or I might never emerge. So I will turn next to a number of bodies of fairly recent origin, of considerable significance in the economic or environmental field. I take them in order of their appearance on the scene. These are the New Town Development Corporations, the Highlands and Islands Development Board, the Countryside Commission for Scotland, the Scottish Tourist Board, and the Scottish Development Agency. The point to keep before us in looking at these bodies is whether their existence is really necessary.

The first New Town Development Corporations were set up in the early post-war years, as instruments for the construction of New Towns in various parts of England and Scotland. I suppose the task could have been entrusted to the existing local authorities, but it was thought — rightly in my view — that no such authority could be expected to devote the concentrated attention to a particular locality necessary to get major developments moving. And since by definition the New Towns were mostly planned for relatively undeveloped areas, election would not have been an appropriate way of setting them up. Appointment by the Secretary of State was therefore natural, although care has always been taken to include (on a personal basis) members also serving on the local authority or authorities affected.

Primarily, the New Town Development Corporations, as the name implies, are development authorities rather than local government authorities; and although they relieve the local authorities of some responsibilities, they depend on the authorities for a good deal of support — e.g. in the provision of services such as water supply and education. General planning control of the New Towns is mainly in the hands of the Secretary of State, operating through approval of master plans and approval — primarily in capital investment terms — of broad programmes in the housing, industrial or commercial fields. The Corporations operate for the most part on money lent by the Government, and in principle they were intended ultimately to become self-supporting. I do not think their work could have been done equally well otherwise, and there is already provision for winding them up when their purpose has been served.

The Highlands and Islands Development Board, set up in 1965, owed something to the New Town experience, but was rather a new kind of animal. It was given a very general remit to prepare and promote measures for the economic and social development of the Highlands and Islands, with specific powers to make grants and loans in support of industry, commerce, or any other relevant activity. Operating wholly on voted money, controlled by annual budgets settled with the Secretary of State, the Board also needed express Ministerial approval for general or specific proposals and for certain particular items such as the acquisition of land. Assistance to industry was governed by formal arrangements approved by the Secretary of State and the Treasury.

While no particular qualifications or consultations were specified for Members of the Board, inevitably appointed by the Secretary of State, the Board was rather unusual in having several whole-time Members including the Chairman. Indeed the statute requires whole-time members to be in the majority, this having been conceded under pressure by the Parliamentary Opposition who argued that only in this way could the effectiveness of the Board be secured. Necessarily these Members had to receive substantial salaries, a situation not arising in any of the other bodies with which I have so far dealt.

Once again Parliament did not fully trust the Secretary

I

of State and the Board to get on with the job without further guidance, and the Act also established the Highlands and Islands Development Consultative Council, to advise the Board on the exercise of their functions. There are some rather peculiar directions about consultations before Members are appointed — inevitably by the Secretary of State — but there are no provisions for salaries or publication of reports. I suppose the Council might not have been set up had there not, for many years before the appointment of the Board, been a non-statutory Council whose task it was to facilitate the co-ordination of the work of government departments and other public agencies designed to promote Highland development.

The Board has in my judgement done a good job, if at times an uneven one, and given the structure of local government at the time it was set up, I do not think its work could have been done so effectively by any other machinery. Now that we have reorganised local government, however, I am not so sure that the Board is indispensable. But I suppose that it is only sensible to wait and see what changes a Scottish Assembly may wish to make in the local government structure, assuming that an Assembly comes to pass.

Next, the Countryside Commission for Scotland. This body made a relatively late entry on the countryside scene, the corresponding English Commission having been set up in 1949 as the National Parks Commission and having done much to stimulate the development of National Parks south of the Border. The original Scottish view had been that separate National Park machinery was not necessary in Scotland. Instead, certain areas were identified as being specially important in this context and were made subject to "special planning control" under the Town and Country Planning Acts. In essence this involved the scrutiny of applications for proposed developments by the Secretary of State as well as by the local planning authority concerned.

However, a variety of interested organisations continued to press the view that something more positive was needed in Scotland. Eventually the Countryside Commission for Scotland was set up by statute in 1967, the year before the National Parks Commission became the English Countryside Commission. Financed by a government grant, it is charged with the broad task of securing the development and improvement of facilities for the enjoyment of the Scottish countryside and for the enhancement of its natural beauty and amenity. This the Commission seeks to do largely by education, persuasion and the provision of expert advice; but it also has limited powers of land acquisition and management, and of making grants and loans to persons other than public bodies.

The Chairman and Members of the Countryside Commission are of course appointed by the Secretary of State, after consultation — as to part of the membership — with local authority associations and organisations representing countryside interests. In this way considerable expertise, associated with enthusiasm and supported by practical experience, is brought to bear on the issues arising. I would not myself assert that equal progress could have been made under purely departmental auspices, without the stimulus of the Commission.

The Scottish Tourist Board was established as a statutory body in 1969. A non-statutory body had operated for many years past, under the joint auspices of the Secretary of State and the Scottish Council, Development and Industry. There was, however, a general feeling that something more effective was needed, with some financial backing from public funds; and the administration of such funds was held to require a statutory Board. Appointed by the Secretary of State, without the usual statutory directions as to consultations, the Scottish Board is part of wider machinery including corresponding Boards in England and Wales, and also the British Tourist Authority (appointed by the Secretary of State for Trade), on which the chairmen of the three Country Boards sit. The Authority concerns itself largely with overseas publicity, mainly using material supplied by the Country Boards.

The Boards have a general remit to promote tourism, and have limited powers to give various forms of financial assistance subject to close Ministerial control. They also have powers to inspect tourist establishments, and there is provision — not yet invoked — for Ministerial orders authorising them to enforce a system of classification. In some ways the Scottish Tourist Board is analogous to the Countryside Commission for Scotland, although in practice it is a smaller body and has less obvious formal expertise among its Members. The case for maintaining it as a separate organisation outside departments is not to my mind so strong, although there could be no question of dismantling the Scottish Board as long as the rest of the Great Britain structure remains.

The last body I have chosen for mention in this context is the Scottish Development Agency. Established under an Act of 1975, this is generally regarded as a very important body in the Scottish economic and industrial scene. Its functions include not only virtually all aspects of economic development, but also the improvement of the environment. Like the New Town Corporations it is financed mainly by loans from the National Loans Fund, although there is also some revenue financing from voted money. Again its members are appointed by the Secretary of State, on a specification calling for experience in a variety of fields relating to its functions without mandatory consultations. Only the Chief Executive — appointed in the first place by the Secretary of State but subsequently by the Agency with the Secretary of State's approval — is a whole-time Member of the Agency with a substantial salary. The present Chief Executive is in fact the Deputy Chairman.

The Scottish Development Agency in some respects took the place of the earlier Scottish Industrial Development Office, an Office set up within the Department of Trade and Industry which had somewhat similar powers in the economic field. Following the 1974 election, however, the view prevailed that many decisions on support for and investment in particular industrial and allied enterprises could best be taken otherwise than in the Civil Service machine. Hence the Scottish Development Agency, which also absorbed the former Scottish Industrial Estates Corporation and the Small Industries Council for the Rural Areas in Scotland. So far as loan finance at commercial rates is concerned, the Council has a fair degree of discretion, and provision is also made for equity participation.

Where selective grants and loans at non-commercial rates are concerned, powers are still reserved in effect to the Secretary of State, although there is a curious arrangement for him to direct the Agency to exercise his powers in specified cases. In this latter field the Secretary of State has the assistance of a statutory advisory body, essentially a continuation of an earlier non-statutory advisory group which operated alongside the Scottish Industrial Development Office. The Agency is not obligated to consult this particular body, but informal contacts are maintained.

It is perhaps early to judge the success of the Scottish Development Agency, but it has been far more effective than some people, at least, expected. Certainly it has had to take decisions of a kind, and on a time scale, that would have been quite impracticable within a Civil Service machine where every issue involves the Minister's accountability to Parliament.

For completeness I should at least say something about the nationalised industries, of which three — the two Electricity Boards and the Scottish Transport Group — operate under the umbrella of the Scottish Office. Ministerial control is limited and indirect; and most of the industries, although operating largely or wholly on capital advanced by the Government, depend on consumers and customers for their income and are under a duty broadly to balance their revenue accounts. Some form of appointment by Ministers has hitherto been regarded as the only possible arrangement, and relatively little criticism is in fact heard of the way this is done in Scotland. However, the developing theme of employee participation indicates a possible future method of identifying some of the members of the Boards.

Ministerial control is in form exercised mainly through capital investment programmes which Boards have to submit for approval, and statutory approval of major schemes. There are statutory powers to Ministers to give general directions, but these powers have proved largely unworkable and ministerial influence is to a considerable extent exerted by informal means. Most nationalised industries are producing corporate plans, i.e. documents setting out their aims and intentions for appropriate periods of years, and these plans serve to assist Ministers in considering investment programmes for more limited periods ahead.

Other restraints on the Scottish Electricity Boards include statutory Fisheries and Amenity Committees appointed by the Secretary of State, advising both Boards and having access to the Secretary of State who can oblige a Board to conform to a recommendation by either Committee. In addition, each Board has a Consultative Council, set up by statute with its chairman a Member of the Board, charged particularly with considering matters of interest to consumers and again having access to the Secretary of State. Although its Members are appointed by the Secretary of State, he is obliged to draw between two-fifths and three-fifths of the Members from a panel of persons nominated by the appropriate local authority association; and the balance, after appropriate consultations, from persons representing agriculture, commerce, industry, labour and the general interests of consumers. Here then is another example of the kind of checks and balances that Parliament imposes.

Moreover, electricity tariffs are subject to scrutiny by the Price Commission, who can delay price increases for detailed investigation under the auspices of the Commission. Most of the Scottish Transport Group's affairs are, however, excluded from the field of the Price Commission, being controlled instead by Ministerially appointed independent statutory Traffic Commissioners who discharge a wide range of licensing and regulatory functions relating to Road Traffic.

It is plain — and grows plainer every day — that government departments, as hitherto understood, are not suitable instruments for running commercial operations. Parliament has recognised this by setting up the Boards, but it does not really trust its instruments to do the job. Hence the inevitable tensions that exist between a Minister and a nationalised industry — inevitable if for no other reason than the different time scales as well as the different value judgments on which Ministers and most of the nationalised industries operate. At the same time it has to be accepted that the nationalised industries cannot in practice be left to operate on purely commercial criteria. A report of the National Economic Development Office in 1976 dealt with all this at some length, and few would claim that the White Paper published in April 1978 has given final answers to all the issues that were or might be raised about control of nationalised industries and their relationships with Ministers.[2]

This paper presents only a brief and necessarily incomplete survey of appointed and *ad hoc* bodies in the field of the Scottish Office. It may, however, be of some assistance to those who seek to identify particular aspects or areas of the subject for study in depth.

REFERENCES

1. For a complete list of appointed and *ad hoc* bodies and their sponsoring departments as listed in the library of the House of Commons, see table in the reference section at the end of the book.
2. *Nationalised Industries in the United Kingdom: their role in the economy and control in the future.* National Economic Development Office. 1976.

10

PUBLIC SUPPORT FOR THE ARTS IN SCOTLAND — THE ROLE OF THE SCOTTISH ARTS COUNCIL

MICHAEL FLINN

Professor of Social History in the University of Edinburgh and Chairman of the Music Committee of the Scottish Arts Council*

Public support for the arts began during the 1939-45 war with the creation of the Council for the Encouragement of Music and the Arts (CEMA). After the war CEMA was replaced by the Arts Council of Great Britain (ACGB), whose remit, as its title implies, extended to Scotland. In 1945, to facilitate its activities in Scotland, ACGB established a committee in Edinburgh which, from 1967, became known as the Scottish Arts Council (SAC). SAC has remained a committee of ACGB, and its chairman and two other members have always been members of ACGB.

The Government, through its education ministry (currently the Department of Education and Science) makes its grant for the support of the arts in the whole of Great Britain to ACGB. ACGB customarily agrees with SAC for a percentage of this grant, based on need, for Scotland (and similarly with WAC for Wales). SAC then has the disposal of this amount entirely at its discretion, subject only to the usual requirements of government accountability and auditing. Thus, in the financial year (1 April to 31 March) 1976-77, the grant made available by DES to ACGB for the support of the arts was £36m. Of this, £4.4m., or approximately 12%, was allocated to SAC. 12%, of course, represents more than Scotland's proportion of the total British population (currently about 9%), the difference being added partly to allow for the higher costs of artists' travel to Scotland's dispersed population, but more particularly in recognition of the

* The views expressed in this article are the author's and not those of the Scottish Arts Council. They are necessarily related to the experience of the Music Committee, and examples and illustrations used in this article are heavily drawn from the work of that committee.

indivisibility of certain basic units like opera and ballet companies and symphony orchestras. Scotland has one each of these, but England, with eleven times the Scottish population, does not need eleven opera companies or even eleven symphony orchestras.

These grants are for current expenditure. The Government, however, also makes some capital available to ACGB for "Housing the Arts", and this is disbursed on a British basis by an ACGB committee on which SAC is represented. "Housing the Arts" capital grants have assisted in the building or improvement of many theatres and galleries in Scotland — the Eden Court Theatre in Inverness, and the MacRobert Centre in Stirling are recent examples of buildings substantially assisted by "Housing the Arts" capital grants. Where very large capital expenditures are involved, as in the adaptation of the Theatre Royal in Glasgow by Scottish Opera as an opera house, or — abortively, in the event — the erstwhile Castle Terrace "opera house" project in Edinburgh, the Government will consider direct applications for "jumbo" capital grants.

Table I

EXPENDITURE BY SCOTTISH ARTS COUNCIL 1976-77

Music	600,439	13%
Opera	1,155,437	25%
Dance	455,500	10%
Drama	887,602	19%
Stage 1	61,043	1%
Art	357,790	8%
Films	14,925	—%
Literature	126,902	3%
Festivals	230,001	5%
Projects, Arts Centres and Clubs	275,605	6%
Operating Costs	256,289	6%
Capital Expenditure	64,937	1%
	4,486,470	97%
Housing the Arts	128,500	3%
	£4,614,970	100%

Table 1 shows the ways the Council spent its grant in 1976-77. These amounts and percentages should be treated with caution. There are reasons why art forms are not equally costly.

There is no reason why the Council's help to projects should be a fixed part of their costs. The categories are not mutually exclusive and government money is channelled into the arts via other agencies, notably local government, education, art galleries and libraries. Nonetheless, the table gives a useful general picture.

The Scottish Arts Council consists of 22 unpaid members appointed by the ACGB and approved by the Secretary of State for Scotland. They are drawn from a wide range of occupations — artists, writers and performers in the arts, businessmen, public administrators, trade unionists, academics and other professionals. All have an interest in, or knowledge of, one or more art form, either professionally, or simply as enthusiasts: those of them who are not professional artists are as representative a group of the artistically informed public as it would be possible to find by any means. For purposes of the detailed consideration of the allocation of the overall grant, SAC divides itself into specialist committees for each principal art form — music, drama, art and literature. In each of these areas the Council is assisted by its professional staff. There are Directors with small (mostly two or three only) staffs for each of the four specialist departments, small "regional development", "tours" and financial departments, the whole under a Director and Deputy Director. In 1976-77, administration accounted for only 6% of the total expenditure.

With certain exceptions, principally in the field of art exhibitions, SAC operates by responding to external initiatives from both individuals and organisations which, where necessary, are solicited by advertisement. There are good reasons for working this way. First, for SAC to launch out into, say, concert promotion or the publication of the work of living Scottish poets would call for a much larger staff: the proportion of the total grant eaten up by administration might rise to unacceptably high levels. Second, and more important, the transfer of the initiative for the expenditure of a significant proportion of the total grant to the Council itself would impose on it a responsibility for determining the direction of development in the arts which many, including SAC itself, would consider to be undesirable. Both ACGB and SAC have studiously eschewed any attempt to dictate the directions in which the arts should develop in order to allow maximum freedom of expression by artists and promoters. "There should be no question", SAC's chairman said in the 1977 House of Lords debate on the arts, "of the Scottish Arts Council imposing a cultural policy from Edinburgh". This, it should be noted, is in marked contrast with forms of state aid to the arts in many countries where financial assistance in cash terms is more generous. It remains the case, however, that the Council and its officers are peculiarly well-placed to observe the *lacunae* left by independent initiative, and the Council has always shown a willingness to stimulate and encourage local, or even national initiative.

It goes without saying that in any year SAC's grant falls a long way short of what is needed to respond adequately to external initiatives. For the Council supports an astonishingly wide range of activities. New members joining the Council are invariably surprised to discover the scope of activities supported, and even the Council's annual report fails to do justice to the variety and ingenuity of methods of support and encouragement. It supports, to an extent sometimes in excess of 50% of their entire revenues, major opera and ballet companies of international reputation; a contracted symphony orchestra; a free-lance medium-scale symphony orchestra, a chamber orchestra and a chamber ensemble under unified management; a full-time string quartet; an international festival and several smaller local festivals; nearly one hundred widely scattered local music and general arts clubs; seven repertory theatre companies and several smaller touring drama companies; many art galleries and centres; and a mobile art gallery. In addition, it provides the chief, if not the sole, source of finance for the commissioning of musical compositions and the writing of plays, for bursaries for artists, writers, and young musicians and dancers, for awards for artists and writers "in residence" in schools, universities, new towns and hospitals, for the publication of poetry and other literature, for the encouragement of the art of film-making, and for the training of producers, designers, instrument repairers and tuners.

With so many competing claims on limited resources, how does SAC decide on its priorities? In part, history comes to the rescue. Once having made possible the launching of a repertory company, a string quartet or an opera company by an initial grant, it would be difficult not to continue at least the same level of support in the following years: to discontinue support that might run to, say, between 25% and 50% of a company's budget would mean almost certain death for that company. Thus, a new major initiative becomes, almost inevitably, a permanent commitment. Not that SAC can ever guarantee continuing support. First, it must, in the public interest, satisfy itself about standards, not only artistic, but also managerial and financial. Second, SAC itself is not guaranteed revenue for years ahead. Before inflation soared in the early 1970s, a system of rolling triennial grants gave some assurance of future levels of grant; but in the face of higher rates of inflation, governments have retreated to annual grants, often announced extremely late. Though there has never in recent years been any serious possibility of the grant being reduced in money terms, in a period of fast inflation what matters is whether the level of grant is maintained in real terms. If it is not, some potential recipients of grants must be disappointed. SAC must safeguard its position by not accepting forward commitments beyond its foreseeable means, which indeed is not permitted by Treasury regulation. The Council's grant was raised by 14.6% for 1977-78 and by 20% for 1978-79. This latter increase should cover inflation and allow for very limited growth in the Council's awards.

Once reassured about standards, SAC is as anxious as anybody to ensure the continuation of a going concern. With only a few exceptions, organisations, once launched, tend not only to stay in existence but also to grow. Thus, a large organisation whose launching initially claimed, say, 1% of SAC's revenue for that year, is likely to go on claiming at least as much in future unless the Council's total grant from ACGB increases in real terms. Many such organisations also wish to expand as time goes on, and their expansion may therefore involve either a constant percentage of an SAC grant growing in real terms, or a rising percentage of a grant held constant in real terms. The growth of a number of major organisations, each dependent upon SAC for an indispensable proportion of their total revenues, necessarily pre-empts a substantial and possibly growing proportion of the Council's total grant. Only substantial growth of the total grant in real terms will prevent the major organisations from encroaching on the residue available for the multitude of smaller or less expensive activities supported by the Council. Table II shows the Council's grants to its 15 major clients for 1978-79 and 1977-78. These organisations receive about 65% of the Council's budget.

Table II

GRANTS TO MAJOR ORGANISATIONS BY THE SCOTTISH ARTS COUNCIL FOR 1978-79 AND 1977-78

	1978-79	1977-78
Scottish Opera	£1,368,000	£1,130,000
Scottish Ballet	570,000	480,000
Scottish National Orchestra	440,000	368,000
Scottish Philharmonic Society	180,000	128,000
Edinburgh Festival Society	260,000	230,000
Royal Lyceum Theatre	250,000	210,000
Glasgow Citizens' Theatre	190,000	167,000
Perth Repertory Theatre	81,000	70,000
Pitlochry Festival Theatre	85,000	69,000
Dundee Repertory Theatre	92,000	77,000
Byre Theatre, St. Andrews	26,000	26,000
Traverse Theatre Club, Edinburgh	81,000	60,000
Eden Court Theatre, Inverness	55,000	48,000
MacRobert Centre, Stirling	64,000	58,000
Third Eye Centre, Glasgow	125,000	90,000
	£3,867,000	£3,211,000
Total budget	£5,950,000	£4,950,000
Percentage of SAC's total allocation	64.9%	64.8%

Note: The total turnover of these bodies exceeds £8,000,000, so that the Council's contribution is slightly less than half their costs.

It is often argued that the existence of these large organisations and their heavy claims on SAC's resources prevent the Council from assisting a much larger number of individual artists and small organisations. In this context it should not be forgotten that SAC receives 3% more of ACGB's overall grant than the strict ratio of Scotland's population would permit at least partly in order to support these large organisations: this, of course, is 25% of the whole of the SAC grant. The initial problem with these large organisations is whether you have them at all or not. If you decide to have them, then, given present levels of government support for the arts, it is almost unavoidable that a substantial proportion of the available resources should be devoted to them. In each of these organisations, SAC's contribution is currently decisive: without it they could not continue.

Leaving aside, however, the question of whether there actually is a substantial number of unsupported individual artists or organisations of an acceptable level of artistic achievement in Scotland at present, the case for devoting so high a proportion of the available resources to a limited number of major organisations is often not fully appreciated. Those who oppose the allocation of resources on this scale to a small number of large organisations should consider the probable state of the Scottish cultural life without an indigenous opera company, symphony orchestra, etc. The only live music of this kind available to Scotland would come from visiting orchestras and opera companies, and then only to the extent that money was available to subsidise visits, and that schedules permitted time for visits. It must be remembered that Scotland possesses neither a single large modern concert hall of the kind which symphony orchestras are used to playing in in places like London, Manchester, Croydon and Sheffield, nor an opera house capable of accommodating an audience of more than 1,600 or an orchestra of the size really required for, say, Wagner and Strauss: these limitations amount to a positive disincentive to visiting companies, however much they are tolerated by the resident companies.

The opera companies and orchestras are based in Glasgow and Edinburgh, and their principal regular series of performances are necessarily confined to the four major cities. If it is assumed that audiences are willing to travel no more than ten miles, these venues, therefore, already make opera and orchestral concerts available to well over half the population of Scotland; and if audiences will travel further (and in many cases they do, as the subscription list of Scottish Opera indicates), then an even higher proportion of the population is served by these venues. Medium-scale opera or orchestras can, moreover, perform in smaller centres, and places like Stirling, Inverness, Ayr and Elgin receive periodic visits from some of these organisations. Most of the major companies have hived off small touring groups that perform even more widely: Scottish Opera have spawned Opera for All for this purpose; the Scottish Philharmonic Society, the Scottish Baroque Ensemble; and Scottish Ballet, Moveable Workshop. But at the end of the day, there will remain a residue of population still without easy access to any kind of live music of the highest quality. The population of some parts of Scotland is sparse and widely scattered and it would be unreal to suppose that it could ever be an economic proposition to take opera or orchestral concerts to it.

More important to the musical life of Scotland, however, is the effect of the sheer presence of 200-250 full-time professional musicians involved in these organisations whose salaries represent the greater part of the grants allocated by SAC. These posts form an important element in the hierarchy of career opportunities for professional musicians in Scotland. Without the opportunity to earn the livings in Scotland provided by these organisations, aspiring professional musicians must emigrate to earn a living. These musicians form an invaluable core to the body of instrumental teachers: without them, instrumental tuition, the foundation of the musical life of any country, would be incalculably poorer. Finally, many of these musicians — orchestral players and singers — form themselves into small chamber ensembles or offer their services as soloists to provide the concerts organised by Scotland's one hundred arts and music clubs: without these soloists and groups, the clubs would have to import more of their concerts more expensively from south of the Border. These arguments apply, *mutatis mutandis*, to much of the support for ballet and drama provision in Scotland.

It would be short-sighted, therefore, to abandon support for the large, centrally based organisations in pursuit of a wider dispersal of limited resources: some increase in provision in the rural areas might result, but it would be at the cost of the overall quality of artistic life in Scotland generally. Money spent in the Central Belt or major cities ultimately benefits the whole country; or, to put it another way, money not spent on the major organisations in these areas would damage, if not destroy, much of the cultural life of the whole country.

But it remains a fact that the large organisations are expensive and that the inflation of their costs in recent years has probably posed the largest single problem confronting the SAC. In the world of arts administration it is commonly asserted that arts costs have tended to inflate faster than prices generally. Attempts have been made to demonstrate this statistically, but the measures employed have not been very satisfactory. The problem of financing the major arts organisations in Scotland in recent years has therefore been one of comparative rates of inflation. Costs have risen at rates largely outwith the control of the companies. Most of the companies have lacked the courage to push up ticket prices as fast, or have claimed to "know" that elasticity of demand for their product was such that to raise ticket prices as fast would only result in falling box office revenue. The ability of SAC, on the other hand, to make good the widening gap was dependent upon the rate at which ACGB's grant from the Government increased from year to year. In addition, there were each year, of course, many new projects looking for support, and the need has been for some increase in the level of the annual grant beyond that necessary to maintain at least the existing level of activity by the major companies. The long run of the whole post-war period has, in the event, witnessed a very substantial "real" increase in the grants provided by successive governments, though there have inevitably been some years when the increase in the annual grant has done no more than cover the inflation of costs of existing activities, as well as years when it has not even done that. In view of all these problems, the amazing fact is that, with very few exceptions, the basic operations of the major organisations in music, ballet, drama, art exhibitions and festivals have both been provided for and permitted in many instances to expand; and that at the same time new activities — some quite large-scale and therefore expensive — have been encouraged by SAC support to start. Among the latter are the Scottish Youth Theatre, the Scottish Photography Group, and the new Festival at Easterhouse in Glasgow.

Quantity is one thing, but the public also looks for some assurances about the quality of the activities supported from taxation. Are the musical compositions commissioned with Arts Council money good music? Do the small literary magazines supported really provide a forum for distinguished poetry? Are the exhibitions that so frequently mystify the public the work of gifted artists or charlatans? Who judges, and by what criteria? The Arts Council's problem is rendered no easier by the fact that in many areas it is necessarily dealing with contemporary art: it is today's composers, artists and writers they are supporting, not yesterday's, and the process of sorting the wheat from the chaff has not been achieved painlessly with the passage of time. In these areas, judgement is difficult and not bound by old conventions; it is better when it is informed, but must remain subjective. The Arts Council can only seek the most informed advice, which it does through expert panels, and try to keep an open mind. Tax and ratepayers and their guardians in central and local government, on the other hand, can afford the luxury of prejudice and closed minds. To absorb the inevitable friction, the Arts Council must interpose itself in the no-man's land between the *avant garde* and those who pay for it. This "buffer" principle is an essential safeguard if any sort of artistic freedom is to be preserved from direct political control.

The considerable achievement of both maintaining the major opera, theatrical and orchestral companies and supporting new and often adventurous developments has been possible, of course, because successive "Ministers for the Arts" have persuaded their governments to provide liberal annual increases that have, in the majority of years, overtaken inflation. But it has also been possible because central government is not the sole source of public support for the arts. In recent years, for example, there has been a move towards support for the arts from industry and commerce. Most of the major arts organisations in Scotland have succeeded in securing some financial support from this sector, while Scottish Opera has recently been particularly successful in enlisting Scottish-based insurance companies as sponsors for new productions of large-scale works. A door has been opened here which it is hoped will lead to a much closer collaboration between the worlds of business and the arts. At present, however, in relation both to total arts revenues in Scotland and to the business resources themselves, the support from this quarter is minimal.

It is to local government that the arts must principally look for partnership with SAC. Local authorities at both district and regional levels are empowered to employ money from the rates for this purpose, and many have set up Leisure and Recreation Committees since re-organisation whose remit includes support for the arts. Since re-organisation, too, Scottish local authorities have created the Convention of Scottish Local Authorities (COSLA). COSLA, which does not publish any annual reports, and about whose activities surprisingly little is publicly known, acts as a forum for the discussion of matters of common concern to local authorities and for the co-ordination of policy at national level. So far as the arts are concerned, this has involved agreement to a basic recommendation that the Regions should accept responsibility for local government support to the national arts organisations, and the Districts for local organisations. There was further agreement to recommend that Regions should set their contributions to each of the national organisations at fixed sums per 1,000 of their populations. This schedule has some importance since it is inevitably regarded by most authorities as a maximum. Since, however, it is also not a minimum, different authorities actually offer varying proportions of the COSLA recommended schedule, some falling a long way short of the recommended contributions.

Thus, at the absolute level, there tend to be wide variations in the contribution of Scottish local authorities to the arts. At the bottom end of the scale, support is minimal. Places seldom or never, for obvious reasons of geography and facilities, visited by the main companies see little immediate advantage to them — in spite of what has been suggested above — in supporting national organisations firmly anchored to Glasgow and Edinburgh, while it is abundantly clear, even to the most culture-conscious councillor, that "there are no votes in opera". At the other end of the scale, some authorities have responded to the call to support the arts with vision and generosity. At the risk of appearing invidious, reference should be made to Edinburgh District's support of the Edinburgh International Festival; to the Highland Region's operation of the Eden Court Theatre; and to the support for Scottish Opera from both Strathclyde Region and Glasgow District. Inevitably the major arts organisations, partly as a consequence of their history, and partly through the chance of their location in this or that region or district, have widely varying experiences of local authority support. The Scottish National Orchestra, for example, as a matter of policy, and also on account of its long history of performance in the major centres, has been particularly success-ful in persuading local authorities to support it. At the other extreme, however, the Third Eye Centre in Glasgow has so far failed to elicit any substantial local government support.

As is well known, the re-organised local authorities (and with them COSLA) were born just in time to experience the chastening economies of expenditure cuts forced on them by

K

central government. In the face of competing claims for local government expenditure in fields like housing, education and social work, it was not to be expected that apparently less urgent areas like the arts would be able to hold their own. Nor did they: by 1978 the COSLA recommended schedule had stood at the same level in money terms for three years, representing a reduction in real terms of 30% or more. Though there have been some exceptions, most authorities have accepted this guidance from COSLA, while not following it in respect of absolute levels. The resultant shortfall in local government support has had the most drastic effect on most of the major organisations, and it is not too much to say that the serious financial situation they find themselves in at present arises almost wholly from the decline in real terms of local government support. Those, like the Scottish National Orchestra, that had been most successful in the past in enlisting local government support have in consequence been the hardest hit. Both the companies themselves and SAC have been strenuous in their endeavours to persuade COSLA and its member authorities to make good the losses, but the pressures on the local authorities by central government understandably make it difficult for them to respond.

The partnership between local government and SAC in the support of the arts in Scotland, while never a partnership of equals, has thus faltered in recent years. This gave added impetus to an enquiry, initiated by SAC in 1974, which resulted in a report on *The Arts in The Scottish Regions* (SAC, Edinburgh, 1976). It followed this up by appointing in 1977 a Regional Development Director with a remit to establish close links with local authorities and to explore every possible way in which local authorities and SAC might collaborate in developing provisions for the arts in all parts of Scotland. It remains to be seen how the local authorities will respond to this initiative. In the meantime the Arts Council itself is under informal pressure from the Government not to use its resources merely to fill the gap left by declining local government support: it is feared that to do so would simply reduce the pressure on local authorities and encourage them further to withdraw their support. Since the decline in local government support is justified by the expenditure cuts forced on them by central government, this advice is rather unhelpful.

While it is easy to conclude from these recent trends that the arts in Scotland are going through something of a crisis at the moment, it would be exaggerated to do so. Though the acute financial problems of many of the arts organisations in Scotland have led to endless agonised discussions round the tables in Charlotte Square and elsewhere, aid to the arts has never been more plentifully supplied than at present. Several major companies have very serious worries about the future, and all are working below capacity and within the tightest budgets; but actual collapse has so far never been closer than just around the corner.

The ultimate uncertainty at the moment for the future of the arts in Scotland, however, arises out of the prospect of devolution. The Bill presently before Parliament will pass responsibility for government support of the arts from London to Edinburgh. Beyond that nothing is known, or is likely to be known for some considerable time after an Assembly is set up, since support for the arts is unlikely to be high in the order of priorities of problems of re-organisation to be tackled by the Assembly. Under an Assembly, SAC could hardly remain a committee of ACGB. Nor would an Assembly necessarily be tied to the present "arts council" type of administrative structure, though most of those with experience of the administration of state aid for the arts believe that it would be unwise to dispense with the "buffer" principle. If the Assembly decided to retain an arts council, however, it would be free to think out its constitution *ab initio*. Here the political colour of the Assembly would have some bearing: there is nothing sacrosanct about the present form of membership and the Labour Party, for example, has recently issued a policy statement, *The Arts and the People,* expressing support for a rather elaborate "representative" structure. Nor is an Assembly tied by any commitment to maintain present scales of state support for the arts. Finally, there is the question of the relations of any Scottish arts council with the future with ACGB, or the English Arts Council as it must become. There may possibly be some scope for a federal British Arts Council. At present, however, SAC's links with ACGB are close and invaluable: it would be a very foolish Assembly that cut these.

11

THE REGIONAL COUNCIL ELECTIONS OF MAY 1978*

J. M. BOCHEL
Senior Lecturer in Political Science, University of Dundee,

D. T. DENVER
Lecturer in Politics, University of Lancaster.

I

The nine Scottish Regional Councils created under the Local Government (Scotland) Act of 1972 constitute the upper tier of the two-tier system of local government in Scotland. The Regions are responsible for a variety of important local government functions including strategic planning, roads and transportation, industrial development, and the police, fire, education and social work services. Though they vary enormously in area, population and resources, the Regional authorities are all large and complex organisations whose performances importantly affect the daily lives of the people they govern.[1]

Regional councillors were first elected in 1974 and it would be fair to say that since then the Regional authorities have been the targets of a good deal of criticism. Generally the complaints have been that they are too large, remote from the ordinary elector, over-bureaucratised, cumbersome and inefficient. There exists quite a strong current of opinion that, in any future reorganisation of local government in Scotland—especially if the proposed Scottish Assembly becomes a reality—the Regions should be abolished. Indeed this is the declared policy of the Scottish National Party. Consequently, in addition to the normal sets of issues that might be found in local government elections, the second round of Regional elections held on 2 May 1978 was seen by many people as an opportunity for

*We are grateful to Brian and Wilma McHardy for their indispensable assistance in the collection and processing of the data upon which this paper is based. Some of the data was collected as part of a larger project on local elections financed by the Social Science Research Council.

electors to pass judgment on the system as well as on the candidates and the parties.

The results of these elections — like the results of all elections — can be studied in a number of ways. The audience to which one is addressing oneself will determine the questions to be asked and hence the nature and depth of the analysis to be undertaken; at least three distinct if overlapping audiences can be identified. Firstly there are those interested in local government and particularly in the Regional Councils, local politicians, candidates, councillors and officials. With these in mind, we present a largely descriptive account of the results, comparing those of 1978 with those for the same authorities in 1974. Secondly, there are national politicians and political commentators who are less interested in the Regional elections *per se* and more concerned with what the results can tell them about trends in electoral opinion in Scotland. In this regard comparisons may be made not just with the last set of Regional elections but also with the last General Election, the District elections of 1977 and intervening by-elections. Finally, the results of the 1978 Regional elections will be of interest to academic political scientists concerned to test and develop hypotheses relating to parties, elections and voting behaviour. We devote relatively little attention to questions of more general academic interest, but we hope that this discussion and our comprehensive collection and analysis of the results which will be published later this year will act as a stimulus to our academic colleagues in this field[2].

II

In describing the Regional election results there are two major themes to consider — participation by candidates, parties and electors, and patterns of party support. We look at each of these in turn.

(i) Participation: parties and candidates

Perceived public apathy towards local elections — as manifested in low turnouts of voters — has long been deplored by public officials, newspaper editors, candidates, party organisers and so on. Less frequently commented upon, but just as surely an indicator of this apathy, has been the unwillingness of people to come forward as candidates and the inability of parties to ensure that local elections are always contested. Uncontested elections have always been fairly common at local level but one of the hopes of the architects of the new structure of local government was that the existence of the larger and, on the face of it, more powerful local authorities, together with the payment of attendance allowances to councillors, would stimulate greater participation by both electors and parties.

In this respect the new Regional authorities got off to an encouraging start in 1974. Interest in the elections was high. Many more divisions were contested than had been the case under the old system and turnout, at 50.6 per cent, was relatively high. The 1978 election results suggest, however, that interest has declined somewhat.

If we consider first the percentage of divisions that were contested, over the whole country, this fell from 90.3% in 1974 to 79.1% in 1978.[3] As Table I shows, however, this decline was not uniform, being particularly marked in the Highland, Borders, Dumfries and Galloway and Tayside Regions. In Highland and Dumfries and Galloway fewer than half the divisions were contested in 1978. On the other hand, there were increases in the percentage of divisions contested in Strathclyde, Lothian and Central — and in the latter two cases every division was contested.

Table I

PERCENTAGE OF DIVISIONS CONTESTED 1974 - 1978

	1974 %	1978 %	Change %
Highland	91.5	46.8	−44.7
Grampian	90.6	73.6	−17.0
Tayside	95.7	73.9	−21.8
Fife	83.3	81.0	− 2.3
Lothian	93.9	100.0	+ 6.1
Central	88.2	100.0	+11.8
Borders	91.3	56.5	−34.8
Strathclyde	97.1	99.0	+ 1.9
Dumfries & Galloway	65.7	42.9	−22.8
Scotland	90.3	79.1	−11.2

At first glance it would not appear to be the parties who are to be "blamed" for the overall decline in competitiveness. The decline is steepest in the Regions in which party competition at local level is least developed and local politics is dominated by Independents. Indeed, as Table II shows, the number of major party candidates in these elections increased as compared with 1974. There was a slight decline in the number of Labour candidates but this was more than counterbalanced by a moderate increase in the number of Conservatives — indicative of the Conservative Party's still growing participation in Scottish local politics — and a substantial rise in the number of SNP candidates. The latter was particularly marked in Strathclyde, where they increased by 46, Lothian, where there was an increase of 21 and Tayside where the SNP contested the Regional election for the first time with 16 candidates. By contrast the number of Independent candidates fell sharply — by almost 50.0% — and declined in each of the nine Regions.

Table II

NUMBER OF CANDIDATES PUT FORWARD BY EACH PARTY
1974 - 1978

	1974	1978	1974 - 78
Con	254	292	+ 37
Lab	303	284	− 20
Lib	83	37	− 46
SNP	126	225	+ 99
Comm	56	38	− 18
Ind	297	152	−143
Others	29	19	− 10
Total	1,148	1047	−101

More detailed analysis of the divisions which were contested in 1974 but not in 1978 corroborates the view that the increase in uncontested returns is mainly a consequence of reduced participation on the part of the Independents. In the 74 divisions which fall into this category, the Conservatives withdrew in 7, Labour in 16, the Liberals also in 16, the SNP in 10 and at least some Independents in 53. In 27 of the divisions it was only Independent candidates who withdrew.

The decline in participation by Independents might have a number of causes. In some areas where the parties have dominated, the Independents might have felt that the struggle against the party machines in elections was too unequal or that they were in an anomalous position in a council run on party lines, and simply withdrawn. In others (for example, Grampian) at least some Independents have reacted to the realities of party-organised local politics by adopting a party label (usually Conservative). But these arguments do not explain the decline in the number of Independent candidates in the Highland Region (−29), Borders (−12) and Dumfries and Galloway (−25) where the parties are still weak. In these Regions — which are very large in area and small in population — it may be that the rewards and satisfactions of local government service are not great enough to outweigh the costs in time and effort. Travel alone for many councillors in the Highland Region, for example, must be a major disincentive.

(ii) Participation: turnout

Turnout in contested divisions in the Regional elections declined from 50.6% in 1974 to 44.6% in 1978. Table III presents turnout figures for each of the nine Regions and it can be seen that there was a decline in every case and that Regional deviations from the overall figure were not, on the whole, very great.

The largest decline was in the Grampian Region — a fall of 9.2% to 33.8%, by far the lowest turnout of any Region. Interestingly, the turnout in Grampian at the 1977 District elections was also the lowest in Scotland at 36.1%, but we can find no satisfactory explanation for the unusually low level of electors' participation in this part of the country.

Table III

PERCENTAGE TURNOUT 1974 - 1978

	1974 %	1978 %	Change %
Highland	52.5	43.9	−8.6
Grampian	43.0	33.8	−9.2
Tayside	47.4	41.3	−6.1
Fife	49.9	46.3	−3.6
Lothian	51.0	43.8	−7.2
Central	57.7	50.4	−7.3
Borders	48.2	41.7	−6.5
Strathclyde	51.7	46.2	−5.5
Dumfries & Galloway	46.9	43.3	−3.6
Scotland	50.6	44.6	−6.0

A variety of hypotheses have been put forward to explain variations in turnout and in turnout change from one election to the next, involving variables such as the weather, the marginality of the electoral division, the choice of candidates, the social structure of the electorate and so on, but we do not have space to pursue these here. We can, however, test an hypothesis specific to these elections. This is that the increased participation by th SNP would lead to higher turnout. This would seem a reasonable hypothesis since intervention by the SNP increases the range of candidates and one would expect that at electoral division level it would lead to greater public awareness since it would mean more extensive advertising, canvassing and general activity. In order to test the hypothesis in a simple way we have isolated those divisions which were contested by the Conservatives and Labour alone of the major parties in both 1974 and 1978 (26 divisions) and those which were contested by the Conservatives and Labour in 1974 but in which the SNP intervened in 1978 (54 divisions). The mean change in turnout in the former group was −9.8%, while in the latter it was −3.5%. It would seem, then, that SNP intervention did have some effect in moderating the decline in turnout.

The overall turnout of 44.6% suggests a marked lack of interest in the Regional Councils on the part of the electorate and supports claims about their remoteness. Despite their greater powers, the Regional Councils had a lower turnout than the District Councils had for their elections in 1977 (47.8%). In only one Region did turnout in 1978 exceed 50% — but this was the case in 22 of the 53 Districts in 1977. After the initial flourish of enthusiasm in 1974 when the novelty of the new system may have quickened interest, and when both District and Regional elections were held on the same day, turnout at Regional level returned in 1978 to a level which is similar to that obtained under the old local government system.

(iii) Patterns of Party Support: Votes

For most people the level of participation in an election is a question of secondary importance. What really matters is who wins votes and seats. Table IV shows the distribution of votes amongst the parties at the 1974 and 1978 Regional elections over Scotland as a whole.

Table IV

PERCENTAGE SHARE OF THE VOTES *

	1974 %	1978 %	Change 1974-78 %
Con	28.6	30.3	+1.7
Lab	38.5	39.6	+1.1
Lib	5.1	2.4	−2.7
SNP	12.6	20.9	+8.3
Comm	1.0	0.5	−0.5
Ind	12.4	4.9	−7.5
Others	1.9	1.4	−0.5

* Figures for each Region are given in the Reference Section at the end of the book.

Though these figures are clearly important and of considerable interest they must be interpreted with caution because of variations in candidatures at the two elections. As we have seen, there were many more SNP candidates in 1978 than in 1974 and fewer Independents. Further, there was an increase in the number of divisions that were not contested at all. Clearly these features complicate any analysis of voting trends. There were, for instance, 12 divisions which Labour took without opposition in 1974 (and were thus credited with no votes) but in which they were opposed in 1978 and gained almost 35,000 votes — more than 60% of the total in those divisions. On the other hand there were no SNP candidates in Tayside in 1974 but in 1978 their 16 candidates obtained almost 15,000 votes, 16.3% of the total. Despite the difficulties presented by changes of this kind, we clearly must consider the pattern of party support in these elections in some detail.

The Labour Party entered the 1978 elections very much on the defensive. The 1974 Regional elections had seen good results for Labour — they were clearly in control of Fife and Strathclyde and were the largest party in Central and Lothian. But those elections had been held at a time when the newly-elected Labour government was still in its "honeymoon" period with the electorate and was enjoying leads of the order of 15% in the national opinion polls. Following the General Election of October 1974, however, the Government became less popular and in the second half of 1976 and throughout most of 1977 Labour trailed badly behind the Conservatives in the polls. in Scotland, Labour's unpopularity was reflected in a series of local government by-election losses and, most strikingly, in the loss of 129 seats in the District council elections in May 1977. In the last few months of 1977 and the first few months of 1978, however, Labour made a substantial recovery in the polls. They nonetheless entered the Regional elections still behind the Conservatives, according to national polls. In these circumstances Labour were generally expected to lose votes and seats as compared with 1974, even if not on the scale of their losses in 1977. But the outcome of the elections must have been a pleasant surprise even to Labour's most optimistic supporters. Despite putting forward slightly fewer candidates than in 1974 and despite a much more extensive challenge by the SNP, Labour increased its share of the vote to 39.6% of the total.

For the Conservatives too, the results of the elections must have been pleasing — if only moderately so. Following the General Election of October 1974 it was not beyond the bounds of possibility that the Conservatives would be fated to become permanently a third party in Scotland. In fact, however, they recovered a good deal in the 1977 District elections and in 1978 they increased their number of candidates and received a higher share of the vote than they had done in 1974 — putting them comfortably ahead of the SNP in terms of popular support.

A reading of the figures given in Table IV would suggest, on the face of it, that the SNP performed splendidly in these elections. They increased their share of the vote by 8.3% and were, indeed, the only party actually to increase the number of votes they received — from about 215,000 in 1974 to 313,000 in 1978. But these elections were a disappointment to the SNP. They had made a major advance in the 1977 District elections, gaining 107 seats and in 1978 they mounted a formidable challenge, increasing substantially the number of candidates they put forward. Before the elections, the SNP were said to be confident of winning a large number of seats in Strathclyde and of taking control of the Central region. In the event they did neither of these, and the increase in their votes is entirely due to the increased number of candidates put forward. This can be seen from the breakdown of the SNP votes given in Table

V. In divisions which they contested on both occasions the SNP vote declined, and more than half of their total in 1978 came in divisions which they had not contested in 1974.

Table V

VOTES OBTAINED BY THE SNP 1974 AND 1978

	1974 Votes	1978 Votes
Divisions contested 1974 only (31)	20,164	—
Divisions contested 1974 and 1978 (94)	195,238	155,982
Divisions contested 1978 only (130)	—	157,037
Total	215,502	313,019

An unusual feature of the performance of the three major parties in these elections is that all of them increased their share of the votes cast. This is due to the decline in votes for Independent candidates from 12.4% in 1974 to 4.9% in 1978. In part this is a reflection of the decline in contested elections in areas where Independents would have obtained most of the votes. Thus, of the 92 seats won by Independents more than half (49) were taken without a contest compared with 17 out of 114 in 1974. In the Highland Region, for instance, Independents increased their number of seats won from 37 to 40 but largely because of uncontested returns their total vote fell from 44,000 to 24,000. In part also, the decline in Independent support reflects increasing domination of the Regional Councils by the political parties — a subject to which we return below. In the six most partisan regions (Grampian, Tayside, Fife, Lothian, Central and Strathclyde) Independent candidates fell from 112 to 34 and their share of the vote from 8.2% to 1.8% between the two elections.

A more accurate picture of the relative performance of the three major parties than is given in Table IV can be obtained from an analysis of those divisions in which the pattern of major party candidatures was the same in both 1974 and 1978. This avoids distortions due to variations in candidatures. Three types of contest are of interest, viz. Conservative v Labour, Labour v SNP, and Conservative v Labour v SNP. The table below shows the division of votes amongst the parties concerned in each of these three kinds of contest.

Table VI

SHARE OF VOTES IN DIVISIONS WHERE MAJOR PARTY CANDIDATES WERE THE SAME IN BOTH ELECTIONS

(i) Con v Lab (36 Divisions)

1974		1978	
Con	Lab	Con	Lab
%	%	%	%
56.7	43.3	58.0	42.0

(ii) Lab v SNP (21 Divisions)

1974		1978	
Lab	SNP	Lab	SNP
%	%	%	%
52.1	47.9	58.0	42.0

(iii) Con v Lab v SNP (56 Divisions)

1974			1978		
Con	Lab	SNP	Con	Lab	SNP
%	%	%	%	%	%
27.4	45.8	26.8	29.1	46.5	24.4

Taking each of these in turn, the first section of the table shows that there was in Con v Lab contests a slight movement from Labour to Conservative between the two elections — a swing of 1.3%. That there was such a movement is not surprising given the change in the two parties' fortunes in the national opinion polls between April 1974 and April 1978. What is surprising is how small the swing was.

In Labour v SNP contests, however, there is a clear and substantial swing from the SNP to Labour (5.9%). When it is remembered that 1974 had been a generally good performance by Labour, their improved position in straight fights with the SNP is a measure of the latter's poor showing.

Finally, where candidates of all three parties were present at both elections there was again a decline in the SNP's share of the three-party vote (−2.2%) while both the other parties improved, the Conservatives gaining slightly more than Labour (+1.7% to 0.7%).

Before we leave this discussion of the voting pattern in 1978 a few words should be said about the minor parties. Firstly, the Liberals are now clearly a very minor party in Scottish local politics. They gained only 2.4% of the votes. This was not simply a reflection of a decline in the number of Liberal candidates. In four Edinburgh divisions, for instance, in which in both 1974 and 1978 Conservative, Labour and Liberal candidates were in competition, the Liberal share of votes dropped from 31.4% to 22.7% and in 6 divisions (3 in Edinburgh and 3 in Inverclyde) where the SNP intervened in 1978 the drop in the Liberal share of the vote (−10.3%) was much larger than that experienced by the other two parties (Conservative −0.2% and Labour −3.8%). Overall, it would seem that the outlook for the Liberals at this level is pretty bleak. The Scottish Labour Party had eight candidates in the field. But, as in 1977, it failed to make any impact. It won no seats and gained only 6,629 votes, almost 75% of these coming from two candidates in Cumnock and Doon Valley, the base of the party's leader, Jim Sillars, MP.

(iv) Patterns of Party Support: Seats

The analysis of voting returns is a fascinating business, but of more practical importance is the number of seats won. Parties and groups seek to win council seats in order to gain control of the authority and thus be able to implement their own distinctive policies. Table VII shows the number of seats won over the whole country in 1974 and 1978.

Table VII

NUMBER OF SEATS WON *

	1974	1978	Change 1974-78
Con	112	136	+24
Lab	172	174	+2
Lib	11	6	−5
SNP	18	18	0
Comm	1	1	0
Ind	114	92	−22
Other	4	4	0
	432	431	

(1 vacant)

* Figures for each Region are shown in the Reference Section at the end of the book.

Labour remains the largest party in Scotland in terms of

Regional council seats. The Conservatives have, however, replaced Independents as the second largest "party". As we have noted, this is partly to be explained by former Independents now accepting a party label. Ten of the twenty-four Conservative "gains" were simply cases in which councillors who had been elected as Independents in 1974 presented themselves in 1978 as Conservatives. There were also, however, a number of cases of Conservative gains against Independent opposition. The overall impression of stability conveyed by Table VII is a little misleading because, of course, gains and losses can cancel each other out. In fact 68 seats changed hands between parties. This is 15.7% of the seats at stake and compared with 21.4% of the seats which changed hands in the District elections of 1977. The Regional election was, therefore, characterised by somewhat less instability than the Districts. The turnover of seats among the parties is shown in Table VIII. (For the purpose of this table we have ignored regional by-elections between 1974 and 1978).

Table VIII

SEATS CHANGING HANDS

Losing Party	Con	Lab	Lib	SNP	Ind	Other	Total Losses
Con	—	2	—	2	3	1	8
Lab	3	—	—	3	3	—	9
Lib	2	—	—	—	4	—	6
SNP	3	6	—	—	—	1	10
Ind	23	3	1	4	—	1	32
Others	1	1	—	1	—	—	3
Total Gains	32	12	1	10	10	3	68

It can be seen that there was some cancelling out of gains and losses. The SNP, for instance, gained 10 seats but lost another 10 thus leaving them with the same number as in 1974. The commonest change was from Independent to Conservative, which we have already touched upon. There were six Conservative gains from Independents in Grampian, 5 in Dumfries and Galloway and 4 in Tayside. Interestingly, only 5 seats changed hands between the Conservatives and Labour.

All of this had important consequences for party control

of individual Regions. The situation in this respect after the 1974 elections and that after the 1978 elections is set out below. Labour now have clear control of all the Regions in the populous central belt while the Conservatives have added Tayside (which they previously controlled with the Independents) to Grampian.

	1974	1978
Independent Control	Highland Borders Dumfries & Galloway	Highland Borders Dumfries & Galloway
Labour Control	Fife Strathclyde	Fife Strathclyde Lothian Central
Conservative Control	Grampian	Grampian Tayside
No overall Control	Tayside (Con largest party) Lothian (Lab largest party) Central (Lab largest party)	

III

Trends in Electoral Support 1974-78

In the national press and on television most comment on local election results is concerned with their implications as indicators of the general state of electoral opinion in the country. They are treated, not unreasonably, as super-opinion polls which give a reliable guide to the popularity of the various parties amongst voters. In this respect the 1978 Regional elections were particularly important because a General Election was expected later in the year. Interest was centred, of course, on the relative performance of the Conservatives, Labour and SNP and because of this, in what follows, we confine ourselves to election results in Strathclyde, Central, Lothian and Fife, for it is only in these Regions that there are enough candidatures by the three parties at local level to make for meaningful analysis. In any event these four Regions contain about 75% of the Scottish electorate and 51 of the 71 Scottish parliamentary constituencies. The overall distribution of votes amongst the three parties in these regions at the elections in 1974, 1977 and 1978 is given in Table IX. The message of the data is clear. The Conservatives effected a substantial recovery between 1974 and 1977 and they managed to improve on this a little betwen 1977 and 1978. Labour experienced a marked drop in popularity between the General Election and the District elections but by 1978 were roughly back at the level of support they had enjoyed in the October 1974 General Election — well ahead of the other two parties. The SNP on the other hand, after maintaining their 1974 level in 1977, dropped back considerably in 1978.

Table IX

THREE-PARTY SHARES OF THE VOTES
(1974, 1977, 1978, Fife, Lothian, Central, Strathclyde)

	General Election 1974 (51 constituencies)	District Elections 1977 (675 wards)	Regional Elections 1978 (227 divisions)
	%	%	%
Con	24.4	30.6	31.3
Lab	44.3	38.2	44.9
SNP	31.3	31.3	23.9

Inevitably, the comparison of the District and Regional elections is complicated by variations in candidatures on the part of the three parties. There were, however, 46 Regional divisions in 1978 in which there were Conservative, Labour and SNP candidates and whose component District wards all had candidates of the three parties in 1977. A comparison of the performances of the three parties in these areas only at the two sets of elections generally confirms the pattern seen in Table IX.

Table X

THREE-PARTY SHARES OF THE VOTES 1977 AND 1978
(selected divisions)

	District Elections 1977 (104 wards)	Regional Elections 1978 (46 divisions)
	%	%
Con	35.0	33.9
Lab	32.7	43.8
SNP	32.3	22.4

Although the figures suggest in this case a slight fall in Conservative support, the Labour recovery and SNP decline are clearly confirmed.

L

To careful observers of Scottish electoral opinion this movement was not entirely unexpected. Following the October General Election, opinion polls in Scotland, which are undertaken and published monthly, showed the three parties running about even in terms of popular support.[4] From the middle of 1977, however, Labour's position, according to these polls, improved. This can be seen clearly in Tabe XI which shows the parties' standing in the polls throughout 1977 and 1978. While Conservative support remained fairly firm, SNP support tended to decline and Labour's to rise very steadily.

Table XI

MEAN SHARE OF VOTE INTENTIONS IN SCOTLAND 1977-78

	Jan-April 1977	May-Aug 1977	Sept-Dec 1977	Jan-April 1978
	%	%	%	%
Con	29.8	28.8	29.3	27.8
Lab	28.0	30.5	34.0	39.5
SNP	32.8	32.5	28.3	26.3

Only three weeks before the Regional elections a firm indication was given in the parliamentary by-election in Glasgow Garscadden that the story being told by these polls was correct. This was the first Scottish by-election of the present Parliament and the SNP had gained all the District seats within the constituency in 1977, taking 44.6% of the three-party vote compared with 36.0% for Labour and 19.4% for the Conservatives. Yet in the by-election Labour held the seat comfortably, gaining 46.9% of the three-party vote compared with 34.0% for the SNP and 19.2% for the Conservatives.

How, then, is one to account for the resurgence of Labour support in Scotland? A variety of reasons have been suggested including the impending success of the Government's devolution bill, the unimpressive performance of SNP councillors at District level, and a tendency for the SNP to rest on its laurels and assume that victories would continue to come its way without undue effort. In our view the real explanation is more general than these. The movement of opinion in favour of Labour is not something peculiar to Scotland. Since mid-1977, national opinion polls have found the Government's standing with the electorate improving steadily. Gallup, for instance, in April-

June 1977 reported a Conservative lead over Labour averaging 15.5%. In April 1978 the Conservative lead was only 2%. Similarly, swings against the Government in by-elections have become smaller through 1977 and 1978 than they were previously. This suggests a more general return of confidence in the Government arising from such general factors as its overall handling of the economy, the electorate's perceptions of the performance of the Prime Minister and so on. Our view has always been that SNP voting has been, to a significant extent at least, a result of disappointment with the performance of governments of both major parties. When the Government was perceived as doing fairly well at least, then it was likely that SNP support would wane and that is what happened in 1978.

IV

As a final comment upon the 1978 Regional elections we want to emphasise the increasingly partisan nature of politics at this level. Writing elsewhere about Scottish local politics we have discussed partisan and non-partisan styles of local politics and noted that the latter is declining.[5] According to our argument the non-partisan style is most likely to be found in small towns and villages electing local councils and we would expect therefore that the Regions would be more likely to be organised upon a partisan basis than the Districts. This is certainly the case. Only the three peripheral Regions of Highland, Borders, and Dumfries and Galloway can now be categorised as non-partisan. The six others are now firmly partisan. The change in these Regions between 1974 and 1978 is illustrated in Table XII.

Table XII

INDEPENDENTS IN PARTISAN AND NON-PARTISAN REGIONS
1974 - 78

	Non-Partisan Regions (3)		Partisan Regions (6)	
	1974	1978	1974	1978
% Candidates Ind	69.3	71.9	12.7	3.9
% Votes Ind	79.1	74.3	9.5	4.3
% Seats Ind	69.2	71.5	7.9	1.8

As can be seen, Independents, from a position of some significance, have now been virtually eliminated in the six partisan Regions. On the other hand, the parties have made little progress in the non-partisan areas. In these the Independent tradition is resilient and looks likely to remain dominant for some time to come.

REFERENCES

1. The nine Regions are shown on the map of Scotland in the Reference section.

2. A comprehensive collection of the election results and a more extensive analysis will be published later in 1978 by the authors and will be available from them. The analysis undertaken in this paper must be regarded as preliminary since it is based upon results given in *The Scotsman* and the *Glasgow Herald* which have not yet been fully checked with the appropriate returning officers.

3. Throughout, we have ignored Division 31 in the Strathclyde Region in which the election was postponed due to the death of the incumbent Labour councillor and candidate, Geoff Shaw.

4. The polls are conducted by System Three (Scotland) Ltd. and published in the *Glasgow Herald*. See table in Reference section for the results of System Three Polls October 1974 - May 1978.

5. Drucker, H. M., and Clarke, M. G. (eds) *The Scottish Government Yearbook 1978* (Edinburgh, 1977), and Bochel, J. M., and Denver, D. T., *The Scottish District Elections 1977* (Dundee, Department of Political Science, University of Dundee, 1977).

REFERENCE SECTION

ACKNOWLEDGEMENTS

We have made use of information from the following:

Civil Service Yearbook 1978
Municipal Yearbook 1978
Times Guides to the House of Commons
Kellas, J., *The Scottish Political System*
Bochel, J. and Denver, J., *The Scottish Local Government Elections* (1974 and 1977)
Keesing's Contemporary Archives
Scotland's Regions 1977/78
Scotsman, "The Bill and its Progress" (weekly series 28. xi. 77 onwards)
Scotsman and *Glasgow Herald* 3 and 4 May 1978 (Regional Election results)
Butler and Kavanagh *British General Election of October 1974*
Butler and Freeman, *British Political Facts*
Economist 6 May 1978
Cook and Ramsden, *By-Elections in British Politics*
Craig, F. W. S., *British Electoral Facts 1885-1975*

SECTION 1

RECENT PUBLICATIONS IN SCOTTISH GOVERNMENT AND POLITICS

C. H. ALLEN,
Department of Politics, University of Edinburgh

The lists below cover material published in the period 1.6.77 to 31.5.78, together with material omitted from earlier lists. I would be grateful if readers would notify me of any items missing from the current lists.

As before, the items are divided into two lists, the first covering books, pamphlets, long articles, memoranda and sets of newspaper features; and the second covering short articles and newspaper features. There is a break in the numbering, with the second part beginning at 400, to allow for easier identification of longer pieces in the Index at the end of the lists.

Certain periodicals have been abbreviated thus:

CCN	Community Council News
Econ.	The Economist
FT	Financial Times
G	Guardian
GH	Glasgow Herald
Orc.	The Orcadian
S	Scotsman
SDE	Scottish Daily Express
Shet. T.	Shetland Times
SI	Scots Independent
ST	Sunday Times
T	Times
WHFP	West Highland Free Press
7D	7 Days

PART 1: BOOKS, PAMPHLETS AND LONGER ARTICLES

1 Adams, F., *The making of urban Scotland*. London: Croom Helm, 1978, 303pp.
2 Alexander, K., "The problems of rural land management in the Highlands", *Landowning in Scotland* 168 (1977), 96-100.
3 Allen, C. H., *Accession list No. 2: Jan.-Dec. 1977*. Edinburgh: Edinburgh University, Unit for the Study of Government in Scotland, 1978, 14pp.
4   "Recent publications in Scottish government and politics", *The Scottish Government Yearbook,* eds. H. M. Drucker and M. G. Clarke. Edinburgh: Paul Harris, 1978, 151-93.
5 Anonymous. "Information developments in Scotland", *BURISA Journal,* Jan. 1978, 1-14.
6   "Regional elections", *South Central Area News* (Edinburgh), 1 (May 1978), 10-13.

7   "Relative performance of incoming and non-incoming industry in Scotland", *Scottish Economic Bulletin* 13 (1977), 14-25.

8   "Strathclyde: BLF survey", *Business Location File*, Nov-Dec. 1977, 30-40.

9   "Structure Plan featuring . . .", *Clydeside Action* 7 (1978), 4-7.

10   Ansdell, I., "Capital scheme's moment of truth", *CCN* 3 (1977), 2-5, 18.

11   Anslics, *Oil: a bibliography*. Aberdeen: Aberdeen and North of Scotland Library and Information Co-operative Service, 1977, 314 pp.

11a   Arthur, P, "The break-up of Britain?" *Parliamentary Affairs*, 31,2 (1978), 220-25.

12   Ascherson, N., "The last of the giants", *Sunday Times Magazine*, 14.5.78, 56-65.

13   Ashworth, G. R. V., *The delimitation of Central Scotland's regions: an appraisal.*. M.Sc. thesis, Strathclyde University, 1976.

14   Bain, D., & Cunningham, R., *Scotland: facts and Comparisons*. Edinburgh: SNP, 1977, 124pp.

15   Ballantine, R. R., *The 'Save Fife' campaign: a case study of a county's fight against local government reform proposals*. B.Phil. thesis, Dundee University, 1975.

16   Barback, R. H., *Devolution and private industry*. London: Confederation of British Industry, 1977, 17pp (revised version of paper to the British Association for the Advancement of Science Conference).

17   Baster, J., *The industrial use of transport in Scotland*. Edinburgh: Scottish Council (Development & Industry), 1978, 15pp.

18   Begg, H. M., & Lythe, C. M.: "Regional Policy 1960-71 and the performance of the Scottish economy", *Regional Studies*, 11,6 (1977), 373-81.

19   Belding, R. K., *Gross migration flows in Scotland*. Canterbury: Urban and Regional Studies Unit, University of Kent, 1977.

20   Bermant, C., "Ghetto city of the poor", *Observer Magazine*, 22.1.78, 20-27.

21   Birch, A. H., *Political integration and disintegration in the British Isles*. London: Allen & Unwin, 1977, 183pp.

22   Blake, C. *The productivity of labour in Scottish manufacturing*. Dundee University, Dept. of Economics, Occasional Paper 5, 1976, 42pp.

23   Blyth, A., "Agriculture in Scotland: III", *Scottish Bankers Magazine*, 69, 274 (1977), 131-7.

24   Bochel, J. M. & Denver, D. T., "Political communication: Scottish local papers and the General Election of 1974", *Scottish Journal of Sociology*, 2,1 (1977), 11-30.

25   "The District Council elections of May 1977", *The Scottish Government Yearbook 1978*, eds. H. M. Drucker & M. G. Clarke, Edinburgh: Paul Harris, 1978, 129-50.

26   *The Scottish district elections 1977*. Dundee: the authors, 1977, 100pp.

27   Bonney, N., "The Scottish Assembly: a proving ground for parliamentary reform?", *Political Quarterly*, 49,1 (1978), 191-9.

28 Bowden, K. et al., *The Scottish Conservative Party: a marketing strategy.* Glasgow: Strathclyde University Department of Marketing, 1975, 52pp.

30 Bradley K & Gelb, A.: *Economic aspects of government intervention into the Scottish Daily News Workers Co-operative.* University of Essex Department of Economics, Discussion Paper 95, 1977, 27pp.

31 British Road Federation: *Trunk roads in Scotland.* London, 1977, 13pp.

32 Brougham, J. E. & Butler, R. W., *The social and cultural impact of tourism: a case study of Sleat, Isle of Skye.* Edinburgh: Scottish Tourist Board, 1977, 103pp.

33 Brown, E.D., " 'It's Scotland's oil'? Hypothetical boundaries in the North Sea, a case study", *Marine Policy,* 2, 1 (1978), 1-21.

34 Budd, S., "Europe and public opinion: the view from Scotland", *Contemporary Review,* 230 (1977), 235-41.

36 Business Scotland, "Fife: a regional report", *Business Scotland,* April 1977, 135-62.

37   "Tayside", *Business Scotland,* Dec. 1977, 481-500.

38   "The Central Region", *Business Scotland,* Sept. 1977, 339-54.

39 Canavan, S. M. M., *Rural planning and the development agency.* M.Sc. thesis, Aberdeen University, 1976.

40 Carty, T., "Oil", *Power and Manoeuverability,* ed. T. Carty & S. McCall Smith, 100-24.

41 Carty, T & Ferguson J., "Land", *Power and Manoeuverability,* ed. T. Carty & S. McCall Smith, 65-99.

42 Carty, T. & McCall Smith, A., *Power and Manoeuverability.* Edinburgh: Q Press, 1978, 185pp.

43 Central Regional Council, *Stirling-Alloa Structure Plan: initial consultations.* Stirling, 1977, 18pp.

44   *Transport policies and programmes,* Stirling, 1977, 63pp.

45 Chalmers, R., *Labour Party politics in Dundee,* Undergraduate thesis, Edinburgh University Politics Department, 1978, 88pp.

46 Crichton Smith, I., "Scottish Gaelic", *Planet* 36 (1977), 17-21.

47 City of Dundee District Council: *Inner City Local Plan: survey reports. 3 Vols: Introduction; Housing; Industry.* Dundee, 1977.

48 City of Edinburgh District Council/Lothian Regional Council, *Gorgie-Dalry: a community and environmental analysis.* Edinburgh: Social and Community Development Programme, 1977, unpag.

49   *Social and Community Development Programme: first annual report summary 1977.* Edinburgh, 1977, 5pp.

50   *'Wester Hailes speaks for itself': involvement of the Community Research Unit in its production.* Edinburgh: Social and Community Development Programme, 1977, 5pp.

51 Clark, A., *Agriculture policy discussion paper,* Edinburgh: Scottish Liberal Party, 1977, 3pp.

52 Clarke, C., "Community councils: power to the people?" *British Political Sociology Yearbook,* Vol. 3, ed. C. Crouch (London 1977), 110-42.

53 Collins, J. B., *Management worker relations in the Scottish woollen industry 1830-1970*. Ph.D. thesis, Bradford University, 1975, 374pp.

54 Commissioner for Local Administration in Scotland: *Report of investigation of a complaint against Angus District Council*. Edinburgh, June 1977, 11pp.

55 . . . *Angus District Council*, Edinburgh, Sept. 1977, 16pp.

56 . . . *Annandale and Eskdale District Council*. Edinburgh, 1978, 2pp.

57 . . . *Banff and Buchan District Council*. Edinburgh, July 1977, 6pp.

58 . . . *Banff and Buchan District Council*. Edinburgh, Jan. 1978, 12pp.

59 . . . *Berwickshire District Council*. Edinburgh, Dec. 1977, 7pp.

60 . . . *Berwickshire District Council*. Edinburgh, Mar. 1978, 11pp.

61 . . . *Caithness District Council*. Edinburgh, Sept. 1977, 10pp.

62 . . . *City of Aberdeen District Council*. Edinburgh, Aug. 1977, 13pp.

63 . . . *City of Dundee District Council*. Edinburgh, June 1977, 7pp + Tab.

64 . . . *City of Dundee District Council*. Edinburgh, Dec. 1977. 7pp.

65 . . . *City of Dundee District Council*. Edinburgh, Mar. 1978, 5pp.

66 . . . *City of Edinburgh District Council*. Edinburgh, Nov. 1977, 10pp.

67 . . . *City of Edinburgh District Council*. Edinburgh, Dec. 1977, 5pp.

68 . . . *City of Edinburgh District Council*. Edinburgh, April 1978, 9pp.

69 . . . *City of Glasgow District Council*. Edinburgh, June 1977, 11pp.

70 . . . *City of Glasgow District Council*. Edinburgh, June 1977, 12pp.

71 . . . *City of Glasgow District Council*. Edinburgh, Aug. 1977, 2pp.

72 . . . *City of Glasgow District Council*. Edinburgh, Nov. 1977, 7pp.

73 . . . *Clydebank District Council*. Edinburgh, Feb. 1978, 3pp.

74 . . . *Clydebank District Council*. Edinburgh, April 1978, 11pp

75 . . . *Cumbernauld and Kilsyth District Council*. Edinburgh, Sept. 1977, 9pp.

76 . . . *Cunninghame District Council*. Edinburgh, 1977, 6pp.

77 . . . *Cunninghame District Council*. Edinburgh, Mar., 1978, 12pp.

78 . . . *Dumfries and Galloway Regional Council*. Edinburgh, Oct. 1977, 12pp.

79 . . . *Dunfermline District Council*. Edinburgh, June 1977, 8pp.

80 . . . *Dunfermline District Council*. Edinburgh, 25 Jan. 1978, 2pp.

81   . . . *Dunfermline District Council,* Edinburgh. 31 Jan. 1978, 5pp.
82   . . . *East Lothian District Council and Lothian Regional Council.*
         Edinburgh, July 1977, 9pp.
83   . . . *Eastwood District Council.* Edinburgh, June 1977, 7pp.
84   . . . *Gordon District Council.* Edinburgh, April 1978, 12pp.
85   . . . *Highland Regional Council.* Edinburgh, Sept. 1977, 17pp.
86   . . . *Highland Regional Council.* Edinburgh, Dec. 1977, 11pp
         + app.
87   . . . *Inverclyde District Council.* Edinburgh, Nov. 1977, 11pp.
88   . . . *Inverness District Council.* Edinburgh, Sept. 1977, 7pp.
89   . . . *Kincardine and Deeside District Council.* Edinburgh. Oct.
         1977, 7pp.
90   . . . *Kincardine and Deeside District Council.* Edinburgh, Mar.
         1978, 14pp.
91   . . . *Kincardine and Deeside District Council.* Edinburgh, April
         1978, 9pp.
92   . . . *Lanark District Council.* Edinburgh, July 1977, 10pp.
93   . . . *Lothian Regional Council.* Edinburgh, Sept. 1977, 2pp.
94   . . . *Lothian Regional Council.* Edinburgh, Oct. 1977, 3pp.
95   . . . *Lothian Regional Council.* Edinburgh, Nov. 1977, 6pp.
96   . . . *Lothian Regional Council.* Edinburgh, Jan. 1978, 8pp.
97   . . . *Midlothian District Council.* Edinburgh, Mar. 1978, 8pp.
98   . . . *Monklands District Council.* Edinburgh, Oct. 1977, 13pp.
99   . . . *Motherwell District Council.* Edinburgh, 1978, 7pp.
100   . . . *Motherwell District Council.* Edinburgh, April 1978, 8pp.
101   . . . *Renfrew District Council.* Edinburgh, June 1977, 5pp.
102   . . . *Ross and Cromarty District Council.* Edinburgh, 1978,
         13pp.
103   . . . *Shetland Islands Council.* Edinburgh, 26 Oct. 1977, 7pp.
104   . . . *Shetland Islands Council.* Edinburgh, 27 Oct. 1977, 7pp.
105   . . . *Stirling District Council.* Edinburgh, Dec. 1977, 8pp.
106   . . . *Stirling District Council.* Edinburgh, April 1978, 2pp.
107   . . . *Strathclyde Regional Council.* Edinburgh, May 1977, 3pp.
108   . . . *Strathclyde Regional Council.* Edinburgh, Aug. 1977, 12pp.
109   . . . *Strathclyde Regional Council.* Edinburgh, Mar. 1978, 11pp.
110   . . . *Strathkelvin District Council.* Edinburgh, June 1977, 9pp.
111   . . . *West Lothian District Council.* Edinburgh, June 1977, 12pp.
112   *Report of the Commissioner . . . for the year ended 31 March
         1977.* Edinburgh, 1977, 16pp.
113 Communist Party of Britain (Marxist-Leninist): *Unity not devolution.*
     London, 1977, 16pp.
114 Condry, E., "The impossibility of solving the Highland problem",
     Journal of the Anthropology Society of Oxford, 7, 31 (1976),
     138-48.
115 C.O.S.L.A., *Memorandum of evidence to Committee of inquiry into
     the system of remuneration of members of local authorities.*
     Edinburgh, 1977, 15pp.
116   *Report of the Layfield committee of inquiry into local govern-
         ment finance (Cmnd. 6453): memorandum of observations by
         the Convention.* Edinburgh, 1977, 16pp.

117 Cook, R. F. (MP), "Parliament and the Scots conscience: reforming the law on divorce, licensing and homosexual offences", *The Scottish Government Yearbook 1978*, eds. H. M. Drucker and M. G. Clarke, Edinburgh: Paul Harris, 1978, 99-112.

118 Cooper, D., *Hebridean connection*. London: Routledge, 1977, 184pp.

119 Cope, E., "Consultation or confrontation? The campaign to save the Scottish Colleges of Education", *The Scottish Government Yearbook 1978*, eds. H. M. Drucker and M. G. Clarke, Edinburgh: Paul Harris, 1978, 88-98.

120 Coppock, J. T., *Second homes: curse or blessing?* Oxford: Pergamon, 1977, 229pp.

121 Corb, R. (Ed.), "Scotland survey", *Investors Chronicle*, 26.5.78, 40pp.

122 Craigen, G. D. & Johnstone W. J. D., "Some sources of finance for industry in Scotland", *Scottish Bankers Magazine*, 69, 274 (1977), 122-30.

123 Crewe, I. et al, "Partisan dealignment in Britain 1964-1974", *British Journal of Political Science*, 7,2 (1977), 129-90.

124 Cumbernauld Development Corporation: *Financing of Cumbernauld New Town*. Cumbernauld, 1978, 20pp.

125 Cunningham, E., *The functional role of the SDA*. Glasgow: SDA, 1977, 12pp.

126 Daiches, D., *Glasgow*. London: Deutsch, 1977, 256pp.

127 Dalyell, T. (MP), *Devolution: the end of Britain?* London: Cape, 1977, 321pp.

128 Danson, M. W. et al, "Social indicators", *Fraser of Allander Institute Quarterly Economic Commentary*, April 1978, 37-62.

129 Darke, R., & Walker, R., *Local government and the public*. London: Leonard Hill, 1977, 255 pp (includes case study on housing in Glasgow).

130 Dartington Amenity Research Trust, *Second homes in Scotland*. Totnes, 1977, 92pp.

131 Dickson, J. W., and White, S., "Individual beliefs and political allegiance: the case of a nationalist party", *Scottish Journal of Sociology*, 1,2 (1977), 111-23.

132 Drucker, H. M., *Breakaway: the Scottish Labour Party*. Edinburgh: Student Publications Board, 1978, 157pp.

133 *The rise and fall of the Scottish Labour Party*. Edinburgh: the author, 1977, 6pp.

134 Drucker, H. M., and Clarke, M. G., (Eds.), *The Scottish Government Yearbook 1978*. Edinburgh: Paul Harris, 1978, 208pp.

135 Duff, D., "Mineral wealth", *The Future of Scotland*, ed. R. Underwood, 36-47.

136 Duncan, T. L. C., and Johnson, R., *Research for planning: a review of research carried out by central government for Scottish planning authorities*. Glasgow: Planning Exchange, 1978, 64pp.

136a Easton, N. (Ed.), *Crann Tara*. Aberdeen, No. 1, 1977.

137 Edinburgh District Council, *District Planning Report*. Edinburgh, 1977.

138 Edinburgh Housing Research Group, *The lid off: the Housing Corporation and housing associations in Edinburgh*. Edinburgh, 1977.

139   Edinburgh University Labour Club, *Red Rag*. Edinburgh, No. 1, 1978.
140   Edmonds, R., "Focus on Strathclyde", *Housing Review*, Mar.-Apr. 1978, 31-37.
141   Elliott, B., et al, *Property and politics: Edinburgh 1875-1975*. Edinburgh: the authors, 1977, 36pp plus tables.
142   Ennew, J., "The changing croft", *New Society*, 16.6.77, 546-8.
143   Erikson, J., "Scotland's defence", *The future of Scotland*, ed. R. Underwood, 153-60
144   Evans, J., "The outlook for industry", *The Future of Scotland*, ed. R. Underwood, 119-27.
145   Fenwick, J. M., "The Shetland experience: a local authority arms itself for the oil industry", *The Scottish Government Yearbook 1978*, eds. H. M. Drucker and M. G. Clarke, Edinburgh: Paul Harris, 1978, 32-50.
146   Ferguson, R., *The writing on the wall: new images of Easterhouse*. Easterhouse: the author, 1977.
147   Fife Regional Council, et al, *An assessment of the Shell Esso proposals for Mossmorran and Braefoot Bay, Fife*. Glenrothes, 1977.
148   Fine, M., *Community planning and community councils*. M.Sc. thesis, Strathclyde University, 1975.
149   Firn, J., and Swales, J. K., "The formation of new manufacturing establishments in the central Clydeside and West Midlands conurbations 1963-72", *Regional Studies*, 12,2 (1978), 199-213.
150   Forrest, R. J., *Regional development and the special problem area: a case study in the Highlands and Islands of Scotland*. M. Soc. Sci. thesis, Birmingham University, 1975.
151   Forsyth, M., and Young, D., *Towards a national Union*. London: Federation of Conservative Students, 1976, 5pp.
152   Francis, J., "The growth of the energy industries", *The Future of Scotland*, ed. R. Underwood, 48-74.
153   Fraser of Allander Institute et al, *Input-output tables for Scotland 1973*. Edinburgh: Scottish Academic Press, 1978, 15pp.
154   Furniss, N., "Internal colonialism: its utility for understanding the development of higher education in Scotland", *Development and Change*, 7,4 (1976), 445-67.
155   Gaskin, M., *The changing prospect*. Edinburgh: Royal Bank of Scotland, 1977, 22pp.
155a Gellner, E., "Review: 'The Breakup of Britain'", *Political Quarterly*, 49,1 (1978), 103-111.
156   Glasgow District Council: *Housing policy proposals to 1983*. Glasgow, 1977.
157   *Multiple deprivation: a report by officers of the Strathclyde Regional Council. Observations by the Director of Planning*. Glasgow, 1977.
158   Glasgow Herald, "Who will rule Scotland?" *GH*, 28.1-2.2.78.
159   Grant, J. S., "The importance of the part-time holding", *The changing fortunes of marginal regions*, eds. P. G. Sadler & G. A. Mackay (Aberdeen University, Institute for the Study for Sparsely Populated Areas), 1977, 148-56.

160 Grant, N., "Scottish education: a brief guide for the perplexed", *Trends in Education,* 1976/4, 4-12.
161 Greater Glasgow Passenger Transport Executive, *Strathclyde rural transport policy study.* Glasgow, 1977.
162 *Study of Islay ferry services: summary and recommendations.* Glasgow, 1977.
163 Grieco, M., "Oil and the Council", *New Shetlander* 119 (1977), 6-9; 120 (1977), 13-17; 121 (1977), 26-28; 122 (1977) 26-29.
164 *Towards a sociology of construction activity in an oil-related context.* Aberdeen: Robert Gordons Institute, 1976.
165 *Towards a sociology of industrial development in peripheral areas.* Aberdeen: Robert Gordons Institute, 1977.
166 Gunn, L., "Devolution: a Scottish view", *Political Quarterly,* 48,2 (1977), 129-39.
167 Gunn, L., and Lindley, P., "Devolution; origins, events and issues", *Public Administration Bulletin,* Dec. 1977, 36-54.
168 Hamilton, D., "Health and health care in West Central Scotland", *The Scottish Government Yearbook 1978,* eds. H. M. Drucker and M. G. Clarke, Edinburgh: Paul Harris, 1978.
169 Hamilton, S. F., "Glasgow's housing policies", *The Scottish Government Yearbook 1978,* eds. H. M. Drucker and M. G. Clarke, Edinburgh: Paul Harris, 1978.
170 Hanby, V. J., "Current Scottish nationalism", *Scottish Journal of Sociology,* 1, 2 (1977), 95-110.
171 Handy, J., *Dundee and the great oil debate.* Dundee: Labour Party, 1978.
172 Handy, J. & Ross, E., *Urban deprivation in Dundee.* Dundee: Labour Party, 1978, unpag.
173 *Dundee: twelve years after the 'National Plan for Scotland',* Dundee: Labour Party, 1978.
174 Handy, J. et. al, *Attracting the chemical industry to Dundee.* Dundee: Labour Party, 1978, 3pp.
175 Hargrave, A., "Trends in the economy", *The Future of Scotland,* ed. R. Underwood, 110-18.
176 Harman, N., "Grasping the thistle: a survey of Scotland", *Economist,* 18.2.78, supplement, 34pp.
177 Harris, P. (ed.), *The D. C. Thomson Bumper Fun Book.* Edinburgh: Paul Harris, 1977, 132pp.
178 Harvie, C., *Scottish nationalism and the Second World War.* Milton Keynes: the author, 1976, 30pp.
179 Hawthorn, J., "Scotland's top registered companies 1977", *Business Scotland,* Aug. 1977, 298-306.
180 Heald, D. A., "Financing the new Scottish local authorities", *Telescope,* Feb., March, April 1976.
181 *Giving the Scottish Assembly financial teeth.* Glasgow: Scottish Fabian Research Paper, 1977.
182 *Whatever happened to devolved taxes?* Political Studies Association Workgroup on Politics of the UK, Aberystwyth, 1977, 12 + xiii pp. Also in *Public Finance and Accountancy,* Nov. 1977, 387-92.

183   Henshaw, P., *A critique of the West Central Scotland Plan*. M.Sc. thesis, Strathclyde University, 1975.

184   Highland Regional Council, *Regional report, part II: settlement policy*. Inverness, 1977, 87pp.

185   H.I.D.B., *Eleventh report* 1976. Inverness, 1977.

186   "Fishing in the Highlands and Islands", *North 7* 26 (Aug. 1977).

187   *Highland agriculture and land use: past activities and future policies of the HIDB*. Inverness, 1977, 28pp.

188   *The Highlands and Islands: a contemporary account*. Inverness, 1977, 16pp.

189   Hill, C. A. J., *Problems of an unequal society: the case of deprived housing estates*. M.Sc. thesis, Edinburgh University, 1975.

190   Gill, D. M., " Neighbourhood councils", *Planning and Administration*, Spring 1978, 27-40.

191   Hobsbaum, P., "The start of an auld sang: the Scots and nationalism", *Encounter*, 49,6 (1977), 71-9.

192   Hobsbawm, E., "Some reflections on 'The Breakup of Britain'", *New Left Review* 105 (1978), 3-23.

193   Hogwood, B. W., *Spatial differentiation of economic and industrial policies in the U.K.* Political Studies Association Workgroup on U.K. Politics, 1976.

194   Honey, R., "Efficiency with humanity: geographical issues in Scotland's local government reform", *Scottish Geographical Magazine*, 93,2 (1977), 109-19.

195   Hood, N., *United States and European manufacturing investment in Scotland*. Paisley College of Technology, Social science working paper, 1975, 24pp.

196,   Hood, N., and Young, S., "Industrial structure and ownership in the Scottish new towns", *Town and Country Planning*, 46,2 (1978), 69-72.

197   "The long term impact of multinational enterprise in industrial geography: the Scottish case", *Scottish Geographical Magazine*, 93,3 (1977), 159-67.

198   Hood, S. C. D., *The SLP, and survey of Aberdeen branch*. Aberdeen University, Politics Department undergraduate dissertation, 1977.

199   House of Commons, *Scotland Bill (1977)*. London, 1977, 89pp.

200   House of Commons Library: *Scotland Bill/Wales Bill*. London, 1977, 10pp.

201   *The devolution debate: regional statistics*. London, 1977, 17pp

202   *The devolution debate: regional statistics (updated)*. London, 1978, 17pp.

203   Horner, D. J., "Erskine new community", *Town and Country Planning*, Feb. 1978, 132-5.

204   Howat, W., et al, "Beyond the first Regional Reports: the family of plans keeps growing", *Corporate Planning*, 4,3 (1978), 9-20.

205   Hughes, M., et al, "Trends in interlocking directorships: an international comparison", *Acta Sociologica*, 20,3 (1977), 297-92.

206   Hunt, D., "The sociology of development: its relevance to Aberdeen", *Scottish Journal of Sociology*, 1,2 (1977), 137-54.

207 Institute of Housing (Scottish Branch): *Observations on 'Scottish housing: a consultative document'.* Edinburgh, 1977.

208 Johnson, R. J., "The electoral geography of an election campaign: Scotland in Oct. 1974", *Scottish Geographical Magazine,* 93,2 1977), 98-108.

209 Johnson, R. W., "Nairn and the Breakup of Britain", *Political Studies,* 26,1 (1978), 119-22.

210 Joint Standing Committee of the S.E.C. and O.D.C.S.: *Scottish industry and offshore markets.* Edinburgh: H.M.S.O., 1977.

211 Jordan Dataquest, *Scotland's top 500 companies:* 1976. London; 1977, 95pp.

212 Keating, M. J., *Nationalism in the Scottish labour movement 1914-74.* Political Studies Association Workgroup on U.K. Politics, Aberystwyth, 1977, 17pp.

213   *A test of political integration: the Scottish Members of Parliament.* Glasgow: Strathclyde University Centre for the Study of Public Policy, 1977, 33pp.

214 Kellas, J. G., *Devolution in British politics.* Glasgow: the author, 1976, 37pp.

214a   *Federalism and quasi-federalism: some Scottish- Canadian comparisons, with special reference to oil.* ECPR/CPSA Symposium on Federalism, Kingston, Ontario, 1977, 15pp.

215   *Scottish Institutions in the Scottish political system: a reappraisal of identity and role.* Scottish-Norwegian conference, Helensburgh, 1975, 6pp.

216   *The application of federalism to the United Kingdom, with special reference to North Sea oil production and revenue.* Glasgow: the author, 1976, 12pp.

217   *The effect of membership of the European Community on representative institutions in Scotland.* London: Hansard Society, 1977, 21pp.

218   *The inevitability of federalism.* Political Studies Association Workgroup on UK Politics, Aberystwyth, 1977, 7pp.

219   "The political response", *The Future of Scotland,* ed. R. Underwood, 161-73.

220 Kellas, J. G., and Owen, R., *Devolution and the political context in Scotland.* Annual meeting of the American Political Science Association, Washington, 1977, 44pp.

221 Kemp, K. A., et al, "Scotland for sale", *S,* 15-19.5.78; 22-25.5.78.

222 Kerr, J., "The failure of the Scotland and Wales Bill: no will, no way", *The Scottish Government Yearbook 1978,* eds. H. M. Drucker and M. G. Clarke, Edinburgh: Paul Harris, 1978, 113-19.

223 Knox, J., and Wilson, E., *Scotland '78.* Alva: Wilson & Knox Ltd., 1977, 262pp.

224 Labour Party (Scottish Council), *Interim report of working group on crime.* Glasgow, 1978, 5pp.

225   *Labour's Scottish Assembly: our case.* Glasgow, 1978, 5pp.

226   *Reply to composite resolution five on the future of local government.* Glasgow, 1978, 6pp.

227   Lanark District Council, *Planning in Lanark: the District Report 1977*. Lanark, 1978.

228   Lang, I., and Henderson, B., *The Scottish Conservatives: a past and a future*. Edinburgh Conservative Political Centre in Scotland, 1975, 20pp.

229   Law Society of Scotland: *Replies by the Law Society of Scotland to questionnaire issued by the Royal Commission*. Vol. 1, Edinburgh, 1977, 162pp; and Vol. 2, Edinburgh, 1978, 227pp, 162pp.

230   Leeds, C. A., *Guide to British Government*. Swanage: Croxton Press, 1975; see "Regionalism, nationalism and devolution", pp. 85-95.

231   Lenman, B., "The Scottish universities and devolution", *Scotia Review* 17 (1977), 11-20.

232   Lipsig-Mumme, J. & C., *Syndicates et referendum: le cas britannique 1971-78*. Montreal: Federation des enseignants quebecoises, 1978, 28pp.

233   Lord, R. F., "Agriculture in Scotland: 2", *Scottish Bankers Magazine*, 69, (1977), 40-45.

234   Lothian Regional Council: *Budget 1976/77: report by the Executive Office*. Edinburgh, 1977, unpag.

235   *Lothian Structure Plan: interim statement for public consultation*. Edinburgh, 1977, 38pp.

236   *Lothian Structure Plan: public participation report*. Edinburgh, 1978, 108 + xvi pp.

237   *Lothian Structure Plan: report of survey*. Edinburgh, 1977, 177pp.

238   Lord President of the Council, *Devolution: financing the devolved services*. London: H.M.S.O., 1977, 23pp.

239   Lythe, C. M., *Shift share analysis and the assessment of Scottish economic performance*. Dundee University, Economics Department, 1976, 28pp.

240   McAleese, D., "Trade", *Power and Manoeuvrability*, ed. T. Carty and A. McCall Smith, 125-42.

241   McDonald, S. T., "The Regional Report in Scotland", *Town Planning Review*, 48,3 (1977), 215-32.

242   McDermott, P. J., *Regional variations in enterprise: electronics firms in Scotland, London and the outer Metropolitan area*. Ph.D. thesis, Cambridge University, 1977, 448pp.

243   McEwen, J., *Who owns Scotland?* Edinburgh: Student Publications Board, 1977, 137pp.

244   McKay, R. R., *The death of regional policy—or resurrection squared*. Newcastle University, Centre for Urban and Regional Studies, 1978.

245   *Regional employment: the influence of regional policy and the national economic situation*. Regional Studies Association conference, Glasgow, 1977.

246   McKechen, W. J., *Schools councils: a missed opportunity*. Paisley College of Technology, Local Government Working Unit, 1977.

247 McKenzie, N., "Centre and periphery: the marriage of two minds". *Acta Sociologica,* 20,1 (1977), 55-74.
248 Mackie, S., *Consultation on national identity,* Dunblane, 1977. N.p.: the author for Church of Scotland, 1977, 3pp.
249 McLean, I., "The politics of nationalism and devolution", *Political Studies,* 25,3 (1977), 425-30.
250 MacLaren, D., "Civil rights and the Scottish Assembly", *Contemporary Review* 230 (June 1977), 296-9.
251 Maclennan, D., *The economics of selling council houses in the Scottish housing system.* Aberdeen University, Political Economy Department, 1977, 31pp.
252 McLetchie, D., and Forsyth, M., *The Scottish Conservative Party: a new model for a new dimension.* London: Federation of Conservative Students, 1975, 11pp.
253 McNeil, D., "A look at Livingston", *Business Scotland,* June 1977, 238-47.
255 McNicoll, I. H., "The impact of local government activity on a small rural economy: Shetland", *Urban Studies,* 14,3 (1977), 399-406.
256 McShane, H., *A life of struggle.* London: Pluto, 1977.
257 Madeley, J. T. S., "Patterns of subordination and strategies of separation: Norway and Scotland compared", *Journal of the Conflict Resolution Society,* 1,1 (1977), 58-69.
259 Maher, G., "The identity of the Scottish legal system", *Juridical Review,* 22, (1977), 21-37.
260 Market and Opinion Research International, *Garscadden by-election same day poll,* 13.4.78. London, 1978, unpag.
261 Markland, J. A., *Some theoretical and empirical considerations of Scottish population migration 1961-71.* Ph.D. thesis, Dundee University, 1976.
262 Marshall, E., *Shetland's oil era.* Lerwick: Shetland Islands Council, 1977, 72pp.
263 Mason, S., *Planning in a Highland area.* M.Sc. thesis. Strathclyde University, 1975.
264 Masterson, M., "Community Councils", *Scolag Bulletin* 19 (1978), 72-74.
265 "Electing the community councils: an interim assessment", *Community Council News* 6 (1977), 8-11.
266 Maxwell, S., "Politics", *Power and Manoeuvrability,* ed. T. Carty and A. McCall Smith, 1-38.
267 Midwinter, A. F., "The implementation of the Paterson Report in Scottish local government 1975-77", *Local Government Studies,* 4,1 (1978), 23-28.
268 Moore, B., and Rhodes, J., *Economic and financial implications of devolution.* British Association for the Advancement of Science conference, 1977, 26pp plus appendices.
269 Moore, B., et al, "The impact of regional policy in the 1970s", *Centre for Environmental Studies Review 1* (1977), 67-77.
269a Mulholland, R., *Scotland's Freedom Struggle.* Strahnairn: the author, 1977, 150 pp.

M

270   Murphy, B., *S.I.I. report: Scottish community newspapers.* Edinburgh: Scottish International Institute, 1978.

271   Mutch, W. E. S., "The expansion of Turnhouse, Edinburgh Airport", *Public Participation in planning,* eds. W. R. D. Sewell and J. T. Coppock (London: Wiley, 1977), 53-58.

272   Nairn, T., *The breakup of Britain.* London. New Left Books, 1977, 368pp.

273   "The SLP", *Planet* 37/8 (1977), 14-17.

274.   Nevis Institute, *Shetland report.* Edinburgh, 1978, 42pp; summary in *Shet. T.,* 7.4.78, 3, 8 and 10; and *S,* 15.4.78, 1,7.

275   Nicolson, J. R., *Traditional life in Shetland.* London: Hale, 1978.

276   North-East Scotland Development Authority: *Annual report 1976/7.* Aberdeen, 1977, 24pp.

277   O'Donnell, J., "District councils — the 1977 elections", *Scottish Marxist* 14 (1977), 27-36.

278   Osborn, F. S., and Whittick, A., *New Towns.* London: Leonard Hills, 1977, 505pp; see pp. 391-452.

279   Osmond, J., *Creative Conflict: the politics of Welsh devolution.* London: Routledge Kegan Paul, 1978.

280   Page, E., *Michael Hechter's 'internal colonialism' model of political development in the British Isles: some theoretical and methodological problems.* Glasgow: the author, 1977, 27pp plus appendices.

281   Parvin, G., and Smith, P., *Political patronage in Scotland.* Glasgow: Scottish Conservative Policy Forum, 1977, 4pp.

282   Paterson, C. F., "Industria floremus", *Scottish Bankers Magazine,* 69, 294 (1977), 138-45.

283   Pearl, M., "Scottish Assembly legislation: pre-assent and post-assent review", *Scots Law Times,* 1978 No. 6, 41-47.

284   Perman, R., et al, "Scotland", *FT* 11, 28.11.77, 16-26.

285   Piggott, C. A., *Population change and the churches in Scotland.* Edinburgh University Geography Department, 1977, 71pp.

286   Planning Exchange, *Conference report: West Central Scotland Plan.* Glasgow, 1975, 102pp.

287   *The social impact of large scale industrial development: a literature review.* Glasgow, 1978.

288   Prattis, J. I., *Economic structure in the Highlands of Scotland.* Glasgow: Fraser of Allander Institute, 1977, 40pp.

289   Purvis, J., "Money", *Power and Manoeuvrability,* eds. A. Carty and S. McCall Smith, 143-77.

290   Reid, L., *Services to elected members: a survey of Scottish local authorities.* Glasgow: Planning Exchange, 1977, 13pp.

291   Residents of Wester Hailes, *Wester Hailes speaks for itself.* Edinburgh: Social and Community Development Programme, Edinburgh District Council, 1977, 36pp.

292   Rich, D. C., *Accessibility and economic activity: a study of locational disadvantage in Scotland.* Ph.D. thesis, Cambridge University, 1976, 396 pp.

293   Rifkind, M., *A new United Kingdom.* Edinburgh: Scottish Conservative Central Office, 1977, 4pp.

294 Risk, C. J., "Devolution: the commercial community's fears", *The Scottish Government Yearbook 1978*, eds. H. M. Drucker and M. G. Clarke, Edinburgh: Paul Harris, 1978, 120-28.

295 Robertson, W., The Scottish Development Agency", *The Scottish Government Yearbook 1978*, eds. H. M. Drucker and M. G. Clarke, Edinburgh: Paul Harris, 1978, 21-31.

296 Rose, R., *The United Kingdom as an intellectual puzzle*. Glasgow: Centre for the Study of Public Policy, 1976, 31pp.

297 Rosen, D. H., and Voorhees-Rosen, R. N., "Shetland and North Sea oil", *New Shetlander* 123 (1978), 6-9.

298 Ross, W., "Approaching the archangelic: the office of Secretary of State", *The Scottish Government Yearbook 1978*, eds. H. M. Drucker and M. G. Clarke, Edinburgh: Paul Harris, 1978, 1-20.

299 Royal Bank of Scotland, *The Royal Bank of Scotland Ltd., 1727-1977*. Edinburgh, 1977, unpag.

300 Sandeman, H., "The North Sea's lenders", *Banker,* May 1977, 80-85.

301 Schiller, P., "New towns poll: the good, the fair and the poor", *Business Location File,* April-May 1978, 7-17.

302 Scotland, J., "The educational system", *The Future of Scotland,* ed. R. Underwood, 98-109.

303 Scottish Association for Public Transport, *Public transport in the Highlands.* Glasgow 1977.

304 *The Stranraer-Dumfries railway: a case for re-opening.* Glasgow, 1977, 21pp.

305 *The Transport White Paper: implications for Scotland.* Glasgow, 1977, 15pp.

306 *Transport in Strathclyde: a submission on the Structure Plan.* Glasgow, 1977.

307 *West Highland transport: future options.* Glasgow, 1978.

308 Scottish Association of Citizens Advice Bureaux, *Memorandum of evidence to the Royal Commission on Legal Services in Scotland.* Edinburgh, 1977, 2vols.

309 Scottish Conservative and Unionist Association, *Conference '77.* Edinburgh, 1977, 100pp.

310 *Constitution, rules and standing orders (as adopted Jan. 1976).* Edinburgh, 1976, 23pp.

316 Scottish Council (Development and Industry): *Annual report 1975-76.* Edinburgh, 1976, 27pp.

317 *Position report: Lord Clydesmuir's statement to the annual general meeting.* Edinburgh, 1976, 7pp.

318 *Review of the industrial situation in Scotland.* Edinburgh, 1977, 13pp.

319 Scottish Council Research Institute: *The economic importance of visitors to Scotland.* Edinburgh, 1978, 18pp.

320 *The framework of industry in Scotland: an analysis of the Scottish input-output table.* Edinburgh, 1977, 10pp plus tables, appendix and chart.

321 Scottish Council of Social Service, *Report of day meeting on 'Review of the management of planning'.* Glasgow, 1977, 21pp.

322 *Workers Co-ops: a Scottish handbook.* Edinburgh, 1977.

323   Scottish Development Agency, *Accounts 1976-77*, London, H.M.S.O., 1978, 26pp.
324   *Annual report 1976/77*. Glasgow, 1977, 64pp.
325   *Evidence to the Committee to review the functioning of financial institutions*. Glasgow, 1977, 32pp.
326   *Opportunity*. Glasgow, 1977, 80pp.
327   Scottish Development Department, *Planning advice note 19: publicity and consultation*. Edinburgh, 1978, 2pp.
328   *Report for 1975 and 1976*. Edinburgh: H.M.S.O., 1977, 33pp.
329   *Review of the management of planning: note of conference . . . Mar. 1978*. Edinburgh, 1978, 6pp.
330   Scottish Economic Planning Department, "The work of the S.E.P.D.", *Scottish Economic Bulletin* 13 (1977), 8-13.
331   Scottish Home and Health Department, *Scottish Health Service Planning Council: report for 1976*. Edinburgh: H.M.S.O., 1977, 24pp.
332   Scottish Information Office, *The Scottish Office*. Edinburgh, 1977, 13pp + table.
333   Scottish Legal Action Group, *Royal Commission on Legal Services in Scotland: memorandum*. Five parts, Dundee, 1977 and 1978.
334   Scottish Liberal Party, *Conference '77*. Edinburgh, 1977, 20pp.
335   *Scottish Liberal Law Reform Group evidence to the Royal Commission on Legal Services in Scotland*. Edinburgh, 1977, 10pp.
336   Scottish National Party, *44th Annual National Conference: agenda*. Edinburgh, 1978, 48pp (includes draft policy documents on structure of government, fishing, economic strategy).
337   *A national forestry policy*. Edinburgh, 1977, 4pp.
338   *Draft policy: law and order*. Edinburgh, 1978, 5pp.
339   *Draft policy paper on self-management enterprises*. Edinburgh, 1978, 5pp.
340   *Notes and commentary on 'A national forestry policy'*. Edinburgh, 1977, 4pp.
341   *Policy document: education*. Edinburgh, 1977, 8pp.
342   *Policy document: environment*. Edinburgh, 1976, 3pp.
343   *Policy document: housing*. Edinburgh, 1977, 4pp.
344   *Policy document: industry*. Edinburgh, 1976, 5pp.
345   *Policy document: taxation*. Edinburgh, 1977, 2pp.
346   *Policy document: the crofting counties*. Edinburgh, 1977, 6pp.
347   *Policy document: transport*. Edinburgh, 1976, 5pp.
348   *Post-independence economic strategy*. Edinburgh, 1978, 7pp.
349   *Poverty amid plenty: the paradox of Scottish employment and resources*. Edinburgh, 1977, 4pp.
350   *Scotland's resources* (Research bulletin, Vol. 5, No. 1). Edinburgh, 1977, 16pp.
351   *Statement of evidence to the Select Committee of the House of Lords on a bill of rights*. Edinburgh, 1977, 2pp.
352   *Submission to the Government's Green Paper on 'Scottish Housing'*. Edinburgh, 1977, 7pp.

353 Scottish Office, *Local government finance in Scotland.* Edinburgh: H.M.S.O., 1977, 23pp.

354 Scottish Special Housing Association, *A chronicle of 40 years 1937-77.* Edinburgh, 1977. 79pp.

355 Scottish Trades Union Congress, *80th annual report 1977.* Glasgow, 1978, 922pp.

356 *Preliminary agenda, 81st annual Scottish trades union congress* (Aberdeen, 1978), Glasgow, 1978, 59pp.

357 Scottish Voluntary Organisations Group: *Partners in care: report of a working party on voluntary organisations and social service in Scotland.* Edinburgh, 1977, 8pp.

358 Scottish Young Conservatives, *Working for a better Scotland: 30th annual conference (Peebles, 1977).* Edinburgh, 1977, 6pp.

359 Sewel, J., *The effects of the centralisation of education in the Highlands and Islands of Scotland.* Ph.D. thesis, Aberdeen University, 1977, 283pp.

360 Sewel, J. et al, *Education and migration: a study of the migration and job expectations of young people and their parents in the Highlands and Islands of Scotland.* Aberdeen University, 1976, 83pp.

361 Sharpe, T., "The constitutional consequences of Mr Smith", *Scolag Bulletin* 18 (1978), 56-58.

362 Shetland Islands Council, *Shetland Structure Plan: written statement.* Lerwick, 1977, 108pp.

363 *Shetland Structure Plan. Vols. 3 and 4.* Lerwick, 1978.

364 Smith, B., "Shetland archives and sources of Shetland's history", *History Workshop* 4 (1977), 203-14.

365 Smith, H. D., *The making of modern Shetland.* Lerwick: Shetland Times, 1977, 94pp (Parts 10 and 11, dealing with the 1970s, also in *New Shetlander* 122 (1977), 9-13 and 123 (1978), 10-12).

366 Smith, R., "Stonehouse: obituary for a new town", *Local Government Studies,* 4,2 (1978), 57-64.

367 "The politics of an overspill policy: Glasgow, Cumbernauld . . .", *Public Administration* 55 (1977), 79-94.

368 Smith, T. B., "The Scottish legal tradition", *Scottish Review* 8 (1977), 30-36.

369 Smout, C., "The Scottish identity", *The Future of Scotland,* ed. R. Underwood, 11-21.

370 Social Science Research Council: *The social impact of North Sea oil developments in Scotland.* London, 1975, 22pp plus appendices.

371 *International register of research on the social impact of offshore oil development.* Aberdeen University, 1977, 53pp.

372 Steed, M., *Devolution: what English dimension?* Political Studies Association Workgroup on UK Politics,Aberystwyth, 1977, 24pp.

373 Strathclyde Regional Council, *Policy review on departmental structures: report on the first phase of the group's investigation.* Glasgow, 1978, 40pp.

374 *Register of research and data inventory.* Glasgow, 1978, unpag.

375   *Strathclyde Structure Plan 1977: consultative draft.* Glasgow, 1977, 95pp.

376   *The first three years.* Glasgow, 1978, 83pp.

377   *Transport policies and programmes 1978-83.* Glasgow, 1978, 170pp.

378   Strathclyde Regional Council, Policy Planning Department, "Priorities and the Regional Report", *Corporate Planning,* 3,2 (1976), 231-34.

379   Tayside Regional Council: *Tayside Structure Plan: report of survey.* Dundee, 1977.

380   Thompson, W., "Review of 'Breakaway: the Scottish Labour Party', by H. M. Drucker", *Scottish Marxist* 16 (1978), 24-30.

381   Thornley, J., "Planning processes in marginal regions", *The changing fortunes of marginal regions,* eds. P. G. Sadler and G. A. Mackay (Aberdeen, Institute for the Study of Sparsely Populated Areas, 1977), 157-63.

382   Thornton, O., "Prospects for transport", *The Future of Scotland,* ed. R. Underwood, 129-37.

383   Turpie, L., "Opposition in local government", *The Scottish Government Yearbook 1978,* eds. H. M. Drucker and M. G. Clarke, Edinburgh: Paul Harris, 1978, 51-60.

384   *Scottish Conservative local government handbook.* Glasgow: the author, 1977, 68pp.

385   Underwood, R. (Ed)., *The Future of Scotland.* London: Croom Helm, 1977, 180pp.

386   Urwin, D., *The alchemy of delayed nationalism.* European Consortium for Political Research Workshop, Louvain, 1976.

387   Wannop, U., *The Strathclyde Region (regional strategies in practice),* Regional Studies Association conference, Glasgow, 1977.

388   Webb, K., and Hall, E., *Explanations of the rise of political nationalism in Scotland.* Glasgow: Strathclyde University Centre for the Study of Public Policy, 1978, 59pp.

389   Wilkinson, M., and Howat, B., *Regional reports and structure plans in Scotland.* Glasgow: Planning Exchange, 1977, 13pp.

390   Wilson, B., "Devolution is appeasement that is bound to fail", *Journalism Studies Review,* 1,1 (1976), 28-30.

391   Wyke, C., *The Scottish Conservative Party: history, organisation, and entry into local government.* Undergraduate thesis, Edinburgh University, Dept. of Politics, 1978, 133 pp.

392   Young, E., *The law of planning in Scotland.* Glasgow: William Hodge, 1978.

PART II: SHORT ITEMS

400   Anon. Opinion polls: *Sunday Mail,* 1.12.77; *GH,* 17.6.77; 25.7.77; 15.8.77; 12.9.77; 10.10.77; 14.11.77; 12.12.77; 30.1.78; 11.2.78; 18.3.78; 11.4.78; 12.5.78; (voting intentions); *GH,* 13.2.78; 20.3.78; 22.5.78 *Sun,* 6.3.78 (devolution); *GH,* 11.4.78; *Sun,* 6.3.78 (Garscadden voting intentions); *Sunday Post,* 14.5.78; *GH,* 29.5.78 (Hamilton voting intentions).

401   "A brave show at the polls", *Forward Scotland* 4 (1977), 8.
402   "A fond kiss, and then we sever", *Econ.*, 4.6.77, 21.
403   "Anti-devolution MPs explain their views", *Shet. T.*, 4.11.77, 1 and 13.
404   "A reply to Tom Nairn", *Scottish Worker*, 4,6 (1977), 10-11.
405   "A Scottish landowner in Europe", *Landowning in Scotland* 167 (1977), 37.
406   "Bad for Nats", *Econ.*, 22.4.78, 24, 26.
407   "Big Daddy", *Clydeside Action* 7 (1978), 15-16.
408   "Claymores drawn in Scotland", *Econ.*, 22.4.78, 23-4.
409   "Comment: the forgotten homeless", *Scoland Bulletin* 18 (1978), 46.
410   "Community councils hold 'post mortem'", *Orc.*, 4.5.78, 3.
411   "Conference 77', *Free Scot* 13 (1977), 9-11.
412   "Could still do better", *Econ.*, 30.3.78, 15.
413   "Devo. gets the green light from a cynical Commons", *Econ.*, 19.11.77, 21.
414   "Don't rig the Scottish poll", *Econ.*, 4.2.78, 21.
415   "High noon for the sheriff", *Econ.*, 3.12.77, 27.
416   "How SSHA built a hundred thousand roofs over Scotland", *Surveyor*, 10.11.77, 12-14.
417   "In the court of the Coffin King", *7D*, 9.12.77, 7 (see also 23.12.77, 7).
418   "It's time to close ranks", *SI* 77 (1977), 1.
419   "Judges and politics", *Scolag Bulletin* 13 (1977), 6-7 (see also 15 (1977), 174-5).
420   "Labour licks Nats in Scotland", *Econ.*, 6.5.78, 20, 23.
421   "Manpower in the local authorities: Scotland", *Department of Employment Gazette*, Dec. 1977, 1372-3.
422   "Mother government in Garscadden", *Econ.*, 8.4.78, 18.
423   "Nats still ride high", *Econ.*, 8.10.77, 25-6.
424   "Nine lives", *Econ.*, 14.1.78, 18-19.
425   "Opinion poll plus Garscadden makes bad news for Nats", *7D*, May 1978, 10.
426   "Problems and prospects in Falkirk", *CCN* 11 (1978), 24.
427   "Raasay riddle that demands an answer", *7D*, 9.12.77, 4.
428   "Reluctant home rulers", *Econ.*, 12.11.77, 16-17.
429   "Report from Cree Valley", *CCN* 8 (1977), 7-8.
430   "Report from Springburn", *CCN* 10 (1978), 6.
431   "Scotland 1984", *Scottish Socialist* 6 (1977), 10.
432   "Scotland points the way, but where to?" *Econ.*, 7.5.77, 19-20.
433   "Scotland: the economics of independence", *Econ.*, 16.7.77, 80-81; see also 20.8.77, 4, 6; 3.9.77, 6.
434   "Scottish Labour Party policy — interview", *Carn* 19 (1977), 4-5.
435   "SNP and denominational schools", *Focus* (Dundee), Sept. 1977, 4.
436   "Special status", *New Shetlander* 121 (1977), 5-6.
437   "Tartan ostrich", *Econ.*, 21.5.77, 25-6.
438   "Thank God for Garscadden", *SI* 86 (1978), 1.

439   "The 'pro-life' lobby", *7D*, 17.2.78, 4.
440   "The three Rs", *Focus* (Dundee), Sept. 1977, 4-5.
441   "The yard that just growed and growed", *WHFP*, 5.5.78, 3.
442   "Will Scots succumb to a rightwinger?" *G*, 18.5.78, 16.
443   Addison, P., "Degrees of devolution", *Times Literary Supplement*, 9.9.77, 1083.
444   Airs, G., "Back to the Glen", *Record*, 22.4.77, 13.
445   Anderson, L., "Battle to save our oil yards", *SDE*, 24.9.77, 11.
446   "SLP — alive and rebellious", *SDE*, 15.10.77, 11.
447   "Why resignation was the only solution", *SDE*, 10.12.76, 12.
448   Arnold R., "New Lanark: a vision of success", *CCN* 3 (1977), 10-11.
449   Ascherson, N., "Aberdeen survey reveals political dissensus", *S*, 27.2.78, 7.
450   "A book worth writing—despite its failings", *S*, 18.1.78, 11.
451   "After Garscadden, the soft sell", *S*, 24.5.78, 13.
452   "An omen for Scotland", *New Statesman*, 24.2.78, 239-40.
453   "Another half loaf — and still no meat", *S*, 5.11.77, 9.
454   "Church hinders reformation", *S*, 9.5.78, 9.
455   "Conservatives to debate law and order", *S*, 11.5.78, 15.
456   "Devolution without industrial power", *S*, 10.6.77, 13.
457   "Drift towards SNP", *Scotsman Half-Yearly Review*, 19.7.77, 1.
458   "Duelling over dualism", *S*, 23.9.77, 13.
459   "Labour's Scottish heavyweight champion", *S*, 11.11.77, 11.
460   "Many a slip before lights go up in Assembly", *S*, 21.11.77, 11.
461   "Nationalists keep quiet", *S*, 26.10.77, 11.
462   "Opinions but no commitment", *S*, 7.4.78, 17.
463   "Poet of the revolution", *S*, 13.12.77, 11.
464   "Revival time for Labour", *S*, 30.5.78, 7.
465   "Shetland and the 'Grimond amendment'," *S*, 10.2.78, 12.
466   "Shetland sets a puzzle", *S*, 5.5.78, 13.
467   "SNP keep cool in a trough", *S*, 4.5.78, 15.
468   "Talking of dead men's votes", *S*, 16.2.78, 11.
469   "The case against centralism", *S*, 19.1.78, 13.
470   "The year in Scotland", *S*, 16.12.77, 12.
471   "Time of political recrimination", *S*, 27.1.78, 13.
472   "Too much on the Assembly agenda", *S*, 30.1.78, 7.
473   "Vision of the plebian Tory", *S*, 12.10.77, 13.
474   " 'West Lothian litany' in perspective", *S*, 28.11.77, 6.
475   Baggott, M., "Day of reckoning for the shipyards", *S*, 30.6.77, 11.
476   "Job prospects grim in the short term", *Scotsman Half-Yearly Review*, 19.7.77, 5.
477   Baggott, M., et al, "Scottish Development Agency", *S*, 28.10.77, supplement.
478   Baird, M., "Clarion call to a new reformation?", *S*, 19.5.78, 12.
479   Balfour, A., "Strathclyde: oil hopes sink", *S*, 1.11.77, 10.
480   Banel, R., "Calling it a day — after 33 years in local authority service", *S*, 14.2.78, supplement p. 3.
481   "Happier liaison between development corporation and local authority", *S*, 8.6.77, supplement p. 3.
482   Barker, D., "Yankee lairds", *G*, 15.8.77, 11.

483 Barr, B., "The stakes are high", *7D,* 3.2.78, 5.
484 Barr, D., "The importance of local investment", *WHFP,* 3.2.78, 2.
485 Bateman, C., "People with glass blocks shouldn't move mountains", *G,* 31.1.78, 7.
486 Bayne, I., Review of 'Scotland and Nationalism', by C. Harvie (London, 1977), *SI* 77 (1977), 8.
487 Beattie, W., and Birrell, G., "Sink or swim for the Scots fishing industry", *SDE,* 18.7.77, 8.
488 Bell, C., "Conflict of opinion over government plan", *S,* 19.10.77, 12
489   "Critical look at Scotland's new towns", *S,* 20.1.78.
490   "How abstainers can bring down the Bill", *S,* 27.1.78, 13.
491   "Mrs Thatcher's Scottish policy", *Spectator,* 14.1.78, 13.
492   "Nationalists apart", *Spectator,* 4.11.77, 11.
493   "Scotch myths", *Spectator,* 18.6.77, 13.
494   "Scotland's political test", *Spectator,* 28.1.78, 15-16.
495   "The restless force", *S,* 30.5.-1.6.78.
496 Bell, D., "No panacea for unemployment", *S,* 21.4.78, 14.
497 Benson, R., "Margo still reaches for the stars", *SDE,* 24.5.78, 10.
498 Birrell, G., "A strict jobs diet that only puts on weight", *SDE,* 7.8.77, 6.
499   "Berwick; the borderline case", *SDE,* 31.4.77, 11.
500   "My Scotland — by Maggie", *SDE,* 18.2.78, 10-11.
501   "The road to red chaos", *SDE,* 9.3.78, 11.
502   "Tories in Blunderland", *SDE,* 13.5.77, 11.
503 Birt, A., "Road to the referendum", *7D,* 23.12.77, 8.
504 Birt A.; Maxwell, S., "Two views of Tam's prophecy", *7D,* 25.11.77, 11.
505 Blair, H., "Scottish plays are no longer death", *Question* 9 (1976), 19-20.
506 Blanden, M., "Why the big four are moving North", *FT,* 21.11.77, 29.
507 Bogdanor, V, "Why the word 'devolution' hides the real power to Scotland", *T,* 6.1.78, 12.
508 Bovey, K., "Road to the referendum", *7D,* 10.2.78, 2.
509 Bowen, M., and Kellner, P., "Scots put jobs before 'freedom'," *ST,* 16.4.78, 4.
510 Bradford, D., "Scotland Bill still a long way from harbour", *S,* 31.1.78, 9.
511   "Sense of foreboding hangs over Scotland Bill", *S,* 6.12.77, 11.
512 Bridgland, F., "Torness a focus for changing instincts", *S,* 5.5.78, 13.
513 Brodie, J., "How Scotland gathers experts to deal with housing problems", *T,* 22.11.77, 20.
514 Brown, G., "The nonsense of nationalism", *7D,* 17.3.78, 2.
515 Brown, H. (MP), "Government's new strategy for housing", *S,* 17.10.77, 8.
516 Brown, W., "The case for four channels for ITV", *S,* 14.1.78.
517 Buchanan, I., "Peterhead's rich new world", *Weekend S,* 18.2.78, 1.
518 Buchanan, N. (MP), "Flaw that could wreck Assembly", *GH,* 13.1.78, 6.

519   "Learning from the electorate", *GH*, 7.4.78, 6.
520   "Road to the referendum", *7D*, 3.2.78, 2.
521   "So sad, this whining racism", *GH*, 23.9.78, 6.
522   "The rationalism of nationalism",*WHFP*, 2.9.77, 7.
523   Buchanan, R., "More autonomy for the regions", *S*, 5.7.77, 9.
524   "Scotland's transport problems", *S*, 27.4.78, 12.
525   Business Scotland, "And send them homewards to think again", *Business Scotland*, March 1977, 13.
526   Burk, G., "End of the road for these travelling people?", *GH*, 8.8.77, 7.
527   Burns, D. J. M., "Districts — who needs them?", *CCN* 13 (1978), 6-7.
528   Burns, J. T., "Housing in Scotland 25 years on . . . and on", *Housing Monthly*, Aug. 1977, 21-23.
529   Campbell, M. C., "The case for public ownership", *WHFP*, 27.1.78, 2.
530   Campbell, D., "Freedom fighters took to the leafy parts of Scotland", *7D*, 28.10.77, 5.
531   Campbell, G., "Is this the end of devolution?", *SDE*, 27.1.78, 11.
532   "Second half and all to play for", *SDE*, 24.2.78, 10.
533   Campbell, G. and Graham C., "Three way voting danger to Labour" *SDE*, 19.1.78, 11.
534   Campbell, J. S., "The new planning procedures", *Scots Law Times*, 1977/22, 137-40 and 1977/24, 149-52.
535   Canavan, D. (MP), "Stirling's vital role", *Campus* (Stirling) 29 (1977), 3.
535a   "The great Burns night fiasco", *S*, 2.2.78, 10.
536   Carmichael, K., "Living in the Fourth World", *Listener*, 17.11.77, 630-31.
537   Clarke, W., "Callaghan will spell out just how much is at stake", *GH*, 17.3.78, 7.
538   "Hamilton casts its shadow", *GH*, 25.5.78, 6.
539   "Message to the White House, the Kremlin, and voters in Dundee", *GH*, 1.8.77, 7.
540   "SNP and the secret formula for separation", *SDE*, 27.5.76, 7.
541   "SNP and Labour go all out for Garscadden win", *SDE*, 3.3.78, 7.
542   "Will the SNP welcome back its rebels?", *GH*, 13.10.77, 7.
543   Clarke, E., "Interview: establishment against the miners", *7D*, 13.1.78, 4.
544   Cochrane, H., "It's hard to find any concrete hope for the empty oil yards, *GH*, 16.2.78, 7.
545   "Job-hunters in a jam-up", *GH*, 18.10.77, 7.
546   "Scotland needs a Neddy", *GH*, 20.12.77, 6.
546a   Colville, J., "Devolution can offer Britain a new design for democracy", *T*, 7.6.77, 10.
547   Comrie, B., "Recipe for success", *SI* 86 (1978), 11.
548   Cook, C., "Britain's concrete hopes that came to nothing", *G*, 4.5.78, 13.
549   Cosgrove, D., "Councillors in East Kilbride", *CCN* 9 (1978), 24-5.
550   Coutts, D., "Declaration of Independence", *S*, 24.5.78, 12.

551 Crawford, D. (MP), "Fair play for the small man", *SI*, 86 (1978), 7.
552 "SDA must be strengthened", *Saltire Newsletter* (Newton Stewart), 1,2 (1977), 8.
553 "The Irish achievement", *S*, 28.9.77, 10.
554 "Cackling Tam", *SI* 81 (1977), 3.
555 Crowther-Hunt, "How to stop the civil service creep", *G*, 22.4.77, 12.
556 "How to stop the government machine running out of control", *T*, 12.4.77, 5.
556a Cunningham, G. (MP), "The case for the 40% test", *S*, 1.2.78, 8.
557 Cunningham, J. (Cllr.), "The continuing disaster of Glasgow's council housing", *GH*, 1.9.77, 7.
558 Cunningham J., "Why the liberal Mr Fairbairn has hardened", *GH*, 21.3.78, 7.
559 Davidson, J., Antiabortionists on the campaign trail", *S*, 6.4.78, 13.
560 "Scotswomen in bondage", *S*, 16.12.77, 13.
561 "The quiet monster exposed to public gaze", *S*, 31.12.77, 6.
562 Dewar, D., "Garscadden: start of the big battle", *7D*, 17.3.78, 2.
562a Dewar, W. McL., "Our representatives", *Times Education Supplement* (Scotland), 25.11.77, 2.
563 Dickenson, I. S., "The Secretary of State and Assembly legislation", *Journal of the Law Society for Scotland*, 23, 3 (1978), 89-90.
564 Donaldson, A., "Along the way", *Focus* (Crieff), 1 (1970), 3.
565 Donaldson, C. T., "Devolution", *Shet. T.*, 24.2.78, 15.
565a "Devolution and Orkney: how I see it", *Orc.*, 16.2.78, 5.
566 Dowle, M., "Devolution and Shetland", *New Shetlander* 118 (1976), 7-8.
567 "Impact of oil development in Shetland", *S*, 24-25.1.78.
568 "Muddling through the 1970s", *Scotsman Half-Yearly Review*, 19.7.77, 8.
569 "Shetlanders remain suspicious of devolution", *S*, 26.1.78, 13.
570 Drucker, H. M., Extracts from "Breakaway: the Scottish Labour Party", *Weekend S*, 14.1.78, 1; *S*, 16.1.78, 9; 17.1.78, 9.
571 Duncan, R., "The impossible dreams of Front man Michael", GH, 8.6.77, 9.
572 Easton, J., "Holiday island in a sea of gloom", *GH*, 27.12.77, 7.
573 Easton, N., "We'll take a break now . . . ", *Crann Tara* 2 (1978), 15.
574 Easton, N. (ed.), "SLP Congress, Ayr 1977", *Scottish Worker* 4, 7 (1977), 4pp.
575 Edwards, R., "Torness: case for a new enquiry", *S*, 1.5.78, 7.
576 Elder, D. G., "£36,000: what's your choice?", *SDE*, 19.8.77.
577 "A farce without any fun", *SDE*, 19.8.77.
578 "Labour launches a secret weapon", *SDE*, 25.2.77.
579 "Scandal o' the isles", *SDE*, 11.4.77.
580 "The jaunts are still on!" *SDE*, 17.8.77.
581 Emery, F., "Personal bitterness characterises by-election manoeuvring between Labour and Nationalists", *T.*, 29.5.78, 2.
582 "Why Labour is beating the drum in Scotland", *T*, 18.3.78, 14.
583 'Eyjarskeggi', "Silence means yea . . . ", *New Shetlander* 115 (1976), 20-21.

584 Fairgrieve, R. (MP), "The right approach to devolution", *SDE,* 6.12.76, 10.
585 Farrell, J., "Glasgow belongs to . . .?", *Question* 30 (1977), 4.
586 Faux, R., "A £220M step in the Cromarty Firth", *T,* 7.11.77, 25.
587   "All sides support Scottish Agency", *T,* 6.3.78, 22.
588   "Argyll puts its trust in a home-grown talent", *T.,* 20.9.77, 3.
589   "Cry from a Scottish heart: enough of this tartan tomfoolery", *T.,* 21.1.78, 14.
590   "Frustrating time for the Liberals", *T,* 22.9.77, 4.
591   "Frustrations of a loyal Labour supporter in Scotland", *T,* 17.2.77, 3.
592   "Future of Shetland", *T,* 5-6.4.78.
593   "Glasgow still in turmoil after the elections", *T,* 14.6.77, 4.
594   "Hope of prosperity from fish farming project", *T,* 26.4.77, 3.
595   "How SNP has eased nationalism on to Scots", *T,* 6.3.78, 4.
596   "Islanders taking well to community radio", *T,* 11.4.78, 5.
597   "Kirk closer to the people than Church of England, Moderator believes", *T,* 30.5.78, 2.
598   "Labour MP who confounds the conventions of politics", *T,* 19.9.77, 3.
599   "Making the best use of the sea to maintain communities in the Western Isles", *T,* 3.10.77, 18.
600   "SNP doubles candidates for a difficult election", *T,* 17.4.78, 3.
601   "SNP drops brash tactics for Hamilton poll", *T,* 26.5.78, 2.
602   "Scottish nationalists begin to count chickens", *T,* 7.3.78, 4.
603   "Scottish views on devolution", *T,* 15-16.11.77.
604   "Tories weigh attractions of voting no on Scotland", *T,* 9.1.78, 2.
605   "The Tory who draws support from council house tenants", *T,* 24.9.77.
606   "Too many cooks spoiling the Scottish broth", *T,* 24.3.77, 25.
607 Fay, S., "The five faces of Jim Callaghan revealed to the unhappy Scots", *ST,* 4.9.77, 4.
608 Fergusson, A., "Burns night and after", *Spectator,* 4.2.78. 15.   ...
609   "But Scotland has devolution now", *Daily Telegraph,* 11.4.77, 10.
610   "Divisive national myths", *Telegraph Sunday Magazine,* 26.6.77, 7.
611 Ferguson, J., and Carty, A., "Controlling the traffic in land", *S,* 17.5.78, 12.
612   "Why Scotland is a target for land buyers", *S,* 16.5.78, 10.
613 Ferris, J. H., Letter: Shetland Chamber of Commerce position on devolution. *Shet. T.,* 27.1.78, 8.
614 Ffitch, G., "The best of British to this campaign", *SDE,* 21.1.78, 11.
615 Fiddick, P., "Screen split", *G,* 23.5.78, 19.
616 Finlay, A., "Turn of the tide for the nationalists?" *GH,* 15.4.78, 5.
617 Finlay, A., et al, "Who wins Scots vote this time?" *GH,* 28.4.77, 7.
618 Finlayson, J., "A testing time: and your vote really counts", *Evening News* (Edinburgh), 2.5.77, 5.
619   "Election countdown", *Evening News* (Edinburgh), 24.4.-2.5.78.

620 Firth, H., "Whither Shetland?" *New Shetlander* 115 (1976), 10-12.
621 Fletcher, A., "Fighting Scots", *SDE*, 2.9.76, 8.
622 Forbes, D., "New roles for the colleges", *S*, 26.7.77, 8.
623 Foulkes, G., "Success of schools councils", *S*, 1.10.77, 10.
624 Fowles, C., "Aberdeen penalised for success in the oil-related business", *T*, 5.12.77, 20.
625 Frame, J., "Six starters: but only two in the race", *Evening News* (Edinburgh), 11.4.78, 9.
626   "Two horse race on card at Hamilton", *Evening News* (Edinburgh), 25.5.78, 9.
627 Freeman, R., "Devolution", *T*, 14.10.77, 14.
628 Fry, M., "£200,000 worth of trade surplus surprises for the economists", *S*, 23.6.77, 11.
629   "Colonialism in the Highlands", *S*, 31.8.77, 11.
630   "Marxist view of nationalism", *S*, 17.6.77, 13.
631   "Labour's problems in Garscadden", *S*, 7.2.78, 9.
632   "Prospects for investment in Scotland reasonably good", *S*, 17.2.78, 14.
633   "The hinge that hardly moved", *S*, 4.5.78, 15.
634   "Time of political calm", *S*, 19.4.78, 14.
635   "Whither the Scottish Tories?", *S*, 27.9.77, 10.
636   "Who will yield the power of the purse?", *S*, 15.8.77, 9.
637   "Willie Ross: architect of the new Scotland", *S*, 15.12.77, 13.
638 J.J.G. Review of 'The Shetland way of oil' by J. Button (Lerwick, 1976). *New Shetlander*, 119 (1977).
639 Gale, G. "How to save the Union", *Spectator*, 3.12.77, 14-15.
640 Gardiner, L. "The SLP devolution bill", *Scottish Worker*, 4, 3 (1977), 5, 11.
641 Gibson, P. "Deserving democracy", *Roof*, Sept. 1977, 160.
642   "The SNP and housing", *Question* 9 (1976), 8-10.
643 Gibson, R., "Gaidhlig Scotland — without reservations", *Scottish Worker*, 4, 3 1977), 4, 12.
644   "It's Scotland's soil", *Crann Tara* 2 (1978), 8-9.
645   "Review of 'The Breakup of Britain', by T. Nairn", *Crann Tara* 1 (1977), 14-15.
646 Gillon, S., "TPP's and you", *CCN* 13 (1978), 14-16.
647 Gow, D., "Idea of an independent Scotland taken seriously by EEC", *Scotsman Half-Yearly Review*, 19.7.77, 6.
648   "Our men in Luxembourg", *S*, 17.4.78, 7.
649 Graham, C., "As ithers see us", *SDE*, 17.2.78, 10.
650   "Bring on the goodies", *SDE*, 10.1.78, 11.
651   "Britain's oil messiah is on the march", *SDE*, 14.9.76, 8.
652   "Bruce fails in numbers game", *SDE*, 4.7.77, 11.
653   "Don't forget — you need us more than we need you", *SDE*, 24.8.76, 8.
654   "Garscadden: a victory message for Maggie", *SDE*, 7.3.78, 10.
655   "It was like watching children playing a maniac's version of cowboys and Indians", *SDE*, 3.3.78, 10.
656   "Labour pains for the SLP", *SDE*, 1.11.76, 2.
657   "Lost weekend", *SDE*, 16.5.77, 11.

658   "Now is the time to get things back in order", *SDE*, 8.12.76, 10.
659   "Scotland's where the action is", *SDE*, 22.3.77, 10.
660   "Shame knocks at a city's door", *SDE*, 27.4.77.
661   "Teddy's target", *SDE*, 11.5.78, 10.
662   "The incredible shrinking city", *SDE*, 17.3.77, 7.
663   "The Garscadden battleground", *SDE*, 13.4.78, 10.
664   "The good, the bad and the ugly face of our public life", *SDE*, 19.4.77, 7.
665   "The great chance for Scotland to stand up and speak as a nation", *SDE*, 13.4.77, 7.
666   "The man alone", *SDE*, 18.4.78, 10.
667   "The programme that's sure to get all of Britain talking", *SDE*, 12.11.77, 10.
668   "The strangled city", *SDE*, 20.5.77, 13.
669   "Time to doff the gloves and don the gauntlet", *SDE*, 3.8.76, 8.
670   "Tories in a turmoil", *SDE*, 24.6.77, 11.
671   "We are sick of this type of politics", *SDE*, 2.3.77.
672   "We've done ourselves a good turn", *SDE*, 5.5.77, 10.
673   "What a way to run a city", *SDE*, 26.8.77, 10.
674   "Who will let Glasgow flourish?", *SDE*, 11.2.78, 11.
675   "Why they can't divide and rule Scotland", *SDE*, 21.1.77, 8.
676   "Why the UK is OK for us all", *SDE*, 7.2.78, 10.
677   "X — the shape of votes to come", *SDE*, 3.5.77, 10.
678   Grant, N., "Respectable gloss on a racist argument", *S*, 13.1.78, 12.
679   Gray, Rev. J. R., "Rich harvest awaits the Kirk", *S*, 9.2.78, 12.
680   Gregory, C. R., "Scottish tourism: boom or blight?", *S*, 22.8.77, 6.
681   Grimond, J. (MP), "Devolution as I see it", *Shet. T.*, 10.2.78, 12.
682   "Scotland Bill: what's it all about?", *Orc.*, 9.2.78, 1, 5.
683   "Statement on Shetland devolution referendum", *Shet. T.*, 11.11.77, 19 (see also 1, 13, 18).
684   Gronneberg, R., "Another view of Shetland's status", *Shet. T.*, 24.2.78, 21.
685   W. H., "Orkney Islands Council: a look at what it does and some of the snags", *Orc.*, 12.1.78, 5.
686   Haggarty, J., "Report from Stirling", *CCN* 11 (1978), 8-10.
687   Hamilton, A., "Indian as Scottish national candidate for local polls", *T*, 29.4.78, 4.
688   Hamilton, D., "Fair share?", *S*, 31.8.77, 11 (see also 13.9.77, 11).
689   "Private medical practice", *Question* 30 (1977), 3.
690   Hannay, D., "Urban clearances: the unacceptable face of socialism", *S*, 20.12.77, 10.
691   Hargrave, A., "Crystal gazing: hazardous but necessary", *S*, 7.9.77, 10.
692   "The beady eye", *7D*, 25.11.77, 7.
693   "The Grampian way ahead", *S*, 8.9.77, 10.
694   "The independence illusion", *S*, 4-5.4.78.
695   "Why I joined the SNP", *Focus* (Dundee), April 1978, 6.
696   Harrison, D., "STUC — origins far from nationalist", *7D*, May 1978, 2.

697 Hart, F., "Scotland's economy and the state", *Scottish Marxist* 16 (1978), 13-16.
697a   "Scottish housing", *Comment*, 29.10.77, 398-9.
698 Harvie, C., "Open letter to an anti-devolutionist MP", *S*, 8.12.77, 13.
698a   "Road to the referendum", *7D*, 13.1.78, 2.
699 Heffer, E. (MP), "The one rock on which devolution could founder", *T*, 29.8.77, 8.
700 Hennessy, P., "Rescuing devolution", *T*, 18-20.7.77.
701 Henry, G. J., "The oilmen cometh", *New Shetlander* 121 (1977), 24-5.
702 Hetherington, A., "Scotland and the BBC", *New Statesman*, 10.6.77, 774.
703 Hetherington, P., "Abortion issue holds key to by-election", *G*, 9.3.78.
704   "A city does its sums and raises £2.2M", *G*, 5.9.66, 4.
705   "A sad lesson in long division", *G*, 28.6.77, 13.
706   "Central vital to Labour and SNP", *G*, 2.5.78, 4.
707   "Drowning the opposition in a sea of words", *G*, 21.9.77, 13.
708   "Gael bait", *G*, 7.12.77, 13.
709   "Getting her trews in a twist", *G*, 11.1.78, 11.
710   "Glasgow is no longer the Mecca for Islanders", *North 7*, March/April 1978, 2-4.
711   "Has Scotland put Labour back on the map", *G*, 4.5.78, 13.
712   "Labour narrows the margin at Gascadden", *G*, 11.4.78.
713   "Nationalists aim at Labour's heartland", *G*, 30.1.78, 4.
714   "Nationalists split over Assembly", *G*, 2.3.78.
715   "Papering over the cracks", *G*, 20.3.78, 11.
716   "Polling book", *G*, 15.3.78, 13.
717   "Scotland demands share in economic boom", *G*, 23.8.77, 2.
718   "Scots play it cool", *G*, 5.11.77, 15.
719   "SNP claims it is catching up confident Labour", *G*, 31.5.78.
720   "Scottish Nationalists try the soft sell", *G*, 26.5.78.
721   "Sound of ferry battle echoes across the isles", *G*, 17.10.77, 2.
722   "Sporran partners", *G*, 25.1.78, 13.
723   "Strathclyde is keynote of SNP poll drive", *G*, 29.4.78, 4.
724   "The end of a steel plant would mean death for a valley", *G*, 21.1.78, 3.
725   "The land that languishes under the feudal system", *G*, 30.6.77, 13.
726   "The loneliness of the rebel baron", *G*, 27.3.78.
727   "The risk business", *G*, 21.4.78, 20.
728   "The unacceptable face of feudalism", *G*, 7.9.77, 12.
729   "Third party risks", *G*, 18.11.77, 15.
730   "When oil begins to make waves", *G*, 15.3.78, 17.
731   "Where friendship nibbles at democracy", *G*, 25.4.78.
732   "Where Tam Dalyell finds anti-home rule faith", *G*, 24.2.78, 15.
733   "Why Mr Callaghan's highland fling could be his last", *G*, 6.9.77, 13.
734 Hewitson, J., "The cases swamping courts", *GH*, 16.1.78, 7.
735 Hobsbaum, P., "The trouble with Glasgow", *GH*, 8.12.77, 7.

736   Hobsbaum, P.: Ritchie, M., "Is Glasgow just a millstone?", *GH*, 3.12.77, 5.
737   Hoggart, S., "Legislation by silent majority", *G.*, 24.1.78, 15.
738   Hood, A., "The Scotland Bill: how your MP voted", *S*, 22.2.78, 13.
739   Horsborough, F., "Make or break on Margo's home ground", *Evening News* (Edinburgh), 24.5.78, 14.
740   "The tough Teddy pulls no punches", *Evening News* (Edinburgh), 11.5.78, 12.
741   Houston, T. & Lang, J., "The disappearing peers", *Record*, 4.11.77, 10-11.
742   Howatson, W., "Labour and a rural seat", *Question* 9 (1976), 11-12.
743   Huckerby, M., "Atomic waste plan brings protests to Scotland", *T*, 6.4.77.
744   Hunter, J., "The unfunny men who own Scotland", *WHFP*, 9.12.77, 2.
745   Hunter, W., "Boadicea of the Nats set for Hamilton battle", *GH*, 26.5.77, 7.
746   "Harry McShane — the working-class history of Scotland in compact form", *GH*, 28.4.77, 6.
747   "The Hamilton by-election candidates", *GH*, 22-23, 26-27.5.78.
748   "The Hamilton enigma", *GH*, 30.5.78, 7.
749   Hunter Gordon, P., "Incentives, not land nationalisation?", *WHFP*, 20.11.78, 2.
750   Hyndman, B., "Operation cash grab", *Record*, 27.6.77, 7.
751   "Still too much too wrong", *Record*, 30.3.78, 12-13.
752   Irving, G., "Can Tartan TV get out of the rut", *SDE*, 4.1.77, 6.
753   Jack, A., "Scotland's special case?", *Business Scotland*, Feb. 1978, 64.
754   "The Western Isles: the economy", *Business Scotland*, Jan. 1978. 18, 21.
755   Jay, P., "If Ben Nevis were solid gold", *T*, 28.4.77, 25.
755a   "Scotland without England", *T*, 3.2.77, 21.
756   Jenkins, P., "Commentary" (on PR), *G*, 9.12.77, 12.
757   "Labour is riding high but the potential is there for the SNP to present a formidable challenge", *G*, 26.5.78, 14.
758   Johnson, P., "Are the Scots all mad?" *New Statesman*, 26.8.77, 267-8.
759   Johnson, R., "A problem shared", *CCN* 5 (1977), 2-4.
760   "Structure Plans — what next?", *CCN* 10 (1978), 20-21.
761   Johnston, R. (MP), "In the middle — and proud of it", *7D*, 20.1.78, 5.
762   Jones, E., "A view from Aberdeen", *Life and Work*, Oct. 1977, 12-14.
763   Jordan, G., "Guillotine headcount", *S*, 5.8.77, 8.
764   Kellagher, I., "No sites: the plight of Scotland's travelling people", *7D*, 4.11.77, 2.
765   Kelly, S., "Antiabortion campaign could lose Labour this crucial Scottish seat", *Tribune*, 7.4.78, 1.
766   Kemp, A., " 'Breakaway' row: Sillars releases text of letters", *S*, 20.1.78.
767   "War of words over SLP documents", *S*, 19.1.78, 13.
768   Kennedy, G., "Defence in Scotland", *Question* 9 (1976), 4-5.

769   "Independence and Edinburgh Central", *SI* 81 (1977), 8.
770   "Why I'm not in the SLP", *Crann Tara* 1 (1977), 5.
771   Kerr, A.: Comrie, B., "How should SNP fight the referendum campaign?", *SI* 83 (1978), 8.
772   Kerr, J., "Far away from the seat of power", *G,* 5.2.77.
773   "Man in the middle", *G,* 18.4.78, 17.
774   Labour Party (Shetland), "Shetland Labour Party's devolution views", *Shet. T.,* 5.8.77, 6.
775   Lawson, G., "Assembly to produce separation", *S,* 25.11.77, 16.
776   Leask, J. W., "A councillor replies", *New Shetlander* 119 (1977), 24-5.
778   Leigh, D., "The members who hold Labour in thrall", *G,* 27.6.77, 11.
779   "The populists", *G,* 27.3.78, 11.
780   Lindsay, S., "Islanders try out new plan for survival", *GH,* 25.5.78, 7.
781   "Oil boom heartache — but it's better than poverty", *GH,* 26.1.78, 5.
782   "Shetland looks to its future", *GH,* 27.1.78, 6.
783   "The changing Islands", *GH,* 9-10.2.78.
785   Lipton, M. (MP), "A piece of my mind", *Sunday Post,* 9.10.77.
786   Lovell, B., "When independence runs out of energy", *T,* 15.11.77, 21.
787   Low, J., "The case for linguistic devolution", *S,* 29.12.77, 8.
788   Macaulay, D., "The Western Isles: a sense of optimism", *Business Scotland,* Jan. 1978, 15.
789   McBay, I., "Conference 1978", *SI* 86 (1978) 5.
790   MacCalman, J., "Glasgow may have to shrink in its battle to survive", *GH,* 25.4.78, 7.
791   McCartney, B., "Schism splits Labour in Dundee", *S,* 5.9.77, 7.
792   "Sir George steps down to tributes", *S,* 26.4.78, 13.
793   "The rural issues get an airing", *S,* 26.9.77, 7.
794   McCartney, S., "The shame of Tullibody", *SDE,* 8.7.77.
795   McConnell, T., "How the Scots economy fares on its own", *GH,* 23.6.77, 7.
796   McCormack, I., "No magic wand for the homeless", *WHFP,* 7.4.78, 2.
797   MacCormick, D. et al., "Would self-government turn the Scots into blue-eyed Arabs?", *Listener,* 12.5.77, 603-4.
798   MacCormick, N., "The referendum: historical parallels", *S,* 6.12.77, 10.
799   "Westminster must beware of pushing the SNP into an all-out battle", *T,* 17.5.77, 14.
800   Macdonald, M., "How the West was won", *S,* 1.12.77, 13.
801   "Hebridean society: a new-found self-confidence", *Business Scotland,* Jan. 1978, 27-8.
802   Macdonald, P., "Assembly 78: a very good year", *S,* 29.5.78, 6.
803   "Subversives in the ministry" *S,* 22.9.77, 11.
804   McElroy, A., "Highlands economy", *G,* 10.11.77, 8.
805   McEwen, J., "Interview", *WHFP,* 11.11.77, 2.
806   McGill, J., "Plutonium independence", *SI* 82 (1978), 8.
807   McGregor, B., "Gypsies hit the oil road again," *SDE,* 16.2.77.
808   McKay, J., "Tensions within the Church", *Weekend S,* 29.4.78, 8.
809   "How 'Bush' made itself a blazing nuisance", *S,* 9.1.78, 7.

N

810   McKay, R., "The forgotten city raises its voice", *7D,* 17.3.78, 4.

811   "Thoughts on Teddy Taylor", *7D,* 13.1.78, 2.

812   Mackenzie, I., "Building prosperity in the five towns", *G,* 21.4.78, 20.

813   McKie, D., "A whole new ball game over the border", *G,* 26.9.77, 13.

814   McKillop, J., "£11M worth of castles, estates, islands on the market", *GH,* 14.7.77, 7.

815   "How Jimmy Reid could cause red faces in Dumbarton Central", *GH,* 20.9.77, 7.

816   "New towns under the microscope", *GH,* 10-11, 13-14.4.78.

817   "The great Dutch landgrab", *GH,* 30.3.78, 7.

818   McKillop, J. & Allan, A., "Will Millan dig into the sandbank secrets?", *GH,* 8.6.77, 9.

819   McKinlay, J., "Shipbuilding's last chance", *GH,* 29.6-1.7.77.

820   Mackintosh, J. P. (MP), "Devolution could end patronage problems", *S,* 13.2.78, 9.

821   "Glasgow belongs to us", *S,* 4.1.78, 8.

822   "How the dynamic of devolution will work", *S,* 16.1.78, 8.

823   "Now what future for the SNP?", *S,* 24.4.78, 10.

824   "Will boredom kill the Devolution Bill?", *S,* 12.9.77, c9.

825   Maclachan, S., "The Garscadden file", *Record,* 31.3.78, 24-5.

826   "Undecided they stand", *Record,* 11.5.77, 16-17.

827   MacLaren, D., "A disease to be watched", *SI,* 78 (1977), 7.

828   MacLaughlin, S., "The rise and fall of a political dream", *GH,* 18.1.78, 6.

829   McLean, B., "Scots unity", *Education Today and Tomorrow,* 30, 1 (1977), 16.

830   Macleod, A., "Highland Board needs more power to purchase land", *S,* 21.6.77 supplement p.11.

831   "Lewis on the dole again", *S,* 19.4.78, 15.

832   "The outer isles: a new realism", *Scotsman Half-Yearly Review,* 19.7.77, 8.

833   Macleod, R., "And councils in Perth", *CCN* 9 (1978), 25-6.

834   McMorrin, D., "Risks the SDA has to take", *GH,* 10.3.78, 7.

835   McMorrin, G., "The fight is on to control foreign investment", *GH,* 16.2.78, 15.

836   McNamara, S., "Scotland . . the nuclear dustbin?", *Sunday Mail,* 15.5.77, 22.

837   Macneacail, A., "On the road to recovery", *WHFP,* 4.11.77, 2.

838   McNicol, I. H. & Roberts, D. C. S., "The economic impact of tourism in Shetland", *New Shetlander* 113 (1975), 16-17, 21.

839   Macpherson, H., "Faces at Westminster: Russell Fairgrieve", *Business Scotland,* Jan. 1977, 11.

840   MacRae, W., "Independence and Ross & Cromarty", *SI* 83 (1978), 4.

841   Mactavish, H., "Boom and bust", *G,* 21.4.78, 20.

842   Main, A., "Triumph in the Highlands", *SDE,* 24.9.77.

843   Manson, T. M. Y., "What relationship and when?", *New Shetlander* 117 (1976), 11.

844   Massey, D. W., "Editorial note: what do we want from planning?", *Town Planning Review,* 48, 3 (1977), 213-4.

845 Masterson, M., "Dundee", *CCN* 2 (1977), 11-13.
846 Mather, A. S. & Armstrong, A. M., "The estate as the land-use unit in the Scottish highlands", *Landowning in Scotland* 168 (1977), 79-81.
847 Mather, I., "SNP watershed in 'desert with windows' ", *Observer*, 9.4.78, 4.
848 Maude, A. (MP), "Devolution in the balance", *Illustrated London News*, Jan. 1978, 25.
849 May, P. & McKenzie, E., "Liberal sees Assembly elections in March 1979", *S*, 5.11.77, 9.
850 'Melampus', "da wadder eye", *New Shetlander* 118 (1976), 18-19.
851 "Vox pop . . ", *New Shetlander* 116 (1976), 20-21.
852 Midwinter, A., "Giving reform a chance", *S*, 21.9.77, 10.
853 Millan, B. (MP), "Millan and the state of Scotland", *SDE*, 4.3.78, 10-11.
854 "My first year in office", *Record*, 7.4.77, 20.
855 Millar, J., "Wish you weren't here", *Record*, 25.9.77, 24-5.
856 Milligan, E., "Road to the referendum", *7D*, 20.1.78, 2.
857 Milne, J., "7 days in the life of . . ", *7D*, 4.11.77, 12.
858 Morrison, I., "Land: are we making the most of it?", *GH*, 17.2.78, 11.
859 "Six Scots farmers who led Green Pound fight", *GH*, 24.2.78, 7.
860 Moulton, M. J., "Ultra-unionist testament", *S*, 23.11.77, 16.
861 Mount, F., "The flying Scots", *Spectator*, 12.11.77, 4.
862 "The uncaring English", *Spectator*, 26.11.77, 4.
863 Mowat, B., "Caithness youngsters face gloomy employment prospects", *North 7*, March-April 1978, 6-7.
864 Mullin, R., "Breakdown of a breakaway", *SI* 83 (1978), 3.
865 Munro, A., "Report from Stanley", *CCN* 13 (1978), 5-6.
866 Munro, N., "Uist School — battle of words goes on", *WHFP*, 19.5.78, 3.
867 Nicholson, J. R., "Fishing is keeping its head above water — just"; "Shetland and oil: a marriage of necessity", *Business Scotland*, Feb. 1978, 61-2, 66.
868 O'Brien, C. C., "Fearsome prospects in Scots dreams", *Observer*, 19.3.78, 12; see also letters, 26.3.78.
869 Osborne, Rev A., "Preaching politics", *SI* 77 (1977), 6-7.
870 "Road to the referendum", *7D*, 27.1.78, 2.
871 Parkhouse, G., "High time for Mrs T. to speak out on Scotland", *GH*, 9.1.78, 6.
872 "Labour machine needs quick repairs", *GH*, 26.9.77, 6.
873 "Salvos and a sour note", *GH*, 3.4.78, 6.
874 "The World Cup and Scottish voters", *GH*, 4.1.78, 6.
875 "Why the Assembly is no mere sideshow", *GH*, 27.6.77, 7.
876 Paterson L., "What kind of Scotland", *Crann Tara* 1 (1977), 3.
877 Payne, G. & Ford, G., "The lieutenant class", *New Society*, 21.7.77, 118-20.
878 Perman, R., "All at sea in the Shetlands", *FT*, 13.4.78.
879 "Devolution: its uncertain effects on Scottish oil", *FT*, 23.12.77.
880 "Goodbye to jobs as well", *FT*, 5.5.78.

881   "Growing competition in a quieter market", *FT*, 19.9.77.
882   "Oil acts as catalyst for Scotland", *FT*, 14.11.77.
883   "Pact fits Borders' view of politics", *FT*, 19.1.78.
884   "Reviving Eigg and Muck", *FT*, 28.10.77.
885   "Scotland's next choice could also be its last", *FT*, 29.4.78.
886   "SNP now has something to defend", *FT*, 30.3.78.
887   "SNP on a slippery slope", *FT*, 24.5.77, 21.
888   "SNP will be judged solely on success", *FT*, 21.2.78.
889   "SNP scotched", *FT*, 15.4.78.
890   "Scottish banking and finance", *FT*, 23.2.78.
891   "Scottish devolution: a cause for concern in Shetland", *FT*, 28.12.77.
892   "Stopping the Scottish rot: a teaser for the Tories", *FT*, 5.1.78.
893   "Strathclyde", *FT*, 25.10.77, 31-35.
894   "The Borders Region", *FT*, 13.4.78.
894a   "The Highland Region", *FT*, 16.2.78.
895   "The SNP gets chance to show its teeth", *FT*, 10.4.78.
896   "Who would own what if Britain split up", *FT*, 10.2.78.
897   Petrie, G., "The rates explosion", *Evening News* (Edinburgh), 30.2.78.
898   Petrie, G. & McGhee, J., "Crisis in the Health Service", *Evening News* (Edinburgh), 26-29.7.77.
899   Philip, G., "Confident SNP put pressure on Labour", *Evening News* (Edinburgh), 9.12.77.
900   Postlethwaite, T. B., "Why I quit!", *CCN* 9 (1978), 4.
901   Pottinger, G., "The ordeal of George Pottinger", *Weekend S*, 22.4.78, 1; *S*, 24-28.4.78.
902   Pulzer, P., "Half shares is the most the SNP can expect in Scotland", *T*, 6.5.77, 16.
903   "Supporters drift back to Labour but it would be wrong to write the SNP's death notice", *T*, 5.5.78, 3.
904   Pym, F. (MP), "Devolution: new proposals but the crucial flaws remain", *T*, 23.8.77, 10.
       "What the Tories would do about devolution", *GH*, 12.5.78, 6.
905   Raison, T. (MP), "Devolution: the great divider", *Daily Telegraph*, 27.10.77, 18.
       "Why the Devolution Bill is unworkable", *ST*, 20.11.77, 14.
906   Rantell, K., "The crazy muddle of Glasgow's housing statistics", *GH*, 10.10.77, 7.
907   Reid, G. (MP), "Building the road to independence", *Campus* (Stirling), 31 (1977), 3.
908   "Keep oan daeing it till ye get it right!", *SI* 82 (1978), 4.
909   Rifkind, M. (MP), "Assembly and PR", *S*, 11.4.78, 10.
910   "Scots MPs will always have a job to do in Westminster", *T*, 17.1.78, 14.
911   Ritchie, M., "BBC Scotland are caught in a financial trap", *GH*, 9.12.77, 7 (but see 17.12.77, 5).
912   "Campbell's kingdom", *GH*, 3.10.77, 7.
913   "Profit game that blights a city", *GH*, 24.4.78, 7.
914   "Why the maverick has become a capitalist", *GH*, 26.10.77, 6.
915   Ritchie, M. et al., "Superscots", *GH*, 12-14.9.77.

916 Robertson, B., "It's the tangle o' the isles", *Record,* 17.2.78, 16-17.
917 Rodgers, P., "Oil rich Orkney wins uranium fight", *ST,* 11.9.77, 59.
918 Rosie, G., "Can Margo rally the failing Nats?", *ST,* 28.5.78, 4.
919 "Death threat claim as Labour's Dundee debacle rolls on", *ST,* 6.2.77.
920 "Dutch buyers join the Grandees", *7D,* 24.2.78, 4.
921 "Dutch land raiders", *WHFP,* 24.2.78, 1, 5.
922 "Highlands lairds go Dutch", *ST,* 19.2.78, 12.
923 "Sold to the fastest bidder!", *WHFP,* 31.3.78, 1.
924 Ross, D., "How to approach Gaelic", *Question* 30 (1977), 3-4.
925 Ross, R., "Scotland's top civil servant hopes to hand over the reins on a winning streak", *GH,* 29.3.78, 7.
926 "Why the Kirk has to face up to the need for change", *GH,* 19.5.78, 7.
927 Routledge, P., "Scottish trade unions trying to make their voices heard", *T,* 18.4.78, 27.
928 Russell, L., "The case against selling council houses", *7D,* 18.11.77, 2.
929 Russell, W., "For a good Scots now is the time", *GH,* 12.12.77, 6.
930 "Road block in Assembly's path", *GH,* 27.1.78, 6.
931 "The doomsday fears of the arch-enemy of devolution", *GH,* 17.11.77, 7.
932 Rutherford, M., "The Scots fulcrum of British politics", *FT,* 18.11.77, 21.
933 Scotsman, "Central Region: focus on industry", *S,* 26.5.78, supplement.
934 "Lothian industry", *S,* 7.10.77, supplement.
935 "The professions", *S,* 19-23.9.77.
936 "The Tayside Region", *S,* 14.2.78, supplement.
937 Scott, D., "Case for giving councillors a salary", *S,* 8.12.77, 13.
938 "Councils conflict over homeless in terms of new Act", *S,* 14.4.78, 15.
939 "Council house test of government sincerity", *S,* 23.5.78, 11.
940 "Council insist on putting its housing in order", *S,* 9.9.77, 13.
941 "Councils keep the gypsies waiting", *S,* 4.4.78, 11.
942 "Explaining benefits of regionalisation", *S,* 28.4.78, 13.
943 "Island councils succeed in sturdy independence", *S,* 1.5.78, 7.
944 "New towns may hold the key to parties' performance", *S,* 2.5.78, 9.
945 "Regions prepare to prove their worth", *S,* 5.5.78, 13.
946 "TAS take the government to task", *S,* 10.2.78, 13.
947 "The burial of a new town", *S,* 30.8.77, 9.
948 "The May Day which will be Labour's distress signal", *S,* 28.2.78, 11.
949 "Wind of change sweeps thru' housing policy", *S,* 1.7.77, 10.
950 Scottish National Party, "Principles for a free Scotland", *SI* 75 (1977), 7.
951 SNP Research Department, "The real victors in District voting", *SI* 75 (1977), 6.
952 Sharp, D., "In search of votes and candidates", *SDE,* 26.5.77, 11.
953 Shirley, R., "Tax: the tangle must go", *Focus* (Crieff), 2 (1977), 3.

954 Shivas, S., "Dear Charles", *Record*, 23.2.78, 18-19.
955 Short, J., "Spending in the regions", *New Society*, 16.3.78, 608.
956 Silk, P., "Consulting in Strathclyde", *CCN* 10 (1978), 18-19.
957   "Social work and community councils", *CCN* 6 (1977), 12-13.
958 Sillars, J. (MP), "Why I'm not in the SNP", *Crann Tara* 1 (1977), 4.
959 Simpson, A., "Still fighting her battle for Easterhouse . . . and Pat
        has no regrets", *GH*, 25.8.77, 7.
960 Simpson, J. & Donald, J., "The few women who rule the roost in
        regions", *GH*, 17.2.78, 7.
961 Skene, D., "Am I a chauvinist paranoid?", *Crann Tara* 2 (1978), 6-7.
962 Smith, G., "Keep Britain United must decide its aims", *T*, 11.5.76.
963   "The Scottish devolution dilemma", *T*, 14.3.78, 18.
964   "Who would topple the government if the Liberals pulled out?",
        T, 12.1.78, 14.
965   "Why a Scottish referendum must be seen to be fair", *T*,
        28.1.78, 14.
966 Smith, J. (MP), "Devolution: half and half home rule" (interview),
        Roof, May 1978, 91-2.
967   Letter: Shetland devolution. *Shet T.*, 2.12.77, 11; for res-
        ponse by Council and others, see 30.12.77, 1, 5, 6; 20.1.78, 15.
968 Smythe, J., "Different problems; same solution", *Roof*, Sept. 1977.
        148-9.
969   "Strategic weaknesses in Green Paper", *S*, 18.10.77, 11.
970 Spens, M., "SNP and devolution", *Shet. T.*, 4.11.77, 14 (see also
        20.1.78, 7; 24.2.78, 15).
971 Steel, D. (MP), "A crisis of confidence for the Tories, not the
        government", *T*, 14.11.77, 14.
972   "Devolution: why Parliament dare not fail again", *GH*, 30.9.77,
        6.
973   "Will the SNP support a new Bill?", *GH*, 8.7.77, 7.
974 Stewart, D. (MP), "Question the nationalists now ponder", *GH*,
        27.1.78, 6.
975 Stewart, D. E., "Lilybank, *SI* 81 (1977), 4.
976 Stewart, F., "Welcoming the world", *G*, 21.4.78, 19.
977 Swan, Rev N., "Change? Yes, but miracles take longer", *Evening
        News* (Edinburgh), 29.5.78, 8.
978   "Wanted: a master plan for the Kirk", *Evening News* (Edin-
        burgh), 19.5.78, 16.
979 Taylor, D., "SSHA: life begins at 40", *Business Scotland*, Nov. 1977,
        459.
980 Taylor, L., "Vote, vote, vote", *S*, 10.5.78, 14.
981 Taylor, T (MP), "Assembly: new Bill with old pitfalls", *GH*, 11.11.77,
        6.
982   "Now let the voice of the people kill this Devo. Bill", *SDE*,
        22.11.77, 10.
983   "Shelling out the sovereign powers", *GH*, 3.2.78, 6.
984   "Scottish economy demands change in housing policy", *GH*,
        16.9.77, 6.
985   "Why it must be 'No' when Assembly is put to the vote",
        GH, 19.5.78, 6.

986   Taylor, W., "Progressive case of asset stripling", *S*, 8.7.77, 11.
987   Thatcher, M. (MP), "My plan for Scotland", *SDE*, 6.5.77, 10.
988   Thomas, D., "Island in the funds", *Listener*, 13.10.77, 471.
989   Thomason, E., "Power in a small pond", *New Shetlander* 117 (1976), 23, 25.
990   Thomson, C., "Minister scotches fears on more reorganisation", *Local Government Chronicle*, 7.4.78, 364-5.
991   "Strathclyde: still waiting for recognition from the 2,500,000 people it represents", *GH*, 23.6.77, 7.
992   Troon, A., "Raasay", *S*, 29-30.12.77.
993   Trotter, S., "Scotland's sporran will still be filled by Westminster", *GH*, 27.7.77, 7.
994   "Sunny for Jim as opposition to devolution crumbles", *GH*, 17.10.77, 9.
995   "The silent march of the Scotland Bill", *GH*, 17.1.78, 6.
996   Utley, T. E., "The big devolution fraud", *Sunday Telegraph*, 20.11.77, 20.
997   Varwell, A., "Relatives and relationships", *CCN* 11 (1978), 11-12.
998   Vielvoye, R., "How North Sea oil is giving new meaning to Sullom Voe", *T*, 25.11.77, 17.
999   Waitelegg, J., "Developing a healthy independence", *WHFP*, 14-21.10.77.
1000 Waterhouse, R., "Grampian's trump card: Aberdeen", *G*, 15.12.77, 8.
1001   "Gusher pushers", *G*, 9.12.78, 12.
1002 Watson, R., "Beavering away in Brussels", *Business Scotland*, Feb. 1978, 70.
1003   "Scottish shipbuilding: a target for European rationalisation", *Business Scotland*, Dec. 1977, 508-9.
1004 Watt, D., "Devolution calculation in Scotland", *FT*, 6.5.77, 23.
1005 Watt, G., "Politics: a danger area for judges", *GH*, 11.11.77, 7.
1006 Weatherhead, Rev. J. L. et al., "The Kirk", *S*, 31-3.2.78.
1007 Weightman, G., "Scottish power", *New Society*, 9.2.78, 314-5.
1008 Wheeler, R. L., "Egilsay — island of change", *Orc.*, 24.11.77, 7.
1009 White, M., "The epic farce of devolution", *G.*, 15.6.77, 3.
1010 Whitehead, P., "A tale of Scottish TV", *New Statesman*, 28.10.77, 573; (see also 4.11.77, 617-8).
1011 Williamson, N., "Scotland 1980: rearranging the furniture", *WHFP*, 17.6.77, 3.
1012   "SLP: a party's fall and fall", *7D*, 20.1.78, 6-7.
1013   "SNP conference: it's Scotland's Queen", *Scottish Socialist* 6 (1977), 7.
1014 Willock, I. D., "Devolution supplement", *Scolag Bulletin* 14 (1977), 2pp.
1015   "The Law Society unveiled",, *Scolag Bulletin* 16 (1978), 12-13.
1016 Wilson, B., "40 years on: Scotland's pensioners battle with dignity", *7D*, 9.12.77, 4.
1017   "A talk with Russell Johnston", *WHFP*, 27.1.78, 3.
1018   "Darnley takes all the knocks", *Observer*, 11.9.77.
1019   "Fate of Scots estates left to a few MPs", *GH*, 26.8.77

1020   "Good cheer from the Board: but no complacency", *WHFP,*
1.7.77, 1.
1021   "Irishmen buy a £300,000 slice of the Outer Hebrides", *GH,*
30.5.78, 7.
1022   "John McEwen, at 90 . . . ", *7D,* 4.11.77, 8.
1023   "Just another Sunday", *7D,* 27.1.78, 2.
1024   "Mr Gray — the art of moderation", *7D,* 23.12.77, 7.
1025   "Nice guys in the middle", *WHFP,* 24.6.77, 3.
1026   "The Labour Party in Scotland", *Scottish Marxist* 14 (1977),
22-5.
1027   "The SNP: a bandwagon in disrepair", *New Statesman,* 21.4.78,
517-8.
1028 Wilson, G. (MP), "Scottish Assembly or Scottish Parliament . . .
the real choice", *Dundee East Gazette,* Oct. 1976, 1.
1029 Wilson, P. et al., "What the parties have to say", *Evening News*
(Edinburgh), 1.5.78, 8.
1030 Wishart, B., "Independence islands: are the politics of Shetland the
politics of greed?", *SDE,* 6.12.76, 10.
1031 Wishart, R., "A tale of two cities", *Record,* 2.10.77, 7.
1032   "It's an election, not a circus", *Sunday Mail,* 9.4.78, 7.
1033 Wood, D., "From an empty Commons — bingo a full House", *T,*
12.12.77, 15.
1034 "The bread and circuses of devolution", *T,* 14.11.77, 15.
1035   "The great referendum gimmick", *T.,* 7.2.77, 15.
1036 Wood, D. (Cllr), "Why socialist housing policy has failed", *S,*
9.1.78, 7.
1037 Wood, E., "Scotch drink in English bottles", *S,* 11.1.78, 9.
1038 Worsthorne, E., "Who wants a break with Britain?", *Sunday Telegraph,* 18.12.77, 8.
1039 Wright, A., "STV 'working hard' to raise standards", *S,* 7.1.78, 6.
1040 Young A., "7 days in the life of . . .", *7D,* 17.2.78, 8.
1041   "The exploitation of Lilybank", *S,* 7.12.77, 12.
1042   "Thoughts after Wembley", *S,* 20.6.77, 11.
1043 Young, E., "Improving Scotland's planning law", *Local Government
Chronicle,* 25.11.77, 959-60.
1044 Young, H., "Home rule: at last we have a straight question", *ST,*
19.2.78, 4.
1045 Younger, G. (MP) & Douglas-Hamilton, J. (MP), "Keep the Forces
British!", *GH,* 8.8.77, 6.

INDEX TO SECTION 1

HIDB: 185-7, 608, 725, 800, 830, 1020.
Housing: 129, 138, 140, 156, 169, 189, 207, 250, 343, 352, 416, 488, 513, 515, 528, 557, 577, 660, 690, 697a, 704, 794, 906, 928, 939-40, 949, 968-9, 984, 1018, 1036.
. . . Homeless (Act): 409, 642, 796, 938.
Independence: 191, 694.
. . . Economic aspects: 33, 40, 135, 240, 289, 348, 431, 433, 755-5a, 786, 797, 1011.
. . . Foreign relations: 40, 42.
. . . Politics of attainment: 257, 540, 799, 907.
. . . Politics after: 266, 336, 647, 769, 840, 868, 950, 1037.
Information services: 5.
'Internal colonialism': see Underdevelopment.
Johnston, R. (MP): 590, 761, 1017.
Judges and politics: 415, 419, 1005.
Kitson, A.: 459.
Labour Party (Scottish Council): 132, 439, 454, 459, 537, 578, 585, 591, 717, 733, 821, 872, 1026, 1040.
. . . Local branches: 45, 501, 598, 732, 742, 791, 815, 919.
. . . Policy: 224-6, 793.
Land, land use: 2, 484, 644, 805, 846, 858, 1019, 1022.
Land ownership, land sales: 41, 118, 121, 221, 243, 529, 611-2, 728, 744, 749, 814, 817-8, 920-3, 961, 1021.
Language (see also Gaelic): 787.
Legal system: 259, 368.
Legal services: 229, 308, 333, 335, 734.
Legal profession: 458, 1015.
Local government: 13, 136, 267, 277, 373, 383.
. . . alleged abuse: 660.
. . . COSLA: 990.
. . . Councillors, salaries: 115, 290, 480, 550, 937.
. . . District-region relations: 409, 938.
. . . Finance: 116, 180, 353, 750, 897.
. . . Planning: see under Planning.
. . . Reforms, reorganisation: 15, 194, 226, 527, 751, 852, 892, 990.
. . . Regions: 942, 945, 991.
. . . Spending, manpower: 421, 498, 580, 855.
Local politics: Aberdeen: 198, 449.
. . . Dundee: 45, 501, 539, 791, 813, 919.
. . . Edinburgh: 138, 141.
. . . Fife: 15 .
. . . Glasgow: 585, 593, 655, 668, 673-4.
. . . Inverness: 417.
. . . New Towns: 944.
. . . Orkney, Shetland: 466, 731.
Lothian Region: 234-7, 934.
Macdonald, Margo: 497, 739, 745, 747, 778.
Macdiarmid, H.: 12, 463.
Media: press: 24, 30, 118, 177, 270.

SECTION 2

SUMMARY OF SCOTTISH OPINION POLLS RELATING TO VOTING INTENTIONS AND CONSTITUTIONAL CHANGE: OCTOBER 1974 - MAY 1978

Dr W. J. A. MACARTNEY
Open University, Scotland

EXPLANATORY NOTES

Selection:

A large number of opinion polls appeared during the period under review, that is, between the October 1974 General Election and May 1978. Some were concerned primarily with non-political questions, others were not carried out by professional polling organisations, while yet others were only partial in their coverage (e.g. covering by-elections or only one religious denomination); polls in these three categories are not included in the tables which follow.

The main interest was taken to centre on the opinion polls about voting intention and constitutional change. In the former case the most valuable series is that carried out by System Three and published in the *Glasgow Herald* every month. It is valuable for comparative purposes because of its regularity, although the method of sampling and the spread of constituencies were both improved during the period under review. This data is reproduced in diagrammatic form in *Tables 1a and 1b*.

Table 2 gives, for comparison, voting intention polls carried out by a number of other polling organisations for various newspapers and television programmes.

Finally, in *Table 3* are to be found results of those polls on devolution which ask for voters' preference on more than two options: the status quo, independence and one or more forms of devolution. This means that one or two polls giving a straight choice — between independence and the status quo, or along the lines of the referendum question proposed in the Scotland Bill — have not been included. The wording of the questions varied from poll to poll but broadly involved some reference to a Scottish Assembly, augmented in some cases by the option of an indirectly elected assembly, an assembly with greater powers and/or a federal or quasi-federal system. It seemed sensible as a form of shorthand simply to indicate the number of options offered under the broad heading of "Assembly".

Acknowledgments:

We would like to thank the following for kind permission to reproduce data: Market & Opinion Research International (MORI), Marplan, National Opinion Polls (NOP), Professional Studies Ltd. (PSL), System Three Scotland; the *Glasgow Herald, The Scotsman,* the *Sun,* the *Sunday Mail;* the BBC, Independent Television News (ITN), Weekend World. I would further like to thank the following for their co-operation in supplying information about other opinion polls: the *Daily Mail,* the *Daily Record,* the *Scottish Catholic Observer,* the Scottish Conservative Party, the *Sunday Post.* The willing assistance of all those above-mentioned eased considerably the task of producing these tables as well as guarding against any unintended omission.

Technical note:

In the tables "Don't Knows" and "Refusals" have been disregarded. The percentages have been rounded.

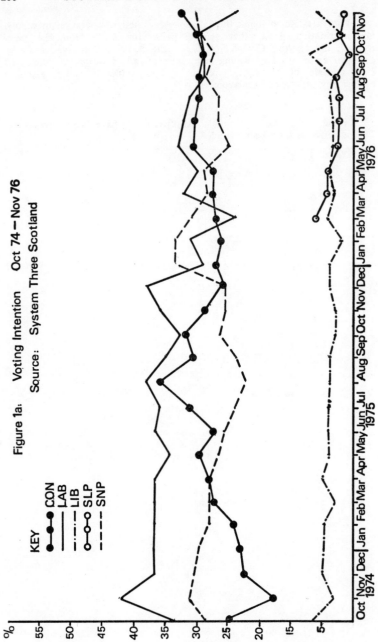

Figure 1a.   Voting Intention   Oct 74 – Nov 76
Source: System Three Scotland

KEY
●—● CON
—— LAB
—·—·— LIB
○—○ SLP
— — — SNP

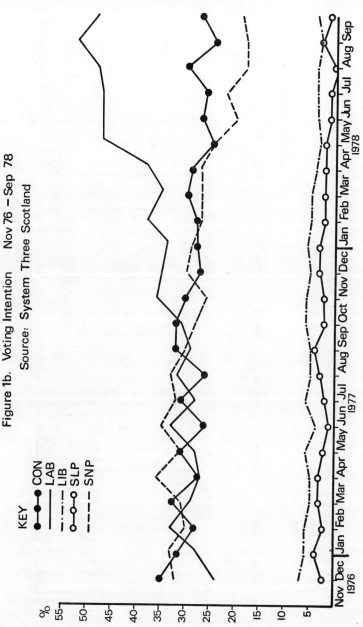

Figure 1b. Voting Intention   Nov 76 – Sep 78
Source: System Three Scotland

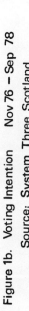

KEY
CON ●━●
LAB ━━━
LIB ━·━·━
SLP ━○━○━
SNP ━ ━ ━

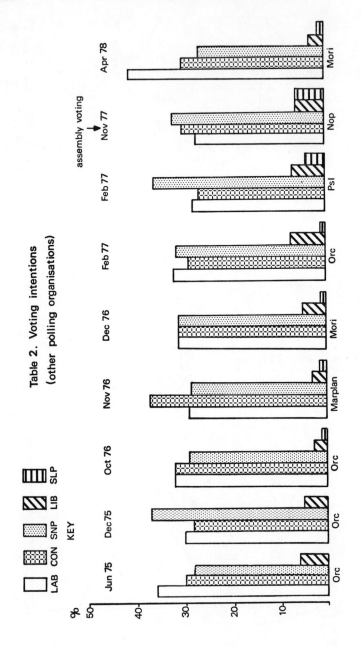

Table 2. Voting intentions
(other polling organisations)

Table 3. Devolution

KEY

Independence

Assembly (x = no. of options)

Status quo

	Jun 75	Oct 75	Dec 75	Apr 76	Oct 76	Oct 76	Nov 76	Dec 76	Jan 77	Feb 77	Feb 77	Mar 77	Apr 78
Source	Orc	Syst 3	Orc	Syst 3	Orc	Marplan	Marplan	Mori	Syst 3	Orc	Psl	Syst 3	Mori
Independence	20	22	22	18	19	21	23	23	20	18	21	26	21
Assembly	3/58	2/59	3/64	2/65	3/57	1/48	1/48	1/55	1/43	3/57	2/52	1/45	1/54
Status quo	22	17	15	17	24	31	29	21	36	25	26	30	26

SECTION 3

CHRONOLOGY OF DEVOLUTION 1885 - 1978

1885   Secretaryship for Scotland established, with responsibility for education, health, poor law, local government, fisheries, police, prisons, roads and public works. (Secretary for Scotland Act).

1897   Scottish Trades Union Congress founded.

1912   Scottish Board of Agriculture founded.

1919   Scottish Board of Health founded, with Parliamentary Under-Secretary.

1926   Scottish Secretary becomes full Secretary of State.

1934   Scottish National Party formed.

1937   Gilmour Committee report on Scottish Administration (Cmd.5563).

1939   Scottish departments (Agriculture, Education, Fisheries, Health, Prisons) vested directly in Secretary of State.

St. Andrew's House, Edinburgh, opened.

1945   Motherwell won by SNP (Robert McIntyre) in April by-election, defeating Labour. Lost in General Election.

Scottish Office takes over forestry, loses National Insurance.

1946   Scottish Council (Development & Industry) formed.

1954   Balfour Commission report on Scottish Affairs (Cmd. 9212).

Electricity transferred to Scottish Office.

1955   Food, animal health, appointment of J.P.s transferred.

1956   Roads and bridges transferred.

1961   Bridgeton by-election, 16th Nov. SNP wins 18.7% of votes.

1962   West Lothian by-election, 14th June. SNP wins 23.3% of votes.

Scottish departments reorganised. Scottish Development Department formed.

1965   Highlands and Islands Development Board founded.

1966   Plaid Cymru wins Carmarthen by-election.

REFERENCE SECTION

1967 Pollok by-election, 9th March. SNP wins 20.2% of vote.

Hamilton by-election, 2nd Nov. SNP (Winifred Ewing) wins seat with 46.1% of vote.

1968 May. Major SNP gains in local elections. They win 37.2% of vote in Glasgow.

May. "Declaration of Perth" — Edward Heath announces establishment of Douglas-Home Committee.

Passenger road transport and sea transport transferred: Scottish Transport Group founded.

December. Crowther Royal Commission on Constitution appointed.

1969 September. Wheatley Commission reports on local government reorganisation (Cmnd. 4150).

Gorbals by-election, 30th Oct. SNP wins 25% of vote.

1970 Ayrshire South by-election, 19th March. SNP wins 20.4% of vote.

General Election. SNP contests 65 seats out of 71 and wins 11.4% of vote. Loses Hamilton but gains Western Isles.

Douglas-Home Committee reports, recommending elected Scottish Assembly.

1971 February. White Paper: "The Reform of Local Government in Scotland" (Cmnd. 4583).

Stirling and Falkirk by-election, 16th September. SNP wins 34.6% of vote.

1973 Scottish Economic Planning Department formed.

Dundee East by-election, 1st March. SNP wins 30.2% of vote.

October. Report of Royal Commission on Constitution (now chaired by Kilbrandon) published, with Memorandum of Dissent by Crowther-Hunt and Peacock (Cmnd. 5460).

Govan by-election, 8th November. SNP (Margo MacDonald) wins with 41.9% of vote.

1974 February 28th. General Election. SNP contest 70 seats, wins 21.9% of vote, loses Govan but gains Argyll, Banff, Aberdeenshire East, Dundee East, Moray and Nairn, Stirlingshire East and Clackmannan.

March. Queen's Speech: Government "will initiate discussions in Scotland and Wales on the report of the Royal Commission on the Constitution and will bring forward proposals for consideration". Lord Crowther-Hunt appointed Minister of State, Privy Council Office with responsibility for devolution.

May. First elections to Scottish regions and districts.

June. White Paper "Devolution within the U.K.: some alternatives for discussion" published.

June 22nd. Scottish Executive of Labour Party rejects devolution proposals.

September. Special Scottish Labour Conference overturns Executive decision.

October 10th. General Election. SNP wins 30.4% of vote, gains Angus South, Dunbartonshire East, Galloway, Perth and East Perthshire.

1975   Scottish Development Agency founded.

Industry powers transferred to Scottish Office.

November 27th. Devolution White Paper "Our Changing Democracy" (Cmnd. 6348) published.

1976   August. "Devolution to Scotland and Wales: Supplementary Statement" (Cmnd. 6585) published.

Main changes: at least two Assembly seats for all constituencies; Assembly alone to nominate Chief Executive; U.K. Government to be able to object to Assembly Bills only if causing "unacceptable repercussions" on non-devolved matters, and unable to take back devolved powers; judicial review of Assembly legislation to be allowed; Assembly power to surcharge rates dropped; SDA operations, administration of the courts, private law, regulation of teaching and legal professions to be devolved.

November 29th. Scotland and Wales Bill published.

December 9th. "Devolution — the English dimension" published.

December 16th. Bill given second reading by 292-247 after Government concedes referenda once Bill is enacted.

1977   January 13th - February 15th. Committee stage of Bill on floor of the House: three clauses and referendum clause approved. Only amendment agreed: Orkney and Shetland each to have one Assembly member.

February 22nd. Motion to guillotine proceedings defeated by 312-283.

April. Manpower services transferred to Scottish Office.

July 26th. Lord President's statement in Commons: separate bills for Scotland and Wales in next session; head of Executive retitled "First Secretary"; premature dissolution of Assembly to be possible on vote of two-thirds of members; legislation on maladministration, teachers' pay and rent regulation to be devolved; block grant to be fixed for "a number of years" by percentage formula; "independent advisory board" on devolution financing; "Joint Council" between Government and Executive proposed.

"Devolution — Financing the Devolved Services" (Cmnd. 6890) published.

November 4th. Scotland Bill published.

November 14th. Bill given second reading by 307-263.

November 16th. Guillotine motion carried by 313-287.

November 22nd. Committee stage begins. Clause I (declaration on unity of U.K.) removed by 199-184.

December 7th. Clause 40 (national pay policy) removed by 290-107.

1978 January 25th. Cunningham amendment that "if it appears to the Secretary of State that less than 40% of the persons entitled to vote in the referendum have voted "Yes" . . . he shall lay before Parliament the draft of an Order in Council for the repeal of this Act" carried 168-142.

Grimond amendment that if Orkney or Shetland vote "No" in referendum "the Secretary of State shall lay before Parliament the draft of an Order in Council providing that . . . the Act shall not apply to them, and providing also for the establishment of a commission to recommend such changes in the government of that area or those areas as may be desirable" carried 204-118.

February 14th. During report stage, Dalyell's new clause stipulating that if Parliament is dissolved before the referendum is held, it must be deferred until three months after polling day, approved 242-223.

Canavan amendment to remove "40% rule" defeated 298-248.

February 22nd. Bill given third reading by 297-257.

March 15th. Bill given unopposed second reading in Lords.

April 4th. During committee stage, Lords vote 155-64 for additional member voting system.

May 17th. Lords' committee stage ends, after Lords vote to withdraw from Assembly responsibility abortion, aerodromes, forestry and afforestation, inland waterways and road passenger service licensing.

SECTION 4

THE STRUCTURE OF THE SCOTTISH OFFICE

The Secretary of State is directly responsible for all the departments making up the Scottish Office. The Scottish Office consists of five departments and a number of "central service" units concerned with such matters as finance, legal services, information and personnel services. The five departments are of equal status and each is in the charge of a Secretary who is responsible to the Secretary of State for the work of his department. A Deputy Secretary (Central Services), who ranks equally with the Secretaries of the five departments, has special responsibilities for the co-ordination of work on devolution and the control of central finance functions, including responsibility for local authority finance.

The Permanent Under Secretary of State is the general adviser to the Secretary of State. Under his chairmanship the Heads of Departments and the Deputy Secretary (Central Services) constitute a Management Group to ensure the co-ordination of the work of the Secretary of State's Departments and to consider common problems across the whole field of Scottish Office responsibilities.

Department of Agriculture and Fisheries for Scotland

This department is responsible for the promotion of the agriculture and fishing industries. Along with the agricultural departments for England and Wales and Northern Ireland, the Department advises Ministers on the formulation of EEC and United Kingdom agricultural policy. The Department implements Government policy for Scottish agriculture by a variety of measures, including the maintenance of agricultural support policy, schemes for capital assistance to agriculture and horticulture, the improvement of livestock and crops, and (through the agricultural colleges and research institutes) the provision of educational, advisory and research services. The Department is also responsible, through the Crofters' Commission, for the development of crofting, and manages on behalf of the nation a large area of state-owned agricultural property. As regards fisheries, duties extend from international relations (including negotiation within the European Community and co-operation in international organisations concerned with the conservation of fish stocks) to domestic matters, such as financial support for the fishing industry, assistance for fishery harbours, scientific research into fisheries' problems and the protection of Scottish fisheries by the department's fleet of fishery cruisers.

Scottish Education Department

This department supervises the public education system in Scotland, in co-operation with the local authorities who are the direct providers of primary, secondary and certain further education within their areas. The Department makes money available for educational buildings, prescribes standards and advises on designs for these buildings, gives guidance on educational curricula and, with the co-operation of the General Teaching Council, is responsible for teacher supply. It exercises certain responsibilities for Scottish Universities, although these, like other Universities in Britain, are primarily the concern of the Department of Education and Science: and its functions also cover youth and community services, adult education, sport, physical recreation and the arts. The Department is responsible for the Royal Scottish Museum and works closely with the National Museums and Galleries and the National Library of Scotland.

The Social Work Services Group, which forms part of the Scottish Education Department has responsibility for the discharge of the Secretary of State's functions under the Social Work (Scotland) Act 1968. These include the administration of grants to the List D (formerly "Approved") Schools, the discharge of the Secretary of State's responsibilities in relation to the children's hearing system and the giving of advice and guidance to social work authorities (the regional and islands councils) and voluntary organisations on the implementation of the 1968 Act. The Group is also responsible for the Secretary of State's functions under other statutory provisions eg. child care, including adoption and fostering. The primary duty placed on social work authorities by the 1968 Act is the promotion of social welfare, the main components of which at present are the care and support in the community of children, the physically handicapped, the mentally disordered, the elderly and other categories of persons in need, together with probation and the after-care of offenders.

Scottish Home and Health Department

This department has two main responsibilities. On the home side it is involved in the administration of the police, fire and prison services: it is concerned with criminal justice, the Licensing Acts and legislation relating to public entertainment: and it is responsible for the law relating to the conduct of parliamentary and local elections and the registration of electors and for a wide range of ceremonial and formal business. On the health side it is responsible for the administration of the National Health Service in Scotland. The Department also exercises on behalf of the Secretary of State, functions deriving from the latter's joint responsibility with the Lord Advocate for law reform and for legal aid.

Scottish Development Department

This department administers Government policy and subsidies in regard to town and country planning, housing, roads and environmental services. It is also responsible for general policy on local government administration, passenger transport policy (including shipping services to the islands), urban renewal, the administration of the community land scheme, conservation, historic buildings and ancient monuments, the rent registration service and the furnished houses rent tribunals service, building control and building standards regulations, public water supplies and sewerage, prevention of air and river pollution, coast protection and flood prevention and nuclear waste management policy. SDD is the sponsoring department for the Scottish Transport Group, the Scottish Special Housing Association and the Countryside Commission for Scotland.

Scottish Economic Planning Department

Set up in 1973, this is the newest of the departments of the Secretary of State. It advises the Secretary of State on matters relating to industrial and economic development in Scotland, including the development of North Sea oil and Scottish aspects of regional policies both in a UK and EEC context. It also has responsibility for direct support to industry through the administration of selective financial assistance under the Industry Act 1972. In this task the department is assisted by the Scottish Industrial Development Advisory Board (SIDAB). It is through the department that the Secretary of State discharges his responsibilities in relation to the Scottish Development Agency, the activities in Scotland of the Manpower Services Commission (including its employment and training services), the generation and distribution of power by the two Scottish electricity boards, the work of the development corporations responsible for the New Towns and the development of tourism in Scotland. The Department also has a general responsibility in relation to Highland development including, in particular, responsibility for the Highlands and Islands Development Board.

SECTION 5

SCOTTISH OFFICE MINISTERS

		Private Secretary
Secretary of State	Rt. Hon Bruce Millan, MP.	K. J. Mackenzie, NSAH, ext. 4001
Ministers of State	Rt. Hon. Gregor Mackenzie, MP. (SEPD matters)	R. H. Scott, NSAH, ext. 4041
	Lord Kirkhill (most SDD matters)	J. A. Rennie, NSAH, ext. 4011
Parliamentary Under Secretaries of State	Hugh Brown, MP. (DAFS matters and housing)	N. Pittman, NSAH, ext. 4005
	Harry Ewing, MP. (SHHD matters and devolution)	P. A. Brady, NSAH, ext. 4024
	Frank McElhone, MP. (SED matters)	P. M. Russell, NSAH, ext. 4010

SECTION 6

SCOTTISH OFFICE DIRECTORY WITH INDICATION OF DEVOLVED AND RETAINED FUNCTIONS UNDER THE SCOTLAND ACT

EXPLANATORY NOTES

Devolution:

The Directory indicates the likely distribution of functions if the Assembly is created. On the basis of the Scotland Act, each division has been marked with one of three initials:

D — devolved to the Scottish Executive

R — retained by the Secretary of State

P — parallel provision likely, or agency arrangement.

Note, however, that in a mainly devolved division there may be elements which are to be retained and vice versa.

Senior Scottish Office Staff:

The organisation and staffing of the Scottish Office down to divisional level are shown here. Heads of Departments are graded as Secretaries. Beneath them are Under Secretaries. The heads of divisions who report to the latter are usually Assistant Secretaries; SP after a name indicates Senior Principal (one grade down). Telephone numbers quoted are enquiry points.

Scottish Office Addresses (all Edinburgh except*):

NSAH   New St Andrew's House, EH1 3SX. 031-556 8400.

SAH   St Andrew's House, EH1 3DB. 031-556 8501.

CH   Chesser House, Gorgie Road, EH11 3AW. 031-443 4020.

WP   16 Waterloo Place, EH1 3DN. 031-557 2090.

JC   James Craig Walk, EH1 3BA. 031-556 8400.

AH   Argyle House, Lady Lawson Street, EH3 9SE. 031-229 9191.

BD   Broomhouse Drive, EH11 3XD. 031-443 4040.

PS   83 Princes Street, EH2 2HH. 031-226 3781.

PH   Pentland House, Robb's Loan, EH14 1TY. 031-443 8681.

AHG*   Alhambra House, Waterloo Street, Glasgow, G2 6AT. 041-248 2855.

THE SCOTTISH OFFICE

		Private Secretary
Permanent Under-Secretary of State	W. Kerr Fraser, C.B. (b. 1929, app. 1978)	C. M. A. Lugton, NSAH, ext. 4023

CENTRAL SERVICES

		Private Secretary
Deputy Secretary	W. K. Reid	J. M. Archer, NSAH,
Central Services	(b. 1931 app. 1978)	ext. 5896

Assistant Under Secretary of State & Head of Liaison Division,		Dover House, Whitehall,
London	J. F. McLellan	London. 01-233-3000

Devolution Division:		
Under Secretary	J. M. Ross	NSAH, ext. 5262
Assistant Secretary	H. H. Mills	

Under Secretary Personnel:
J. A. Ford, M.C., C.B.

Head of Division

P Personnel (General): Management information, manpower planning, personnel planning for devolution, industrial relations — G. J. Murray, WP, ext. 267

P Personnel Management (Administration Group) — J. Inglis, WP, ext. 287

P Personnel Management (Professional, technical and industrial staff) — J. Smith (SP), WP, ext. 225

P Personnel Services: pay, pensions, security, hospitality, VIP visits — J. R. Gordon (SP), JC, ext. 4227

Under Secretary Management Services: J. S. Gibson

P Manpower and Organisation — H. Macnamara, WP, ext. 295

P Accommodation and Office Services — W. J. S. Scott (SP), JC, ext. 5733

P Computer Service — J. S. Robertson, BD, ext. 212

P Telecommunications — A. F. Harrison

P Library — H. A. Colquhoun (Chief Librarian)

CENTRAL SERVICES—*Continued*

Head of Division

Under Secretary Principal Finance
Officer: P. C. Rendle

R   General Financial Questions
(Devolution, PESC)   P. McKinlay, NSAH, ext. 5082

P   Accounting and Central   F. B. Drysdale (SP), CH,
Services Finance   ext. 2149

P   Audit   I. S. Scott (SP), 132 Rose
Street. 031-226-5783, ext. 15
P   Accountancy Services   I. Nicholson (SP), JC, ext. 4445

Under Secretary Finance B:
J. E. Fraser

D   Local Government Finance
Policy, Income & Statistics
(including valuation and
rating)   G. B. Baird, NSAH, ext. 4312

D   Local Government Expenditure including Rate Support
Grant   D. A. Leitch, NSAH, ext. 5416

R   Public Expenditure: Trade,
Industry & Employment;
Nationalised Industries   I. R. Duncan, NSAH, ext. 5636

D   Roads & Transport; Housing;
Other Environmental Services;
Procurement Policies   I. R. Duncan, PS, ext. 274

D   Public Expenditure: Education,
Libraries, Science & Arts;
Forestry   W. A. M. Good, NSAH,
ext. 4161
R   Agriculture & Fisheries   W. A. M. Good, CH, ext. 2341

R   Public Expenditure: Law,
Order and Protective Services   A. H. Mitchell, NSAH, ext. 5289

D   Health & Personal Social
Services   A. H. Mitchell, SAH, ext. 2373

P   Director, Scottish Information
Office: Charles MacGregor

CENTRAL SERVICES—*Continued*

Head of Division

Deputy Director (London):	D. T. Fawell, Dover House. 01-233-7319
Chief Press Officer:	D. C. M. Beveridge, NSAH, ext. 5652

Senior Information Officers:

SEPD matters	J. F. Lindsay, NSAH, ext. 4432
SDD matters	C. M. McPhail, NSAH, ext. 5876
SED matters	M. Q. Jardine, NSAH, ext. 4128
DAFS matters & housing	A. H. Sutherland, NSAH, ext. 5334
SHHD matters and devolution	D. W. Stewart, NSAH, ext. 4856
Manpower Services	W. H. Gunn, NSAH, ext. 5424

P	Chief Statistician	C. M. Glennie, NSAH, ext. 4425
D	Chief Inquiry Reporter	A. J. Hunt, 44 York Pl. EH1 3JJ. 031-556-9191, ext. 274
P	Solicitor	R. W. Deans, NSAH, ext. 4740
	Deputy Solicitors	A. G. Brand, NSAH, ext 5285
		C. J. Workman, NSAH, ext. 5285

Divisional Solicitors and main responsibilities:

(SHHD)	J. L. Jamieson, NSAH, ext. 4244
(SED)	Miss M. Y. Walker, NSAH, ext.5435
(DAFS)	A. J. F. Tannock, NSAH, ext. 4662
(SDD)	D. Cunningham, NSAH, ext. 4464
(DOE)	H. D. Glover, NSAH, ext. 5679
(HIDB)	J. E. Taylor, NSAH, ext. 4238
(DI)	E. S. Robertson, NSAH, ext. 5343
(SEPD)	J. A. Stewart, NSAH, ext 4063

DEPARTMENT OF AGRICULTURE AND FISHERIES FOR SCOTLAND

Secretary:
J. I. Smith, C.B., (b. 1924 app. 1972)

Private Secretary:
Mrs J. Niven, CH, ext. 2478

Head of Division

Under Secretary Agriculture I:
W. W. Gauld

R Capital Grants, Loans, Farm
Structure

S. H. Wright, CH, ext. 2771

Part D Land Tenure, Land use,
Forestry

I. G. F. Gray, CH, ext. 2788

R Agricultural Education,
Advisory Services, Research
D Crofting Development

G. S. Murray, CH, ext. 2074

D Estate Management

T. M. Brown (SP), CH,
ext. 2642

Under Secretary Agriculture II:
R. D. Cramond

R Crops, Plant Health,
Pest control

L. V. McEwan, CH, ext. 2527

R General Agricultural Policy,
EEC co-ordination, hill
farming and other subsidies,
co-operation and marketing

B. Gordon, CH, ext. 2450

R Agricultural labour, animal
health, epidemics, livestock
improvements and animal
welfare

A. I. Macdonald, CH, ext. 2124

R Livestock products: fat-stock,
milk, poultry, eggs, dairy
hygiene, slaughterhouses

L. P. Hamilton, CH, ext. 2436

Under Secretary Fisheries:
J. Cormack

R Fisheries I: regimes (EEC and
international) Law of the Sea;
fish conservation

F. H. Orr, CH, ext. 2157

DEPARTMENT OF AGRICULTURE AND FISHERIES FOR SCOTLAND — *Continued*

Head of Division

D Fisheries II: salmon and
   freshwater fish, fisheries
   harbours, offshore oil and
   marine pollution of fish   H. G. Robertson, CH, ext. 2176

R Fisheries III: fishing industry
   structure and finance, EEC
   marketing, protection and
   enforcement, DAFS fleet   J. F. Laing, CH, ext. 2580

Chief Agricultural Officer   C. Mackay, CH, ext. 2091

Director of Agricultural Scientific   J. M. Todd, East Craigs, EH12
Services   8NJ. 031-339-2355

Chief Agricultural Economist   J. M. Dunn, CH, ext. 2045

Director of Fisheries Research   B. B. Parrish, Torry, Aberdeen.
                                     0224-876544

Chief Inspector of Sea Fisheries   M. J. MacLeod, CH, ext. 2024

SCOTTISH DEVELOPMENT DEPARTMENT

Secretary: Private Secretary:
E. L. Gillett (b. 1920 app. 1976)   S. Brotchie, NSAH, ext. 4202

Under Secretary Planning:
T. L. Lister

Chief Planning Officer:
W. D. C. Lyddon
                                    Head of Division

D Planning I: Grampian,
   Highlands, Borders and
   Dumfries & Galloway regions,
   Islands areas   D. G. Mackay, NSAH,
R Oil-related planning   ext. 5386

D Planning II: legislation, land,
   policy and procedures   J. Lonie, NSAH, ext. 5171

D Planning III: Strathclyde, Tay-
   side, Fife, Central and Lothian N. G. Campbell, NSAH,
   regions; planning appeals   ext. 5785

P

SCOTTISH DEVELOPMENT DEPARTMENT — *Continued*

Head of Division

D   Building Control and Standards   N. E. Sharp, 125 George St. EH2 4LE. 031-226-6981, ext. 218

D   Ancient Monuments   N. E. Sharp, AH, ext. 5259

D   Historic Buildings and Conservation Areas   N. E. Sharp, 25 Drumsheugh Gardens, EH3 7RN. 031-226-3611

D   Urban Renewal Unit (Glasgow Eastern Area Renewal, Urban Aid Programme)   J. Hamill, WP, ext. 343

Under Secretary: W. W. Scott

D   Roads and Transport I: Local transport planning, local roads, Greater Glasgow transport, bus support, freight grants   G. F. Hendry, NSAH, ext. 5757

D   Roads and Transport II: Scottish Transport Group, shipping, air, bridges, road safety   D. Connelly, NSAH, ext. 4894

D   Roads and Transport III: motorways and trunk roads   J. Leithhead (SP), NSAH, ext. 4576

D   Local Government (structures, procedures, manpower)   M. H. Orde, NSAH, ext. 4069

D   Water, Sewerage and Pollution (including coast protection, waste disposal, noise, clean air)   J. Kerr, PH, ext. 222

Under Secretary Housing:
I. D. Penman

D   Housing I: local authority finance management, rent rebates, private building, statistics and research   J. W. Sinclair, PS, ext. 296

D   Housing II: rehabilitation and improvement, Housing Associations, private rented sector   S. C. Aldridge, PS, ext. 313

SCOTTISH DEVELOPMENT DEPARTMENT — *Continued*

Head of Division

D   Housing III: local authority
standards, plans and project
approvals, housing for special
groups, Scottish Special
Housing Association   J. B. More, PS, ext. 295

Chief Architect and Director of
 Building   B. P. Beckett, NSAH, ext. 4329
Chief Research Officer   Miss B. D. Baker, NSAH,
                                         ext. 4440
Chief Estates Officer   P. H. Miller, NSAH, ext. 4843
Chief Quantity Surveyor   A. Y. Hamilton, PS, ext. 264
Chief Engineer   S. C. Agnew, PH, ext. 691
Chief Roads Engineer   J. A. M. MacKenzie, NSAH,
                                         ext. 4800
Chief Industrial Pollution Inspector   W. McCamley, PH, ext. 247

SCOTTISH ECONOMIC PLANNING DEPARTMENT

Secretary: Private Secretary:
T. R. H. Godden, C.B. (b. 1927 app.   E. B. Miller, NSAH, ext. 5139
1973)

Under Secretary and Chief Economic
Adviser: R. G. L. McCrone

                                       Head of Division

R   Regional Development I: Oil   Miss J. L. Ross, NSAH,
development, regional policy,   ext. 5169
EEC co-ordination

R   Regional Development II:
Industrial co-ordination
(including shipbuilding, steel);   J. Glendinning, NSAH,
Government dispersal   ext. 5132

D   Regional Development III:
Scottish Development Agency
R   Manpower and Careers service
policy   R. F. Butler, NSAH, ext. 4388

Under Secretary: J. A. Scott

R   Electricity and Energy Policy   D. J. Essery, NSAH, ext. 4224

D   Highland Development
D   Tourism
R   Peterhead Bay Harbour   H. Robertson, NSAH, ext. 5685

SCOTTISH ECONOMIC PLANNING DEPARTMENT — *Continued*

Head of Division

D   New Towns — J. Fullerton, NSAH, ext. 4935

Under Secretary,
Industrial Development:
A. G. Manzie

R   Industrial Development I:
Steering of industry, inward
investment, financial assistance
policy, SDA liaison — R. Burns, AHG, ext. 386

R   Industrial Development II:
selective financial assistance — L. C. Roberts (SP), AHG,
ext. 251

R   Industrial Development III:
industrial policy, oil technology,
planning agreements — T. M. Band, AHG, ext. 476

R   Industrial Development IV:
export promotion — J. E. Milne, AHG, ext. 276

SCOTTISH EDUCATION DEPARTMENT

Secretary:
J. A. M. Mitchell (b. 1924 app. 1976)

Private Secretary:
R. T. M. Berry, NSAH,
ext. 5005

Under Secretary: Miss P. A. Cox

Head of Division

D   I: Primary and Secondary
Schools (Organisation, cur-
riculum, religious education,
Pack committee) — A. M. Macpherson, NSAH,
ext. 5441

D   II: Local government, special
education, independent schools,
meals and milk, employment
of children — B. J. Fiddes, NSAH, ext. 5615

D   III: Planning, research,
technology, examinations,
Munn and Dunning reports — W. J. Fearnley, NSAH,
ext. 5074

Under Secretary: I. L. Sharp

D   IV: Formal Further Education — J. J. Farrell, 8 George St.
EH2 2PF. 031-226-3521,
ext. 14

SCOTTISH EDUCATION DEPARTMENT — *Continued*

Head of Division

D   V: Higher Education (Central institutions, universities, and educational endowments)

W. A. P. Weatherston, 8 George St. EH2 2PF. 031-226-3521, ext. 26

R   Student Awards

A. J. C. Mitchell (SP), Haymarket Ho., Clifton Terr., EH12 5DR. 031-337-2477

D   VI: Informal Further Education, adult and community education, arts, libraries, museums and galleries, sport and recreation

J. Kidd, 113 Rose St. 031-266-5016, ext. 27

Under Secretary: I. M. Wilson

D   VII: Supply and training of teachers: recruitment, distribution, staffing standards, General Teaching Council

A. K. Forbes, SAH, ext. 2049

D   VIII: Teachers' salaries and conditions of service; administration of Colleges of Education

R. E. Smith, SAH, ext. 2925

D   IX: Educational building programme and approvals

I. D. Hamilton, AH, ext. 5494

Under Secretary, Social Work Services Group: A. F. Reid

D   X: Children's Panels, probation, after-care, research, training, staffing

G. Murray, SAH, ext. 2607

D   XI: List D Schools

R. J. W. Clark, SAH, ext. 2759

D   XII: Local authority social work services

R. D. Jackson, SAH, ext. 2175

D   XIII: Child care, adoption, fostering

Mrs E. Craghill (SP), SAH, ext. 3227

HM Senior Chief Inspector of Schools

J. F. McGarrity, NSAH, ext. 5459

SCOTTISH EDUCATION DEPARTMENT — *Continued*

Head of Division

Chief Social Work Adviser   Miss B. Jones, SAH, ext. 2672
Chief Statistician   D. Wishart, SAH, ext. 2412

SCOTTISH HOME AND HEALTH DEPARTMENT

Secretary: Private Secretary:
A. L. Rennie (b. 1924 app. 1977)   G. Mowat, NSAH, ext. 4014

Under Secretary, Group I:
E. U. Elliot-Binns, C.B.

Head of Division

P   Scottish Office Superannuation   Miss M. A. McPherson, BD, ext. 301

R   Police   R. R. Hillhouse, NSAH, ext. 5138

D   Fire
R   Home Defence and Civil Emergencies   G. P. H. Aitken, NSAH, ext. 2600

Under Secretary, Group II:
D. J. Cowperthwaite

Mostly D Law and General (land tenure, civil law, legal aid, Boundary Commission, minor local regulatory powers)   A. T. F. Ogilvie, NSAH, ext. 4509

D   Prisons   J. Scrimgeour, BD, ext. 647

Mostly D Criminal justice, criminal law, liquor licensing, protection of birds   N. J. Shanks, NSAH, ext. 3897

Under Secretary Health Services (Care): J. B. Hume

D   Health Boards administration and planning   W. P. Lawrie, SAH, ext. 2200

D   Primary care: prevention; environmental health; health education; family planning, maternity, adoption, patients' interests   E. Redmond, SAH, ext. 2319

SCOTTISH HOME AND HEALTH DEPARTMENT — *Continued*

Head of Division

D Mentally and physically
disabled; alcoholism, misuse
of drugs   G. Robertson, SAH, ext. 3128

D Scientific and information
services; emergency services,
blood transfusion, liaison with
Common Services Agency,
devolution (health questions)   T. H. McLean, SAH, ext. 2331

Under Secretary Health Services
(Resources): J. Walker

D Doctors and dentists, medical   Miss M. Maclean, SAH,
and dental education   ext. 3101

D Nursing, administrative and
professional staff   D. Stevenson, SAH, ext. 2244

D Ancillary and domestic services
and staff, control of drugs,
food standards   F. H. Cowley, SAH, ext. 2951

D Capital allocations and
approvals, project control,
land, building and design
guidance, supplies policy   A. H. Bishop, SAH, ext. 2540

HM Chief Inspector of Constabulary D. Gray, NSAH, ext. 4516
Chief Medical Officer   J. J. A. Reid
Chief Scientist   Sir Andrew Watt Kay, Trinity
                                   Park House, EH5 3SF
                                   031-552-6255
Chief Nursing Officer   Miss M. G. Arnold, SAH,
                                   ext. 2219

SECTION 7

LIST OF NOMINATED AND AD HOC BODIES AND THEIR SPONSORING DEPARTMENTS AS LISTED IN THE LIBRARY OF THE HOUSE OF COMMONS

Department	Name of Body	Total No. Appoints. in each	No. of Unpaid Appoints.	No. of Civ. Servs. incl. in Col. 2
SHHD	Advisory Committee on Community Medicine Establishments	6	6	1
SHHD	Advisory Committee on Dental Establishments	9	9	4
SHHD	Advisory Committee on Hospital Medical Establishments	15	15	6
SHHD	Advisory Committee on the Irradiation of Food	14	14(a)	
SHHD	Advisory Committee on the Protection of Birds for Scotland	19	19	
	Advisory Committee on Scotland's Travelling People	12	12	
SED	Advisory Council on Social Work	24	24	
	Agricultural Research Council	21	2(a)&(b)	
	Agricultural Training Board	27	5(b)&(c)	
SDD	Ancient Monuments Board for Scotland	13	13	
SHHD	Ancillary Dental Workers Committee of the General Dental Council	4	1(c)(d)(k)	
DAFS	Animals Board of the Joint Consultative Organisation (JCO)	18	17(a)	
	Animal Diseases Research Association: General Purpose & Finance Committee	11	1	
	Animal Virus Research Institute	8	8(a)	
DAFS	Arable Crops and Forage Board of the Joint Consultative Organisation	17	3(a)	
SED	Board of Governors — Duncan of Jordanstone College of Art, Dundee	23	2	
	Board of Governors — Dundee College of Technology	23	2	
	Board of Governors — East of Scotland College of Agriculture	16	5	

Department	Name of Body	Total No. Appoints. in each	No. of Unpaid Appoints.	No. of Civ. Servs. incl. in Col. 2
	Board of Governors — Edinburgh College of Art	26	2	
	Board of Governors — Glasgow School of Art	27	2	
	Board of Governors — Leith Nautical College	23	2	
	Board of Governors — North of Scotland College of Agriculture	16	4	
	Board of Governors — Paisley College of Technology	22	2	
SHHD	Board of Governors — Scottish Police College	16	16	6
	Board of Governors — Queen Margaret College	26	2	
	Board of Governors — Queen's College, Glasgow	26	2	
	Board of Governors — Royal Scottish Academy of Music & Drama	22	2	
	Board of Governors — Scottish College of Textiles	24	2	
	Board of Governors — West of Scotland College of Agriculture	21	5	
SHHD	Board of Management for the Schemes of Pensions for the Widows and other Dependants of Teachers in Scotland	13	2	
	Board of Management of Scottish Agriculture Development Council	15	4	
	Board of the Scottish Society for Research in Plant Breeding	30	4	
SHHD	Boundary Commission for Scotland	4	2	
SDD	Building Standards Advisory Committee	15	15	
SED	Central Council for Education and Training in Social Work	63	11(b)(c)(d)(e)&(f)	
SED	Central Institutions Academic Staffs Salaries Committee	30	30	
SHHD	Central Midwives Board for Scotland	16	7	
SED	Children's Panels — Borders Region	47	47	
	Central	85	85	

Department	Name of Body	Total No. Appoints. in each	No. of Unpaid Appoints.	No. of Civ. Servs. incl. in Col. 2
	Dumfries & Galloway	42	42	
	Fife	102	102	
	Grampian	103	103	
	Highlands	76	76	
	Lothian	180	180	
	Orkney Islands	10	10	
	Shetland Islands	13	13	
	Strathclyde	890	890	
	Tayside	123	123	
	Western Isles	17	17	
	Children's Panel Advisory Committees —			
	Borders	5	3	
	Central	5	3	
	Dumfries & Galloway	5	3	
	Fife	5	3	
	Grampian	5	3	
	Highland	5	3	
	Orkney Islands	5	3	
	Children's Panel Advisory Committees —			
	Shetland Islands	5	3	
	Lothian	5	3	
	Strathclyde	10	6	
	Tayside	5	3	
	Western Isles	5	3	
SDD	Clean Air Council for Scotland	21	21	
SHHD	Committee for Clinical Nursing Studies	12	12	
	Committee of Appeal	10	10	5
SED	Committee on Mathematics for General Education	12	12	
	Committee to Review Classification of Courses	28	28	5
DAFS	Consumers' Committee for Great Britain	12	12(a)&(c)	
DAFS	Consumers' Committee for Scotland	7	7	
	Council for National Academic Awards	26	26(b)	
	Council for Training and Education of Health Visitors	31	5(b)(d)(e) &(i)	
	Council of Management of the Hannah Research Institute	8	2	

Department	Name of Body	Total No. Appoints. in each	No. of Unpaid Appoints.	No. of Civ. Servs. incl. in Col. 2
	Council of Management of the Macaulay Institute of Soil Research	15	3	
SDD	Countryside Commission for Scotland	12	10	
SHHD	Departmental Committee on Criminal Procedures	11	11(j)	
	Departmental Committee on Reparation by the Offender	13	13(j)	
SHHD	Eastern Area Nurse Training Committee	13	2	
	Educational Panel Independent Schools Tribunal	12	12	
SEPD	Electricity Consultative Council for North of Scotland District	31	31	
SEPD	Electricity Consultative Council for South of Scotland District	29	28	
	Engineering & Building Board of the Joint Consultative Organisation	16	16(a)	
DAFS	Farm Animal Welfare Advisory Committee	17	17(a)	
	Fisheries Research & Development Board	14	14(a)	
DAFS	Food Science & Technology Board of the Joint Consultative Organisation	17	17(a)	
SHHD	General Nursing Council for Scotland	28	12	
SHHD	General Practice Finance Corporation — Scottish Advisory Committee	10	10	6
	General Purpose & Finance Committee of Animal Diseases Research Association	11	1	
SED	General Teaching Council for Scotland	49	4	
SHHD	Glasgow Area Nursing Training Committee	13	2	
	Governing Body of Grassland Research Institute	13	13(a)(b)	
	Governing Body of Hill Farming Research Organisation	15	15(a)	
	Governing Body of National Vegetable Research Station	23	5(a)(b)	
	Governing Body of Scottish Horticultural Research Institute	16	16	

Department	Name of Body	Total No. Appoints. in each	No. of Unpaid Appoints.	No. of Civ. Servs. incl. in Col. 2
	Governing Body of Scottish Institute of Agriculture Engineering	8	2(a)(b)	
	Health Boards —			
	Argyll & Clyde	21	20	
	Ayrshire & Arran	21	20	
	Borders	14	13	
	Dumfries & Galloway	19	18	
	Fife	21	20	
	Forth Valley	18	17	
	Grampian	20	19	
	Greater Glasgow	23	22	
	Highland	19	18	
	Lanarkshire	23	22	
	Lothian	23	22	
	Orkney	15	14	
	Shetland	15	14	
	Tayside	19	18	
	Western Isles	15	14	
	Her Majesty's Commissioners for the Government of Queen Victoria School (Dunblane)	19	6	1
DAFS	Herring Industry Advisory Council	33	33(a)(c)(i)	
SEPD	Highlands & Islands Development Board Consultative Council	39	39	
DAFS	Hill Farming Advisory Committee for Scotland	13	13	1
SDD	Historic Buildings Council for Scotland	10	9	
DAFS	Horticulture Board of the Joint Consultative Organisation	17	16(a)	
SHHD	Local Review Committees (Parole Scheme)	59	59	10
DAFS	Meat & Livestock Commission — Consumers Committee	10	7(a)(c)	
DAFS	Meat & Livestock Commission — Distribution Committee	26	25(a)(c)	
DAFS	Meat & Livestock Commission — Production Committee	19	18(a)(c)	
SED	National Committee for the In-Service Training of Teachers	27	27	
	National Galleries of Scotland Board of Trustees	7	7	

Department	Name of Body	Total No. Appoints. in each	No. of Unpaid Appoints.	No. of Civ. Servs. incl. in Col. 2
SHHD	National Medical Manpower Committee	9	9(d)	
	National Museum of Antiquities of Scotland Board of Trustees	24	12	
SHHD	National Optical Consultative Committee	22	4	
SHHD	North Eastern Area Nurse Training Committee	13	2	
SEPD	North of Scotland Hydro Electric Board	9	1	
SHHD	Northern Area Nursing Training Committee	13	2	
SEPD	Nuclear Safety Advisory Committee	16	16(e)	
SEPD	Oil Development Council for Scotland	28	28	
SHHD	Parole Board for Scotland	15	3	
SEPD	Peterhead Bay (Management) Co. Ltd.	7	7	
	Police Advisory Board for Scotland	33	33	
	Police (Scotland) Examinations Board	8	8	1
SDD	Red Deer Commission	13	12	
	River Purification Boards —			
	Clyde	17	17	
	Forth	12	12	
	Highland	8	8	
	North East	6	6	
	Solway	5	5	
	Tay	6	6	
	Tweed	5	5	
SHHD	Scottish Central Fire Brigades Advisory Council	20	1	1
SED	Scottish Certificate of Education Examination Board	38	38	
	Scottish Council for Educational Technology	52	11	
	Scottish Council for Postgraduate Medical Education	30	9	2
SED	Scottish Council for Research in Education	22	5	
SED	Scottish Committee for Schools/ Industrial Liaison	21	3	
SEPD	Scottish Economic Council	20	20	
	Scottish Electricity Boards: Amenity Committee	5	5	

Department	Name of Body	Total No. Appoints. in each	No. of Unpaid Appoints.	No. of Civ. Servs. incl. in Col. 2
	Scottish Electricity Boards: Fisheries Committee	6	6	
SHHD	Scottish Food Hygiene Council	19	19	
SHHD	Scottish Health Service Planning Council	26	26	6
	Scottish Hospital Endowment Research Trust	7	7	
SHHD	Scottish Hospital Trust	8	8	
	Scottish Housing Advisory Committee	20	20	
SED	Scottish National Camps Association	14	14	
SHHD	Scottish National War Memorial Board of Trustees	19	3	
	Scottish Office Discussion Group on Inquiries	10	10	1
SHHD	Scottish Records Advisory Council	11	11	
SDD	Scottish River Purification Advisory Committee	19	19	
SED	Scottish Sports Council	20	17	
SHHD	Scottish Standing Committee on Prostethics	12	12	2
SDD	Scottish Standing Committee for the Calculation of Residual Values of Fertilizers and Feeding Stuffs	5	5	
	Robert Gordon's Institute of Technology — Standing Committee	22	2	
	Scottish Advisory Committee on Top Grant Scientific Posts	11	11	3
SED	Scottish Advisory Committee to the Central Council for Education & Training in Social Work	13	13	
SHHD	Scottish Advisory Committee to the Council for the Training & Education of Health Visitors	13	13	
SDD	Scottish Agricultural Advisory Council	12	12	1
SDD	Scottish Agricultural Consultative Panel	36	36	1
SDD	Scottish Agricultural Development Council	15	5	

Department	Name of Body	Total No. Appoints. in each	No. of Unpaid Appoints.	No. of Civ. Servs. incl. in Col. 2
SDD	Scottish Agricultural Wages Board	17	12	
	Scottish Business Education Council	22	22	
SED	Scottish Central Committee on Mathematics	16	16	2
SED	Scottish Central Committee on Primary Education	18	18	2
SED	Scottish Central Committee on Physical Education	12	12	1
SED	Scottish Central Committee on Science	18	18	3
SED	Scottish Central Committee on Social Subjects	18	18	3
SED	Scottish Central Committee on Technical Education	18	18	2
	Scottish Central and Local Government Statistics Liaison Committee	26	26	10
SED	Scottish Studentship Selection Committee	10	10	
SED	Scottish Teachers Salaries Committee	37	27	2
	Scottish Technical Education Council	22	22	
	Scottish Transport Group	11	1	
	Scottish United Services Museum Advisory Committee	10	10	2
	Scottish Valuation Advisory Council	15	15	
SED	Secondary Mathematics Committee	13	13	2
	Sheriff Court Rules Council	14	1	
SEPD	South of Scotland Electricity Board	9	1	
	South Eastern Area Nurse Training Committee	13	2	
	Standing Consultative Council on Youth and Community Service	22	22	
SHHD	State Hospital Management Committee	16	16	4
SHHD	Visiting Committees (HM Borstal Institutions)	51	51	
SHHD	Visiting Committees (HM Detention Centre, Glenochil)	15	15	
SHHD	Visiting Committees (HM			

Department	Name of Body	Total No. Appoints. in each	No. of Unpaid Appoints.	No. of Civ. Servs. incl. in Col. 2
	Young Offenders' Institutions)	51	51	
SHHD	West Central Area Nurse Training Committee	13	2	
SHHD	Western Area Nurse Training Committee	13	2	
SDD	White Fish Industry Advisory Council	54	54(a)(c)(i)	
	Working Group on the Devlin Report	5	5(j)	
	Working Party on Civic Government	15	15	
SED	Working Party on Music	15	15	1
	Governing Body of Rowett Research Institute	15	5	

Appointments made jointly by the Secretary of State for Scotland and other Ministers:

(a) Minister of Agriculture, Fisheries and Food.
(b) Secretary of State for Education and Science.
(c) Secretary of State for Wales.
(d) Secretary of State for Social Services.
(e) Secretary of State for Energy.
(f) Secretary of State for the Home Department.
(g) Secretary of State for the Environment.
(h) Secretary of State for Employment.
(i) Secretary of State for Northern Ireland.
(j) Lord Advocate.
(k) Minister of Health for Social Services in Northern Ireland.

SECTION 8

THE STRUCTURE OF SCOTTISH LOCAL GOVERNMENT

Local government in Scotland was re-organised in May 1975. A large number of small authorities with a mixture of functions were replaced by sets of regional, district and island councils with more ordered responsibilities. The three island councils — Shetland, Orkney and the Western Isles — are all-purpose authorities. Mainland Scotland is then divided into nine regions — Borders, Dumfries and Galloway, Lothian, Strathclyde, Tayside, Fife, Central, Grampian, and Highland — and each region sub-divided into districts of which there are 53 in all. The boundaries are drawn to have regard to social, economic and recreational pattern rather than size. Hence half the population of Scotland lives in one region — Strathclyde — compared with only 100,000 in the Borders Region. Glasgow City District has over ¾ million population and therefore has more people than any region apart from Strathclyde; in contrast there are a number of districts with around 30,000 people. Each council is composed of councillors elected by geographical area and is served by officers responsible for the particular services and functions. In 1977-78 68% of revenue income came to local authorities via the Treasury's Rate Support Grant. The balance came mainly from local taxation (the rate levy or tax on property) with a small amount from rents and service charges.

Regional Authority Functions

Major planning and related services:
>   Strategic planning; industrial development; transportation: roads, traffic management and road safety, passenger transport, ferry services, airports; water, sewerage, flood prevention and arterial drainage; countryside and tourism.

Education; Social Work; Police; Fire; Coast protection; Consumer protection; Weights and measures; Food standards and labelling; Disease of animals; Community centres, parks and recreation*; Museums and art galleries*; Registration of births, deaths and marriages; Registration of Electors.

District Authority Functions

Local planning and associated services:
>   urban development; countryside**.

Building control**; Housing; Community centres, parks and recreation*; Museums and art galleries*; Libraries**.

Environmental health, including:
>   cleansing; refuse collection and disposal; food hygiene; Shops Act, etc.; clean air; markets and slaughterhouses; burial and cremation.

Regulation and licensing, including:
>   cinemas and theatres; betting and gaming; taxis; house-to-house collections.

*Exercised concurrently by regional and district authorities.
**Except in Highland, Dumfries and Galloway and Borders regions where the functions concerned are regional.

Q

Islands Authority Functions
    The islands authorities exercise all of the above functions subject to joint arrangements in the case of police and fire.

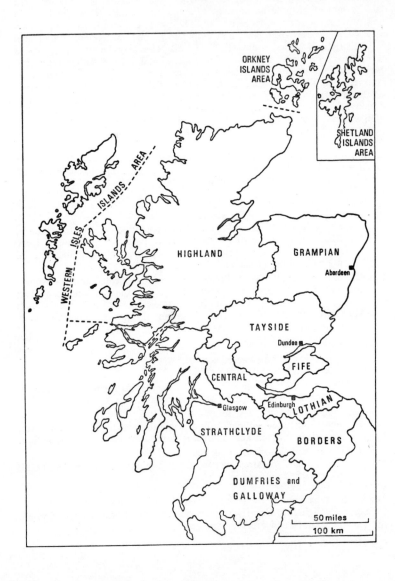

SECTION 9

REGIONAL COUNCILS:

Names and addresses of Conveners and Chief Officers

	Convener Population	Chief Executive	Director of Administration	Director of Finance	Director of Education	Director of Social Work	Director of Planning	Director of Roads
BORDERS Newtown St Boswells TD6 0SA 083 52 3301	John Askew (Con) 99,000	K J Clark	A R Napier	H Hall	J McLean	D A Macdonald	D P Douglas	R I Hill
CENTRAL Viewforth Stirling 0786 3111	James Anderson (Lab) 270,000	E Geddes	P W Buchanan	J Broadfoot	I Collie	H M Garland	F Bracewell	J F Keith
DUMFRIES & GALLOWAY Council Offices Dumfries 0387 3141	John Niven (Ind) 144,000	L T Carnegie	D A Lyle	D Y Booth 0387 62323	J K Purves 30 Edinburgh Rd Dumfries 0387 63822	J W Barbour 8 Gordon St Dumfries 0387 63022	A H Dobbie	H D B Murray
FIFE Fife House North Street Glenrothes 0592 754411	Robert Gough (Lab) 339,000	J M Dunlop	D P McLean	R Venters	I S Flett Wemyssfield Kirkcaldy 0592 62351	M A Gillespie Queensway Glenrothes 0592 756901	M E Taylor County Bldgs Cupar 0334 3722	R J Storie (Engineering) Craig Mitchell House Flemington Road Glenrothes 0592 756541
GRAMPIAN Woodhill House Ashgrove Road West Aberdeen AB9 2LU 0224 23401	Alexander Mutch (Con) 454,000	J D Macnaughton	I Miller	T E Carter	J A D Michie	Miss M Hartnoll	T F Spott	W Turner
HIGHLAND Regional Buildings Glenurquhart Road Inverness 0463 34121	Ian Campbell (Ind) 186,000	F G Armstrong	F F Bruce R H Stevenson	J W Bremner	R Macdonald	J G Bailey	D W M Calder	G K M Macfarlane

	Convener Population	Chief Executive	Director of Administration	Director of Finance	Director of Education	Director of Social Work	Director of Planning	Director of Roads
LOTHIAN George IV Bridge Edinburgh EH1 1UQ 031-229 9292	John Crichton (Lab) 755,000	R G E Peggie	A L McNicoll	B Grosset	W D C Semple 40 Torphichen St Edinburgh EH3 8JJ	J G Gardner Shrubhill House Shrub Place Edinburgh EH7 4PD 031-554 4301	F P Tindall 1 Parliament Sq Edinburgh EH1 1TU	A S Crockett 19 Market St Edinburgh EH1 1BL
STRATHCLYDE Melrose House 19 Cadogan Street Glasgow G2 6HR 041-204 2800	Charles O'Halloran (Lab) 2,489,000	L Boyle	G Carlton	R Paterson	E Miller 25 Bothwell St Glasgow G2 6NR	F E Edwards McIver House 51 Cadogan St Glasgow G2 7QB 041-204 2727	H D B Torrance McIver House 51 Cadogan St Glasgow G2 7QB 041-204 2727	W S McAlonan McIver House 51 Cadogan St Glasgow G2 7QB 041-204 2727
TAYSIDE Tayside House 26-28 Crichton Street Dundee 0382 23281	William Fitzgerald (Con) 402,000	A H Martin		G A McFee	D G Robertson	S O Moxley	H Ramsay	A R Mollison

ISLANDS COUNCILS

	Convener Population	Chief Executive	Director of Administration	Director of Finance	Director of Education	Director of Social Work	Director of Planning	Director of Roads
ORKNEY County Offices Kirkwall 0856 3535	Edwin Eunson (Ind) 18,000	H A G Lapsley	R M Ross	R H Gilbert	A Bain Albert Street Kirkwall	A R MacKinnon Mounthoolie Lane Kirkwall	M Sargent The Strynd Kirkwall	
SHETLAND Town Hall Lerwick 0595 3535	Alexander Tulloch (Ind) 19,000	E Urquhart	P B Regan County Bldgs Lerwick	C V Ennis 4 Market St Lerwick	R A B Barnes Brentham St Harbour St Lerwick	P Malcolmson 64 St Olaf St Lerwick	J M Fenwick Victoria Bldgs Esplanade Lerwick	*Housing* H Darnley
WESTERN ISLES Council Offices South Beach Stornoway 0851 3773	Rev Donald Macaulay (Ind) 30,000	R MacIver	A W S Rae	D G Macleod	A Macleod 0851 3992	0851 3664	R Haworth	

SECTION 10

REGIONAL ELECTIONS:
SEATS WON BY EACH PARTY IN EACH REGION IN MAY 1978

	Lab	Con	SNP	Lib	Ind	Others	Vacant	Total	Uncontested in 1978
BORDERS	0	9 from Lib: Hawick E	1 from Ind: Hawick N	1 from Ind: Forest	12 from Lib: Galashiels E Galashiels NW	0	0	23	10
CENTRAL	18 from SNP: Stirling (Causeway-head), St Ninians, Camelon N & S, Inchyra & Bowhouse	6 from SNP: Falkirk West & Middle; from Ind: Trossachs	6 from Ind: Banknock	0	2	2 Dem Nat from SNP: Lauriston. 1 Ind Lab	0	34	0
DUMFRIES & GALLOWAY	1 from Ind: Kirkconnel	5 from Ind: St Mary's, St Michael's	1 from Con: Palmerston	0	26 from Progressive: Sanquhar & Queensberry	0	0	35	19
FIFE	24 from Con: Kirkcaldy 7-10. from Ind: Dunfermline 11-12.	14 from Ind: Kirkcaldy 1-2, St Monans, Newport. from Lab: Kirkcaldy 3-4.	1 from Lab: Glenwood	0	2 from Con: Leslie	1 Comm	0	42	8

	Lab	Con	SNP	Lib	Ind	Others	Vacant	Total	Uncontested in 1978
GRAMPIAN	13	33 from Ind: Ugie & Cruden, Mearns; from Lib: Don-Ury	2 from Con: Peterhead W/Boddam, Peterhead E	1	3	1 Ind Lib from Con: S Gordon	0	53	14
HIGHLAND	3 from Ind: Dalneigh	1	2	1	40	0	0	47	25
LOTHIAN	26 from Con: Links/Lorne from SNP: Armadale, Slateford/ Hailes	18	3	1	1	0	0	49	0
STRATH-CLYDE	72 from SNP: Kilsyth/ Cumbernauld NW, Calderwood/ St Leonard's, Irvine; from Ind: Tinto.	25 from Lab: King's Park/ Castlemilk; from SNP: Kirkintilloch, Bishopbriggs, Murray/ Avondale	2 from Con: Mid-Argyll/ Islay	2	0	1 Ind Ratepayers	1	103	1
TAYSIDE	15 from Con: Arbroath E	25 from Lab: Perth 2-3; from Ind: Montrose, Dunkeld	0	0	6 from Con: Scone	0	0	46	12

Details of party gains do not include changes of allegiance by sitting member.
Islands Councils are all non political: also elected May 1978.

REGIONAL ELECTIONS:
PROPORTION OF VOTES WON BY EACH PARTY IN EACH REGION IN MAY 1978

	Con	Lab	Lib	SNP	Comm	Ind	Others
HIGHLAND	2.6	5.3	2.6	6.0	—	83.4	—
GRAMPIAN	43.1	28.5	6.2	14.4	0.1	5.8	1.8
TAYSIDE	42.8	34.4	1.6	16.3	0.9	3.4	0.7
FIFE	32.7	44.0	0.3	15.4	4.0	3.6	—
LOTHIAN	33.2	40.3	4.3	20.3	0.4	1.5	—
CENTRAL	14.4	41.7	—	35.0	0.4	5.1	3.9
BORDERS	16.3	9.5	14.6	2.9	—	56.8	—
STRATHCLYDE	30.0	43.0	1.8	22.6	0.3	0.7	1.8
DUMFRIES & GALLOWAY	13.3	13.2	—	3.7	—	67.4	2.4

SECTION 11

REGIONAL ELECTIONS:
DETAILED RESULTS FOR GLASGOW AND EDINBURGH

EXPLANATORY NOTES

In the following tables, the share of the vote by party is given for Glasgow and Edinburgh wards, arranged by parliamentary constituencies. 1978 votes and turnout are in *italic type*.

1974 figures refer to the first regional election and those for 1977 are calculated from the results in the two district wards that comprise each regional one.

Where a party contested only one of the district wards in 1977 this is shown thus *

A councillor's name is in *italic* when he has gained the seat for his party compared to the 1974 result.

Percentage of votes won by each party in each ward in regional elections of 1978 and 1974 and district election of 1977; names of district and regional councillors; turnout.

EDINBURGH

Parliamentary Constituency	District Councillor elected 1977	Ward	Regional Councillor elected 1978	Party percentage share of vote					Turnout
				Lab	SNP	Con	Lib	Others	
CENTRAL EDINBURGH	B C Rutherford Lab R Cairns Lab	Holyrood/ Meadows	G Foulkes Lab	*49.0*	*17.8*	*28.6*	*4.5*	—	*37*
				1977: 43.0	23.5	30.7	2.8*	—	38
				1974: 53.6	33.2	—	—	13.2	43
	W K MacFarlane Con J A Mitchell Lab	Lochrin/ Tron	W J Taylor Lab	*47.2*	*16.1*	*36.7*	—	—	*38*
				1977: 38.7	13.3*	48.0	—	—	37
				1974: 45.5	—	40.7	13.8	—	41
	Ms M Moss SNP Ms E R MacKenzie Lab	Dalry/ Tynecastle	Ms J W Buchanan Lab	*43.9*	*26.8*	*23.9*	*5.4*	—	*39*
				1977: 32.7	30.1	27.2	—	10.0*	41
				1974: 41.7	22.6	23.2	12.5	—	45
	J C Wilson Lab J G Gray Lib	Moat/ Polwarth	Ms C Filsell Lab	*44.1*	—	*20.6*	*35.4*	—	*37*
				1977: 28.8	13.2*	22.5	30.5	5.0*	42
				1974: 40.4	—	22.7	36.9	—	47

Parliamentary Constituency	District Councillor elected 1977	Ward	Regional Councillor elected 1978	Party percentage share of vote					Turnout
				Lab	SNP	Con	Lib	Others	
SOUTH EDINBURGH	K G Ferguson Con Mrs N H Mansbridge Con	Churchhill Braid	A H Lester Con	10.8 1977: 9.6 1974: 6.9	— — —	66.5 66.8 52.2	22.8 23.6 40.9	— — —	48 53 60
	E M Kean Con R Brereton Con	Sciennes/Marchmont	W G Reid Con	17.7 1977: 12.7 1974: 13.8	— — —	60.0 58.3 57.0	22.3 27.8 29.2	— 1.2 —	46 50 56
	D Ritchie Con Ms M E S Houston Con	Prestonfield/Mayfield	Ms A Huggins Con	30.4 1977: 26.3 1974: 30.3	— 12.0* —	56.4 61.6 51.1	13.2 — 18.6	— — —	43 47 54
	J C Campbell Lab R M Lonie Lab	Inch/Gilmerton	P Wilson Lab	60.7 1977: 51.9 1974: 76.4	23.6 28.7 —	15.7 19.4 23.6	— — —	— — —	45 46 45
	A P Metcalfe Con B R MacKenzie Lab	Alnwickhill/Kaimes	Ms J Rogan Lab	39.7 1977: 36.8 1974: 55.4	18.1 15.3* —	37.1 42.8 44.6	5.1 5.1* —	— — —	46 46 45
PENTLANDS	J F Walls Con J D MacLennan Con	Merchiston/Colinton	J Gilchrist Con	10.5 1977: 7.8 1974: 8.1	— 5.6* 18.7	69.6 60.8 53.5	19.9 25.8 29.8	— — —	47 53 59
	B A Meek Con Ms G Barton Lab	Fairmilehead/Firrhill	B A Meek Con	28.5 1977: 25.7 1974: 26.1	16.9 22.0 18.7	54.6 52.3 43.7	— — 11.5	— — —	50 56 58
	(B.E. 2.5.78) J Mackay Lab D F Renton Lab	Sighthill/Stenhouse	E Milligan Lab	53.3 1977: 43.1 1974: 68.3	26.3 34.6 —	20.4 22.2 30.2	— — —	— — 1.6	42 43 44

Parliamentary Constituency	District Councillor elected 1977	Ward	Regional Councillor elected 1978	Lab	SNP	Con	Lib	Others	Turnout
	Ms E Alves Con	Slateford/	J P Mulvey Lab	39.2	36.8	23.9	—	—	37
	N R MacCallum SNP	Hailes		1977: 31.2	40.3	28.5	—	—	39
				1974: 42.4	28.1	29.5	—	—	44
WEST EDINBURGH	J B Carson SNP	Pilton/	N Lindsay Lab	58.1	35.4	6.5	—	—	33
	Ms E T McLaughlin Lab	Muirhouse		1977: 50.5	45.3	—	4.3*	—	31
				1974: 70.0	—	12.7	14.9	2.4	31
	J G R Crombie Con	Craigsbank/	D C E Gorrie Lib	9.8	9.3	36.2	44.7	—	55
	I G Anderson Con	Carrickknowe		1977: 10.5	11.7*	46.9	30.9	—	55
				1974: 14.0	—	37.2	48.8	—	58
	A J McLernan Con	Corstor-	G A Theurer Con	20.0	23.1	42.7	14.2	—	46
	N M Irons SNP	phine/		1977: 17.4	22.6*	41.5	18.5	—	55
		Drumbrae		1974: 25.9	—	41.5	32.6	—	58
	Ms R V MacArthur Con	Murrayfield/	R M Knox Con	11.8	12.2	75.9	—	—	50
	R M Knox Con	Blackhall		1977: 11.5	—	80.3	8.2	—	53
				1974: 10.8	—	71.9	17.4	—	58
	A I MacKintosh Con	Cramond/	J A Thomson Con	16.7	16.5	66.8	—	—	45
	J E D Sanderson Con	Barnton		1977: 11.1	24.2	61.2	3.5*	—	53
				1974: 22.2	—	57.4	20.4	—	54
NORTH EDINBURGH	V Lindsay Lab	Drylaw/	Ms W E Donaldson	28.3	21.1	50.6	—	—	43
	T Morgan Con	Comely Bank	Con	1977: 23.8	28.2	48.0	—	—	49
				1974: 43.6	—	56.4	—	—	52
	D Drummond-Young Con	Dean/	I A Cramond Con	29.1	—	70.9	—	—	34
	Ms S A Pringle Con	St Andrews		1977: 22.8	8.5*	68.7	—	—	39
				1974: 18.8	—	59.9	23.3	—	43

Party percentage share of vote

Parliamentary Constituency	District Councillor elected 1977	Ward	Regional Councillor elected 1978	Party percentage share of vote					Turnout
				Lab	SNP	Con	Lib	Others	
	A G Jackson Con	Pilrig/	J Cook Lab	45.9	15.8	38.3	—	—	47
	G McKinnon Lab	Calton		1977: 35.1	13.8*	51.0	—	—	44
				1974: 54.2	—	45.8	—	—	47
	Ms K E MacFie Con	Broughton/	W R V Percy Con	24.2	14.2	43.5	18.2	—	44
	R R Dalgety Con	Inverleith		1977: 13.0*	11.6*	45.4	30.0	—	44
				1974: 26.1	—	48.7	25.3	—	49
LEITH	G M Monies Lab	Royston/	R Brown Lab	57.5	25.0	17.5	—	!	49
	P E McGhee Lab	Granton		1977: 46.6	33.0	20.5	—	—	49
				1974: 49.0	30.5	20.5	—	—	51
	D C Dow Con	Trinity/	H A Nicholson Con	35.7	—	64.3	—	—	46
	Ms M M McAlpine Con	Newhaven		1977: 28.0	—	63.3	8.6*	—	50
				1974: 35.3	—	64.7	—	—	55
	J Hastie Lab	Harbour/	J A Crichton Lab	58.0	20.6	21.4	—	—	38
	J W Kerr Lab	Bonnington		1977: 44.8	26.5	25.6	—	3.1	39
				1974: 70.8	—	29.2	—	—	42
	C Waugh Con	Links/	Ms M G S Monies Lab	43.6	19.9	36.5	—	—	46
	A Burton Lab	Lorne		1977: 30.8	22.9	38.5	6.5*	1.3	49
				1974: 44.5	—	55.5	—	—	51
EAST EDINBURGH	H M Taylor Con	Willowbrae/	Ms P Herriot Lab	50.8	16.1	33.1	—	—	48
	R Imrie Lab	Craigentinny		1977: 39.2	26.0	34.9	—	—	—
				1974: 62.2	—	36.2	—	1.6	49
	G V McAra Con	Jock's Lodge/	I J Berry Con	29.3	20.1	50.6	—	—	51
	K W Borthwick Con	Portobello		1977: 23.3	26.5	50.3	—	—	54
				1974: 37.5	—	62.6	—	—	53

Parliamentary Constituency	District Councillor elected 1977	Ward	Regional Councillor elected 1978	Party percentage share of vote					Turnout
				Lab	SNP	Con	Lib	Others	
	J S Cavaye Con W D Roe Lab	Duddings- ton/ Milton	N Henderson Con	45.3 1977: 41.5 1974: 47.1	— — —	54.7 58.5 53.0	— — —	— — —	42 45 49
	D H Brown Lab Ms W D Black Lab	Niddrie/ Craigmillar	P W Nolan Lab	60.2 1977: 65.7 1974: 75.6	29.3 23.8 22.2	8.5 (regional by-election) —	— — —	2.0 2.1	34 37 41

GLASGOW

Parliamentary Constituency	District Councillor elected 1977	Ward	Regional Councillor elected 1978	Party percentage share of vote				Turnout
				Lab	SNP	Con	Others	
SHETTLESTON	Ms H McGregor Lab	Tollcross/	D Laing Lab	39.0	19.1	22.8	19.0	47
	Ms S Baird Lab	Parkhead		1977: 38.3	28.2	30.4	3.0	45
				1974: 50.7	24.8	23.2	1.3	47
	H Macrae Lab	Carntyne/	D Marshall Lab	58.2	26.2	15.6	—	40
	A McTaggart Lab	Camlachie		1977: 43.9	29.7	21.4	5.0	41
				1974: 57.2	24.5	16.8	1.5	42
PROVAN	Ms P Kennedy SNP	Easterhouse/	A Viola Lab	59.6	28.7	7.9	3.8	34
	E Hendry SNP	Garthamlock		1977: 39.8	43.2	12.9	4.1	39
				1974: 57.8	31.7	6.4	4.2	36
	N Stobo Lab	Wellhouse/	A J Long Lab	61.9	26.6	9.2	2.3	39
	Ms M McGhee SNP	Queenslie		1977: 46.4	39.2	11.9	2.5	44
				1974: 57.6	34.4	6.6	1.4	45
	C Gilbert Con	Riddrie/	Ms A L Ballantyne Lab	51.1	21.3	26.3	2.3	40
	D Mason Lab	Lethamhill		1977: 36.9	34.5	25.3	3.3	43
				1974: 54.0	27.3	18.7	—	46
CENTRAL	T Ennis Lab	City/	W Lindsay Lab	64.0	13.2	22.9	—	37
	P O'Rourke Lab	Townhead		1977: 64.0	30.3	5.6*	—	37
				1974: 69.7	15.1	15.2	—	41
	J McQueenie Lab	Calton/	J D Cannell Lab	68.4	17.7	13.9	—	35
	J Mullen Lab	Dalmarnock		1977: 59.0	40.9	—	—	36
				1974: 60.7	14.3	13.1	11.9 (Lib)	39
SPRINGBURN	M J Martin Lab	Balornock/	P Trainer Lab	60.0	26.6	13.4	—	39
	J Chatham Lab	Robroyston		1977: 49.7	38.1	12.3	—	45
				1974: 53.8	34.8	9.7	1.7	47

Parliamentary Constituency	District Councillor elected 1977	Ward	Regional Councillor elected 1978	Party percentage share of vote				Turnout
				Lab	SNP	Con	Others	
	C Moore Lab J Henderson Lab	Cowlairs/Petershill	R Gould Lab	62.6 1977: 56.0 1974: 57.8	21.6 44.0 29.6	15.8 — 11.3	— — 1.2	37 40 42
	W L Wightman Lab R McKay Con	Milnbank/Dennistoun	P McEachran Lab	50.4 1977: 37.9 1974: 44.5	18.4 29.9 24.9	29.8 31.3 29.5	1.4 0.9 1.1	42 45 49
MARYHILL	S M Ewing SNP R Gray Lab	Summerston/Wyndford	L McGarry Lab	57.0 1977: 39.3 1974: 66.7	23.9 40.1 —	15.9 18.1 30.5	3.2 2.5 2.8	41 46 44
	D Hodge Lab J Kernaghan Lab	Ruchill/Milton	G McGrath Lab	57.5 1977: 46.1 1974: 53.3	27.4 43.4 35.4	13.4 8.2* 9.9	1.7 2.3 1.3	40 42 47
	R Innes Lab Ms J A McFadden Lab	Possilpark/Cowcaddens	W Harley Lab	65.4 1977: 62.0 1974: 59.3	21.5 36.0 30.7	11.9 — 8.3	1.2 2.0 1.8	36 40 42
KELVINGROVE	Ms M Goldie Con A T Keter Con	Botanic Gardens/Park	G Rennie Con	33.2 1977: 25.9 1974: 41.8	17.4 25.1 —	49.4 45.8 58.2	— 3.3 —	36 38 45
	G Rennie Con Ms C Morris Con	Kelvin/Woodside	J Gray Lab	52.0 1977: 32.0 1974: 49.8	15.4 22.1 —	32.6 40.8 36.8	— 5.1 13.4	42 47 46
	D Wood Con R McTaggart Lab	Partick East/Anderston	M Green Lab	52.4 1977: 32.6 1974: 40.5	16.5 29.3 24.1	29.4 35.7 33.1	1.7 2.1 2.2	47 44 50

Parliamentary Constituency	District Councillor elected 1977	Ward	Regional Councillor elected 1978	Lab	SNP	Con	Others	Turnout
HILLHEAD	W Aitken Con	Anniesland/ Kelvinside	L Turpie Con	16.5	16.5	67.0	—	45
	R N S Logan Con			1977: 9.0	19.9	63.5	7.7 (Lib)	51
				1974: 9.3	9.0	49.1	32.6 (Lib)	57
	S Taylor Con	Scotstoun/ Partick West	Ms J S Browning Con	34.5	16.4	49.1	—	50
	A Hodgins Con			1977: 29.3	27.9	42.8	—	54
				1974: 30.8	22.8	40.2	6.3	57
GARSCADDEN	Ms M Crawford SNP	Drumry/ Summerhill	J Hemphill Lab	55.7	32.4	7.8	4.1	36
	J O'Brien SNP			1977: 39.6	55.3	—	5.1	41
				1974: 57.4	32.7	7.7	2.2	42
	J C Whyte SNP	Blairdardie/ Knightscliffe	Ms C A Judge Lab	45.3	24.6	28.8	1.3	44
	C Darroch SNP			1977: 32.0	38.3	28.4	1.3	52
				1974: 42.8	33.3	22.5	1.4	53
	D McLean SNP	Yoker/ Knightswood	W Perry Lab	51.8	23.7	23.1	2.4	43
	J Bain SNP			1977: 33.9	38.3	23.9	3.9	51
				1974: 49.1	29.1	19.8	2.0	51
QUEEN'S PARK	J Lavelle Lab	Gorbals/ Hutchesontown	J Wray Lab	58.1	22.3	9.4	10.2	37
	G McAulay SNP			1977: 43.0	41.5	8.4*	7.1	35
				1974: 63.3	20.2	12.8	3.8	40
	A Green Con	Crosshill/ Prospecthill	T Murphy Lab by-el 29.6.78	46.2	17.3	33.7	2.8	34
	W McGuinness SNP			1977: 35.3	41.3	20.7	2.7	46
				1974: 45.4	25.6	27.6	1.4	50
GOVAN	H S McNeill Lab	Drumoyne/ Fairfield	J Davidson Lab	59.4	21.3	19.3	—	40
	J McDonald Lab			1977: 49.4	36.0	14.0*	0.6	46
				1974: 50.2	35.3	13.6	1.0	49

Parliamentary Constituency	District Councillor elected 1977	Ward	Regional Councillor elected 1978	Party percentage share of vote				Turnout
				Lab	SNP	Con	Others	
	A McMahon Lab / B A Maan Lab	Ibrox/ Kingston	Ms A McLean Lab	*53.7*	*26.3*	*20.0*	—	*39*
				1977: 44.8	33.4	16.9	4.8	46
				1974: 48.0	33.3	18.7	—	48
CRAIGTON	M Kelly Lab / Ms C R Campbell Con	Hillington/ Bellahouston	F McLean Lab	*47.6*	*15.7*	*36.7*	—	*49*
				1977: 35.3	27.5	37.2	—	52
				1974: 46.6	18.0	34.2	1.2	58
	A MacKenzie Con / T R Hamilton Lab	Cardonald/ Crookston	W Timoney Lab	*55.6*	*18.0*	*26.4*	—	*45*
				1977: 37.6	28.6	31.2	2.6	48
				1974: 53.6	20.6	24.3	1.4	53
POLLOK	I J A Dyer Con / Ms J M Hamilton Con	Pollok-shields/ Strathbungo	J Mair Con	*23.3*	*15.7*	*55.4*	*6.6*	*46*
				1977: 16.4	23.2	55.8	4.6	52
				1974: 21.8	18.6	55.9	3.7	53
	J K Richmond Con / *Ms M Hodgins* Con	Camphill/ Pollokshaws	Ms A A McCurley Con	*35.4*	*15.2*	*49.4*	—	*48*
				1977: 25.4	24.4	47.7	2.5	54
				1974: 33.7	19.7	40.9	5.6	58
	F Duffy Lab / *F Hannigan* SNP	Nitshill/ Darnley	J F Dunnachie Lab	*56.5*	*34.5*	*9.0*	*6.6*	*39*
				1977: 38.2	45.6	10.1	6.1	41
				1974: 61.4	27.9	8.8	1.8	45
CATHCART	J Young Con / D Mason Con	Newlands/ Mt Florida	J Hicks Con	*19.7*	*11.1*	*69.1*	—	*51*
				1977: 14.8	15.1	68.7	1.4	50
				1974: 26.2	—	73.8	—	61
	M Toshner Con / G Manson Lab	King's Park/ Castlemilk	*Ms J M Mason* Con	*38.4*	*18.1*	*42.3*	—	*45*
				1977: 25.6	30.4	39.7	4.3	49
				1974: 41.0	15.0	39.2	4.8	43
	L Gourlay Con / *Ms B Johnson* SNP	Linn/ Cathkin	J Fitch Lab	*45.3*	*18.7*	*36.1*	—	*43*
				1977: 30.9	30.3	37.7	2.1	45
				1974: 50.8	14.3	33.2	1.7	49

Percentage of vote won by each party in Regional Elections of 1978 and District Elections of 1977 and 1974 in Glasgow and Edinburgh

		Lab	SNP	Con	Lib	Others
GLASGOW	1978	46.7	20.8	29.9	1.7	0.9
	1977	35.1	32.7	28.7	1.9	1.7
	1974 (district)	47.7	19.2	28.8	2.2	2.1
EDINBURGH	1978	33.6	17.1	42.5	6.6	0.2
	1977	26.6	19.3	44.8	7.9	1.3
	1974 (district)	36.2	6.7	41.4	13.5	2.2

SECTION 12

DISTRICT COUNCILS

Seats won by each party in each district in May 1977. Names and address of Conveners and Chief Executives. Population ('000s) in brackets after district name.

	Lab	SNP	Con	Lib	Other	Ind/non party	Uncontested in 1977	Convener/Provost	Chief Executive
BORDERS									
Berwickshire (17)	—	—	11	—	—	1	8	J R Ford	R Christie District Offices, Duns, TD11 3DU (03612 2231)
Ettrick & Lauderdale (32)	—	—	1	1	—	14	5	A L Tulley	D H Cowan Council Chambers, Paton Street Galashiels, TD1 3AS (0896 4751)
Roxburgh (36)	1	—	1	2	—	12	10	Rev R S Blakey	J F A Richardson District Offices, High Street Hawick TD9 9EF (0450 5991)
Tweeddale (14)	—	—	—	—	—	10	7	T Blyth	G Gardiner District Offices, Peebles (0721 20153)
CENTRAL									
Clackmannan (48)	3	8	1	—	—	—	0	J Clement	A E O'Neill The Whins, Alloa (0259 722160)
Falkirk (143)	8	22	2	—	—	4	5	A Crawford	J P H Paton Municipal Buildings Falkirk FK1 5RS (0324 24911)

	Lab	SNP	Con	Lib	Other	Ind/non party	Uncontested in 1977	Convener/Provost	Chief Executive
Stirling (79)	7	4	8	—	—	1	1	Mrs L M McCaig	D M Bowie Municipal Buildings Corn Exchange Road Stirling FK8 2HU (0786 3131)
DUMFRIES & GALLOWAY									
Annandale & Eskdale (35)	—	—	—	—	—	16	9	R G Greenhow	G F Murray High Street, Annan (04612 3311)
Nithsdale (56)	4	4	—	—	—	20	11	W B Simpson	G D Grant Municipal Chambers Dumfries, DG1 2AD (0387 3166)
Stewartry (22)	—	—	—	—	—	12	4	J Nelson	W L Dick-Smith Council Offices Kircudbright DG6 4PJ (0557 30291)
Wigtown (30)	—	1	—	—	—	13	8	D R Robinson	D R Wilson Sun Street, Stranraer, DG9 3JJ (0776 2151)
FIFE									
Dunfermline (125)	19	2	7	—	—	2	0	L G Wood	G Brown City Chambers, Dunfermline (0383 22711)
Kirkcaldy (149)	16	8	5	—	5	2	8	J Edmiston	W C Hogg Town House, Kirkcaldy KY1 1XW (0592 61144)

	Lab	SNP	Con	Lib	Other	Ind/ non party	Uncon- tested in 1977	Convener/ Provost	Chief Executive
North-East Fife (65)	—	—	14	1	—	3	6	D M Russell	H Farquhar County Buildings Cupar, KY15 4TA (0334 3722)
GRAMPIAN City of Aberdeen (210)	22	2	17	7	—	—	5	W J Fraser	J M Wilson Town House Aberdeen, AB9 1AQ (0224 23456)
Banff and Buchan (76)	—	2	—	—	—	16	9	W R Cruik- shank	W S McAlister St Leonards Sandyhill Road, Banff (026 12 2521)
Gordon (51)	—	—	3	2	—	7	4	J B Presley	A C Kennedy 3 High Street Inverurie, AB5 9QA (0467 20981)
Kincardine & Deeside (36)	—	—	2	—	—	10	5	I M Frain	Miss E M G Cockburn Arduthie Road Stonehaven, AB3 2DQ (056 92 62001)
Moray (81)	—	3	—	—	—	15	7	J M Anderson	J P C Bell High Street, Elgin, IV30 1BX (0343 3451)
HIGHLAND Badenoch & Strathspey (9)	—	—	—	—	—	10	9	A C Robertson	H G McCulloch High Street, Kingussie (054 02 555)
Caithness (29)	—	—	—	—	—	15	6	J M Young	A Beattie Council Offices, Wick (0955 3761)

	Lab	SNP	Con	Lib	Other	Ind/ non party	Uncon- tested in 1977	Convener/ Provost	Chief Executive
Inverness (55)	4	—	—	—	—	20	12	I C Fraser	C J Will Town House, Inverness IV1 1JJ (0463 39111)
Lochaber (20)	2	2	—	—	—	8	8	Miss Maclean	J McGhee Tweedale, Fort William (0397 3881)
Nairn (10)	—	2	—	—	—	8	7	H. McLean	J R McCluskey 4 Court House Lane Nairn IV12 4DR (0667 52056)
Ross & Cromarty (42)	—	—	—	—	—	20	12	W S Fowlie	T M Aitchison County Buildings Dingwall IV15 9QN (0349 3381)
Skye & Lochalsh (10)	—	—	—	—	—	10	7	L Mackinnon	D H Noble Dunvegan Road, Portree (0478 2341)
Sutherland (12)	—	—	—	—	—	14	8	D F Mackay	D W Martin District Offices Golspie KW10 6RB (040 83392)
LOTHIAN									
City of Edinburgh (467)	23	5	34	1	—	1	2	K W Borthwick	E G Glendinning City Chambers, High Street Edinburgh, EH1 1YJ (031-225 2424)
East Lothian (79)	9	—	8	—	—	—	3	T Wilson	D B Miller Council Buildings Haddington EH41 3HA (062 082 4161)

	Lab	SNP	Con	Lib	Other	Ind/non party	Uncon-tested in 1977	Convener/ Provost	Chief Executive
Midlothian (85)	7	5	2	—	—	1	3	D R Smith	D W Duguid 1 White Hart Street, Dalkeith (031-663 2881)
West Lothian (124)	9	9	—	—	1	2	0	J Clark	D Morrison South Bridge Street, Bathgate (Bathgate 53631)
STRATHCLYDE									
Argyll & Bute (66)	—	1	4	—	—	19	13	E T F Spence	M A J Gossip Kilmory, Lochgilphead (0546 2127)
Bearsden & Milngavie (38)	1	—	6	—	—	3	1	T H N Young	A R Rae Boclair, Bearsden, G61 2TQ (041-942 2262)
Clydebank (56)	3	5	1	—	1	—	0	W Johnston	J M Brown Municipal Buildings Clydebank, G81 1XQ (041-952 1103)
Cumbernauld & Kilsyth (48)	3	7	—	—	—	—	0	G S Murray	R Kyle Bron Way, Cumbernauld (02367 22131)
Cumnock & Doon Valley (48)	6	—	1	—	2	1	3	J Paterson	D T Hemmings Lugar, Cumnock KA18 3JQ (0290 22111)
Cunninghame (133)	5	11	5	—	—	3	1	M Brown	J M Miller Cunninghame House Irvine, KA12 8EE (0294 74166)
Dunbarton (81)	3	4	5	—	1	2	1	W Petrie	L Mackinnon Crosslet House, Dunbarton (0389 65100)

	Lab	SNP	Con	Lib	Other	Ind/ non party	Uncontested in 1977	Convener/ Provost	Chief Executive
East Kilbride (83)	1	11	2	—	—	1	0	J Marshall	W G McNay Civic Centre, East Kilbride (035 52 28777)
Eastwood (51)	—	—	10	—	2	—	6	I S Hutchison	M D Henry Cotton Street, Paisley (041-889 5454)
City of Glasgow (856)	30	16	25	1	—	—	0	D Hodge	C Murdoch City Chambers Glasgow, G2 1DU (041-221 9600)
Hamilton (107)	10	6	1	2	—	1	0	C Brownlie	W Johnston 102 Cadzow Street Hamilton ML3 6HH (069 82 21188)
Inverclyde (104)	8	1	1	13	—	—	0	A D Fletcher	I C Wilson Municipal Buildings, Greenock (0475 24400)
Kilmarnock & Loudon (83)	7	2	7	—	—	—	0	Mrs M G Parker	J C W Nicol Civic Centre Kilmarnock, KA1 1BY (0563 21140)
Kyle & Carrick (112)	7	1	17	—	—	—	6	A D Paton	J R Hill Burns House, Ayr (0292 81511)
Lanark (55)	4	3	—	—	3	4	1	R C M Monteith	R G Dalkin District Offices Lanark, ML11 7JT (0555 61331)

	Lab	SNP	Con	Lib	Other	Ind/non party	Uncontested in 1977	Convener/Provost	Chief Executive
Monklands (108)	13	2	5	—	—	1	6	T Clarke	J S Ness Dunbeth Road Coatbridge ML5 3LF (0236 24941)
Motherwell (161)	19	3	5	1	1	—	1	V Mathieson	F C Marks PO Box 14, Motherwell (0698 66166)
Renfrew (209)	14	3	11	—	1	3	4	R Cowper	W McIntosh Cotton Street, Paisley (041-889 5400)
Strathkelvin (81)	4	6	4	—	—	—	0	D Stark	A W Harrower PO Box 4 Kirkintilloch, G66 1PW (041-776 7171)
TAYSIDE Angus (90)	3	—	12	—	—	7	7	M Struthers	W S McCulloch County Buildings Forfar, DD8 3LG (0307 5101)
City of Dundee (194)	20	—	21	—	2	1	3	W C Vaughan	G S Watson City Chambers, Dundee (0382 23141)
Perth & Kinross (118)	3	2	19	—	—	5	9	N T Renfrew	R T Blair 1-3 High Street, Perth (0738 24241)

SECTION 13

SCOTTISH PARLIAMENTARY BY-ELECTIONS SINCE 1945

Date	Seat	Con	Lab	SNP	Lib	Others	Turnout	Comment
9/4/45	Scottish Universities	71.2 (Ind)			28.8 (N. Lib)		44.6	Independent gain from National Liberal
12/4/45	Motherwell		48.6	51.4			54.0	SNP victory in absence of Con candidate
General Election of 1945, seats:		27	37	0		7		
3/10/45	Edinburgh, East	38.4	61.6				51.0	
7/2/46	South Ayrshire	36.4	63.6				69.0	
12/2/46	Glasgow, Cathcart	52.5	37.1	10.4			55.6	
29/8/46	Glasgow, Bridgeton	21.6	28.0			34.3 ILP 16.1 Others	53.3	ILP held seat against Labour
22-27/11/46	Scottish Universities	68.2	11.5		8.0	12.3	50.7	
26/11/46	Aberdeen, South	54.8	45.2				65.6	
5/12/46	Kilmarnock	32.5	59.7	7.8			63.4	Willie Ross enters Parliament
27/11/47	Edinburgh, East	34.3	50.6	5.0	10.1		63.0	
28/1/48	Glasgow, Camlachie	43.7	42.1		1.2	6.4 ILP 6.6 Others	56.8	Conservative gain
18/2/48	Paisley	43.2	56.8				76.0	
30/9/48	Glasgow, Gorbals	28.6	54.5				50.0	
7/10/48	Stirling & Falkirk Burghs	42.8	49.0	8.2			72.9	
25/11/48	Glasgow, Hillhead	68.4	31.6			16.9 Comm	56.7	

(Thirteen of the fifty-one by-elections between the 1945 and 1950 General Elections were fought in Scotland. This is much greater than Scotland's percentage of seats).

		Con	Lab	SNP	Lib	Others	Turnout
General Election of 1950, seats:		31	37	0	2	1	
25/4/50	Dunbartonshire, West	49.6	50.4				83.4
25/10/50	Glasgow, Scotstoun	50.8	47.3			1.9	73.7

R

Date	Seat	Con	Lab	SNP	Lib	Others	Turnout	Comment
General Election of 1951, seats:		35	35	0	1			
17/7/52	Dundee, East	35.6	56.3	7.4		0.7	71.5	
8/4/54	Edinburgh, East	42.4	57.6				61.8	
14/4/54	Motherwell	39.3	56.4			4.3	70.5	
21/12/54	Inverness	41.4	22.6		36.0		49.2	
27/1/55	Edinburgh, North	59.4	40.6				46.4	
General Election of 1955, seats:		36	34	0	1			
8/12/55	Greenock	46.3	53.7				75.3	
29/5/57	Edinburgh, South	45.6	30.9		23.5		65.8	
13/3/58	Glasgow, Kelvingrove	41.6	48.0			10.4	60.5	
12/6/58	Argyll	46.8	25.7		27.5		67.1	
20/11/58	Aberdeenshire, East	48.6	27.1		24.3		65.9	
9/4/59	Galloway	50.4	23.9		25.7		72.7	
(The SNP did not contest by-elections in the 1950, 51 or 55 Parliaments)								
General Election of 1959, seats:		31	38	0	1	1		
19/5/60	Edinburgh, North	54.2	30.3		15.5		53.8	
20/4/61	Paisley	13.2	45.4		41.4		68.1	
8/11/61	Fife, East	47.5	26.4		26.1		67.3	
16/11/61	Glasgow, Bridgeton	20.7	57.5	18.7		3.1	41.9	SNP challenge begins. Gain Tory votes
14/6/62	West Lothian	11.4	50.9	23.3	10.8	3.6	71.1	
22/11/62	Glasgow, Woodside	30.1	36.1	11.1	21.7	1.0	54.7	Labour gain with Lib help
7/11/63	Kinross & West Perthshire	57.4	15.2	7.3	19.5	0.6	76.1	
21/11/63	Dundee, West	39.4	50.6	7.4		2.6 Comm	71.6	
12/12/64	Dumfriesshire	40.9	38.5	9.7	10.9		71.6	
14/5/64	Rutherglen	44.5	55.5				82.0	

Date	Seat	Con	Lab	SNP	Lib	Others	Turnout	
General Election of 1964, seats:		24	43	0	4			
24/3/65	Roxburgh, Selkirk & Peebles	38.6	11.3		49.2		82.2	Lib gain from Con.
General Election of 1966, seats:		20	46	0	5			
9/3/67	Glasgow, Pollok	36.9	31.2	28.2	1.9	1.8	75.7	Con win from Lab with SNP help
2/11/67	Hamilton	12.5	41.5	46.0			73.7	First SNP breakthrough
30/10/69	Glasgow, Gorbals	18.6	53.4	25.0		3	58.5	Much Lab relief at holding seat
19/3/70	South Ayrshire	25.6	54.0	20.4			76.3	More Lab relief
General Election of June, 1970, seats:		23	44	1	3			
16/9/71	Stirling & Falkirk	18.9	46.5	34.6			60.0	Impressive SNP performance
1/3/73	Dundee, East	25.2	32.7	30.2	8.3	3.6	70.6	
8/11/73	Edinburgh, North	38.7	24.0	18.9	18.4		54.5	
8/11/73	Glasgow, Govan	11.7	38.2	41.9	8.2		51.7	Immense boost to SNP morale
General Election of Feb., 1974, seats:		21	40	7	3			
General Election of Oct., 1974, seats:		16	41	11	3			
13/4/78	Glasgow, Garscadden	18.2	45.4	32.0		3.1	72.0	Immense boost to Labour morale
31/5/78	Hamilton	13.0	51.0	33.4	2.6			

SECTION 14

GENERAL ELECTIONS IN SCOTLAND SINCE 1945: PARTY SHARES OF VOTES AND SEATS

	Lab	Con	Lib	Others	SNP	SNP seats contested	% of vote in contested seats
1945	47.6%	41.1%	5.0%	5.1%	1.2%		
	37	29	0	5	0	8	7.6%
1950	46.2%	44.8%	6.6%	2.0%	0.4%		
	37	32	2	0	0	3	7.4%
1951	47.9%	48.6%	2.7%	0.5%	0.3%		
	35	35	1	0	0	2	12.2%
1955	46.7%	50.1%	1.9%	0.8%	0.5%		
	34	36	1	0	0	2	14.5%
1959	46.7%	47.2%	4.1%	1.2%	0.8%		
	38	31	1	0	0	5	11.4%
1964	48.7%	40.6%	7.6%	0.7%	2.4%		
	43	23	4	0	0	15	10.7%
1966	49.9%	37.7%	6.8%	0.6%	5.0%		
	46	20	5	0	0	23	14.1%
1970	44.5%	38.0%	5.5%	0.6%	11.4%		
	44	23	3	0	1	65	12.2%
Feb. 1974	36.6%	32.9%	7.9%	0.5%	21.9%		
	40	21	3	0	7	70	21.9%
Oct. 1974	36.2%	24.7%	8.3%	0.3%	30.4%		
	41	16	3	0	11	71	30.4%

SECTION 15

GENERAL ELECTION RESULTS: OCTOBER AND FEBRUARY 1974, AND JUNE 1970 *

EXPLANATORY NOTES

In the following table the percentage of the vote won by each party is given for each constituency for the last three General Elections: where no figures are quoted for 1970, major boundary changes prevent comparison.

%OO and %CT: the percentage of owner-occupiers and council tenants in the constituency according to the 1971 census.

Electorate: 1977 figures. An asterisk denotes that it is over 125% of the Scottish average (53,000), so entitling the constituency to a third seat in the Scottish Assembly under the Scotland Act, other constituencies having two. The first Assembly seats will be fought on a constituency-wide basis; thereafter each parliamentary constituency will be divided into two or three Assembly constituencies by the Boundary Commission.

MP: 'e' is date when last entered Commons.   C: Communist

Percentage of votes won by each party in each constituency in the General Elections of October and February 1974 and June 1970; turnout; size of constituency; proportion of council tenants and owner occupiers; names of MPs

%OO	%CT		Date	% Turnout	Party Percentages					Maj	Member of Parliament
					Lab	SNP	Con	Lib	Other		
16	65	Aberdeen North 65,000	1974 Oct	70	50.9	29.7	11.3	8.1	—	9,621	Robert Hughes
			Feb	76	47.7	23.3	16.7	12.3	—	11,856	(b.1932, e.1970) — Lab
			1970 June	70	62.1	8.4	22.0	6.3	1.2C	17,900	
44	34	Aberdeen South 66,000	1974 Oct	76	34.8	20.1	35.5	9.6	—	365	Iain Sproat
			Feb	82	33.2	13.7	39.6	13.4	—	3,558	(b.1938, e.1970) — Con
			1970 June	77	43.3	5.3	45.4	6.0	—	1,089	
37	39	Aberdeenshire East 52,000	1974 Oct	71	9.4	48.5	35.5	6.6	—	4,371	Douglas Henderson
			Feb	77	6.7	50.8	35.0	7.5	—	5,699	(b.1935, e.Feb.74) — SNP
			1970 June	69	18.0	29.8	40.9	11.3	—	3,489	
42	32	Aberdeenshire West 64,000	1974 Oct	77	12.2	22.2	35.7	29.9	—	2,468	Russell Fairgrieve
			Feb	81	10.5	15.4	38.9	35.2	—	1,640	(b.1924, e.Feb.74) — Con
			1970 June	76	15.5	5.3	46.6	32.5	—	5,549	

* For names and votes of all candidates in October 1974 see Scottish Government Yearbook 1978.

%OO	%CT	Constituency	Date	% Turnout	Lab	SNP	Con	Lib	Other	Maj	Member of Parliament
36	34	Angus North & Mearns 41,000	1974 Oct	72	12.3	34.2	43.6	9.9	—	2,551	Alick Buchanan-Smith (b.1932, e.1964) — Con
			Feb	79	12.8	23.3	48.8	15.1	—	7,451	
			1970 June	75	18.4	16.9	53.1	11.6	—	9,595	
33	34	Angus South 57,000	1974 Oct	75	10.5	43.8	39.2	6.5	—	1,824	Andrew Welsh (b.1944, e.Oct.1974) — SNP
			Feb	80	13.8	36.6	49.5	—	—	5,343	
			1970 June	74	20.7	23.1	56.1	—	—	12,030	
37	35	Argyll 43,000	1974 Oct	72	13.6	49.7	36.7	—	—	3,931	Iain MacCormick (b.1939, e.Feb.1974) — SNP
			Feb	77	12.6	48.8	38.6	—	—	3,288	
			1970 June	74	25.2	29.9	44.8	—	—	4,482	
42	49	Ayr 54,000	1974 Oct	79	34.6	16.7	42.1	6.3	—	3,219	George Younger (b.1931, e.1964) — Con
			Feb	83	38.6	11.0	50.4	—	—	5,098	
			1970 June	82	42.1	5.2	52.7	—	—	4,450	
25	67	Ayrshire Central 65,000	1974 Oct	79	45.1	24.5	24.8	5.6	—	9,555	David Lambie (b.1925, e.1970) — Lab
			Feb	82	49.0	15.0	36.0	—	—	6,277	
39	46	Ayrshire North & Bute 50,000	1974 Oct	71	28.8	25.9	38.9	6.4	—	3,506	John Corrie (b.1935, e.Feb.1974) — Con
			Feb	77	27.8	16.3	45.7	10.2	—	6,730	
			1970 June	74	35.4	10.9	53.6	—	—	6,394	
19	69	Ayrshire South 51,000	1974 Oct	77	56.2	19.8	18.6	5.4	—	14,478	James Sillars (b.1937, e.1970)—Scottish Labour Party
			Feb	79	57.2	16.4	26.4	—	—	12,450	
			1970 June	77	61.8	8.0	30.2	—	—	12,235	
42	37	Banff 33,000	1974 Oct	73	7.3	45.9	37.9	8.9	—	1,851	Hamish Watt (b.1926, e.Feb.1974) — SNP
			Feb	76	6.4	46.1	34.5	13.0	—	2,785	
			1970 June	70	17.4	22.9	38.7	21.0	—	3,451	
26	52	Berwick & East Lothian 61,000	1974 Oct	83	43.3	13.2	37.6	5.9	—	2,740	John Mackintosh (b.1929, e.Oct.1974) — Lab
			Feb	86	42.3	14.2	43.4	—	—	540	
			1970 June	84	45.6	10.2	44.2	—	—	641	
25	49	Bothwell 61,000	1974 Oct	77	48.7	24.5	17.9	8.9	1.2C	10,948	James Hamilton (b.1918, e.1964) — Lab
			Feb	81	46.8	14.1	26.7	11.2	—	9,601	
34	42	Caithness & Sutherland 30,000	1974 Oct	78	35.3	23.9	18.8	22.0	—	2,560	Robert MacLennan (b.1936, e.1966) — Lab
			Feb	83	36.1	16.1	21.5	26.2	—	2,352	
			1970 June	83	36.7	15.5	22.4	25.4	—	2,705	

%OO	%CT	Constituency / Electorate	Date	% Turnout	Lab	SNP	Con	Lib	Other	Maj	Member of Parliament
11	85	Coatbridge & Airdrie 60,000	1974 Oct	75	51.6	27.9	17.2	3.3	—	10,568	James Dempsey (b.1917, e.1959) — Lab
			1974 Feb	78	54.1	17.3	28.6		—	11,783	
33	45	Dumfries 64,000	1974 Oct	77	26.5	26.4	38.8	8.3	—	5,828	Hector Monro (b.1922, e.1964) — Con
			1974 Feb	80	25.8	18.6	44.0	11.4	—	8,968	
			1970 June	76	33.5	13.4	53.1		—	9,106	
23	68	Dunbartonshire Central 50,000	1974 Oct	80	40.2	29.1	17.2	4.8	8.7C	4,385	Hugh McCartney (b.1920, e.1970) — Lab
			1974 Feb	83	40.4	14.5	24.0	6.3	14.6C	6,664	
40	57	Dunbartonshire East 69,000*	1974 Oct	81	30.3	31.2	31.1	7.3		22	Margaret Bain (b.1945, e.Oct.1974) — SNP
			1974 Feb	85	29.6	22.3	36.1	11.4		3,676	
29	54	Dunbartonshire West 55,000	1974 Oct	78	38.1	33.7	23.2	5.0		1,814	Ian Campbell (b.1926, e.1970) — Lab
			1974 Feb	80	39.6	27.2	33.2			2,609	
23	57	Dundee East 65,000	1974 Oct	73	32.7	47.7	16.8	2.8		6,983	Gordon Wilson (b.1938, e.Feb.74) — SNP
			1974 Feb	81	33.7	39.5	26.3		0.4	2,966	
			1973 Mar (by-election)	71	32.7	30.2	25.2	8.3	3.6	1,141	
18	62	Dundee West 64,000	1970 June	76	48.3	8.9	42.3		0.4	2,798	Peter Doig (b.1911, e.1963) — Lab
			1974 Oct	74	41.0	35.1	18.5	4.6	0.8C	2,802	
			1974 Feb	81	43.0	25.1	30.5		1.3C	6,448	
			1970 June	76	51.5	8.7	38.1		1.6C	6,822	
25	60	Dunfermline 64,000	1974 Oct	76	40.1	28.6	23.0	8.2		5,291	Adam Hunter (b.1908, e.1964) — Lab
			1974 Feb	81	39.3	17.8	30.3	12.6		4,410	
14	83	East Kilbride 73,000*	1974 Oct	79	41.9	36.7	16.3	5.1		2,704	Maurice Miller (b.1920, e.1964) — Lab
			1974 Feb	81	43.9	25.9	28.9		1.3C	7,968	
47	11	Edinburgh Central 39,000	1974 Oct	68	40.3	24.8	26.0	8.9		3,953	Robin Cook (b.1946, e.Feb.1974) — Lab
			1974 Feb	74	37.8	13.6	34.6	13.9		961	
34	56	Edinburgh East 58,000	1974 Oct	76	44.9	25.6	23.1	5.9	0.5C	8,456	Gavin Strang (b.1943, e. 1970) — Lab
			1974 Feb	81	43.7	15.4	31.6	8.6	0.6C	5,549	
45	25	Edinburgh Leith 38,000	1970 June	74	51.9	8.2	39.0		0.9C	5,514	Ronald King Murray (b.1922, e.1970) — Lab
			1974 Oct	75	39.7	26.1	28.0	6.2		3,445	
			1974 Feb	79	40.6	21.1	38.3			721	

%OO	%CT	Constituency	Date	% Turnout	Lab	SNP	Con	Lib	Other	Maj	Member of Parliament
58	10	Edinburgh North 46,000	1974 Oct	69	25.9	23.5	39.3	11.2	—	4,391	Alex Fletcher (b.1929, e.1973) — Con
			Feb	76	26.2	12.7	45.8	15.3	—	7,013	
39	46	Edinburgh Pentlands 59,000	1974 Oct	76	30.9	24.5	33.9	10.6	—	1,257	Malcolm Rifkind (b.1946, e.Feb.1974) — Con
			Feb	80	31.1	11.4	41.7	15.8	—	4,602	
49	36	Edinburgh South 58,000	1974 Oct	74	28.2	21.7	35.9	14.2	—	3,226	Michael Clark Hutchison (b.1914, e.1957) — Con
			Feb	81	27.5	12.8	41.7	17.9	—	6,381	
			1970 June	74	36.5	6.9	48.1	8.4	—	4,780	
53	27	Edinburgh West 55,000	1974 Oct	77	25.2	20.2	38.2	16.4	—	5,202	Lord James Douglas-Hamilton (b.1942, e.Oct.1974) — Con
			Feb	82	24.4	9.9	44.2	21.5	—	8,477	
16	82	Fife Central 61,000	1974 Oct	74	51.9	33.4	12.3	—	2.4C	7,986	William Hamilton (b.1917, e.1950) — Lab
			Feb	79	53.2	22.5	19.8	—	4.4C	14,094	
39	40	Fife East 59,000	1974 Oct	74	16.9	31.7	38.8	12.6	—	2,914	Sir John Gilmour (b.1912, e.1961) — Con
			Feb	79	15.0	19.4	47.9	17.6	—	12,579	
			1970 June	74	24.6	11.8	54.6	9.0	—	11,863	
39	36	Galloway 41,000	1974 Oct	77	9.0	40.3	40.2	10.5	—	30	George Thompson (b.1928, e.Oct.1974) — SNP
			Feb	78	10.2	30.7	43.9	15.3	—	4,008	
36	48	Glasgow Cathcart 50,000	1970 June	72	20.3	20.5	50.3	8.8	—	8,280	Teddy Taylor (b.1937, e.1964) — Con
			1974 Oct	77	38.1	16.4	42.7	2.8	—	1,757	
			Feb	81	40.6	13.6	45.8	—	—	2,095	
15	44	Glasgow Central 21,000	1974 Oct	57	63.6	19.2	13.0	4.2	—	6,441	Tom McMillan (b.1919, e.1966) — Lab
			Feb	63	58.6	13.8	21.4	6.1	—	5,965	
16	76	Glasgow Craigton 45,000	1974 Oct	76	50.5	24.3	20.0	—	—	8,781	Bruce Millan (b.1927, e.1959) — Lab
			Feb	80	51.3	17.9	30.7	5.1	—	7,238	
6	91	Glasgow Garscadden 53,000	1978 Apr (by-election)	69	45.4	32.9	18.6	—	3.1	4,552	Donald Dewar (b.1937, e.1978) — Lab
			1974 Oct	71	50.9	31.2	12.9	4.9	—	7,626	
			Feb	74	52.3	21.8	24.3	—	—	11,264	
26	33	Glasgow Govan 28,000	1974 Oct	72	49.5	41.0	7.0	1.9	1.6C	1,952	Harry Selby (b.1914, e.1973) — Lab
			Feb	75	43.2	40.9	12.7	3.2	0.4	543	
47	23	Glasgow Hillhead 41,000	1974 Oct	72	28.2	22.8	37.1	11.9	—	2,696	Tam Galbraith (b.1917, e.1948) — Con
			Feb	79	24.4	11.3	43.9	20.3	—	6,381	

%OO	%CT	Constituency	Date	% Turnout	Lab	SNP	Con	Lib	Other	Maj	Member of Parliament
32	9	Glasgow Kelvingrove 37,000	1974 Oct	63	42.8	23.2	27.6	6.4	—	4,119	Neil Carmichael (b.1921, e.Feb.1962) — Lab
			Feb	69	44.5	19.2	36.3	—	—	2,398	
10	77	Glasgow Maryhill 51,000	1974 Oct	66	57.6	29.9	9.3	3.1	—	9,418	Jim Craigen (b.1938, e.Feb.1974) — Lab
			Feb	70	56.6	24.9	18.5	—	—	11,383	
31	53	Glasgow Pollok 60,000	1974 Oct	72	43.5	24.3	27.0	5.3	—	7,091	James White (b.1922, e.1970) — Lab
			Feb	78	46.1	14.4	38.7	—	0.8C	3,406	
			1970 June	73	46.2	8.9	44.8	—	—	603	
1	97	Glasgow Provan 55,000	1974 Oct	64	58.6	30.2	9.8	—	1.4C	9,974	Hugh Brown (b.1919, e.1964) — Lab
			Feb	69	61.6	19.6	16.8	—	2.0C	15,787	
28	39	Glasgow Queen's Park 36,000	1974 Oct	67	56.1	21.8	17.0	3.7	1.4C	8,914	Frank McElhone (b.1929, e.1969) — Lab
			Feb	73	56.2	26.6	15.5	—	1.6	8,366	
21	48	Glasgow Shettleston 34,000	1974 Oct	64	54.3	28.5	14.4	2.8	—	6,349	Sir Myer Galpern (b.1903, e.1959) — Lab
			Feb	69	53.6	22.0	24.4	—	—	7,736	
21	57	Glasgow Springburn 44,000	1974 Oct	67	54.6	28.3	13.3	2.7	1.1C	8,395	Richard Buchanan (b.1912, e.1964) — Lab
			Feb	70	53.7	22.8	22.1	—	1.4C	10,395	
16	70	Greenock & Port Glasgow 62,000	1974 Oct	71	48.2	21.1	11.3	19.4	—	11,955	J. Dickson Mabon (b.1925, e.1955) — Lab
			Feb	67	48.3	11.4	18.5	20.6	1.1C	11,776	
26	68	Hamilton 52,000	1978 May (by-election)	72	51.0	33.4	13.0	2.6	—	6,492	George Robertson (b.1945, e.1978) — Lab
			1974 Oct	81	47.5	39.0	9.5	4.0	—	3,332	
			Feb	80	48.0	31.9	20.1	—	—	6,378	
37	42	Inverness 62,000	1974 Oct	71	15.6	29.6	22.0	32.4	—	1,134	Russell Johnston (b.1932, e.1964) — Lib
			Feb	76	17.9	16.6	26.7	38.7	—	5,223	
			1970 June	72	27.7	—	32.9	39.5	—	2,395	
24	68	Kilmarnock 61,000	1974 Oct	80	45.7	30.2	18.9	5.2	—	7,529	William Ross (b.1911, e.1946) — Lab
			Feb	83	47.2	15.3	27.7	9.8	—	9,727	
41	26	Kinross & West Perthshire 38,000	1974 Oct	75	7.6	41.5	41.7	9.2	—	53	Nicholas Fairbairn (b.1933, e.Oct.74) — Con
			Feb	78	9.9	23.1	52.9	14.0	—	8,082	
			1970 June	74	15.2	18.6	57.4	8.8	—	9,764	
21	65	Kirkcaldy 61,000	1974 Oct	75	45.4	32.0	16.5	6.1	—	6,101	Harry Gourlay (b.1916, e.1959) — Lab
			Feb	79	46.9	25.7	27.3	—	—	9,382	

%OO	%CT	Constituency	Date	% Turnout	Lab	SNP	Con	Lib	Other	Maj	Member of Parliament
26	63	Lanark 50,000	1974 Oct	82	37.6	35.8	23.2	3.4	—	698	Judith Hart (b.1924, e.1959) — Lab
			Feb	84	41.7	21.8	36.5	—	—	2,100	
34	58	Lanarkshire North 56,000	1974 Oct	80	46.2	26.9	22.5	4.4	—	8,341	John Smith (b.1938, e.1970) — Lab
			Feb	83	48.4	18.5	33.1	—	—	6,784	
22	66	Midlothian 96,000*	1974 Oct	77	41.5	35.6	16.0	6.9	—	4,084	Alex Eadie (b.1920, e.1966) — Lab
			Feb	82	44.6	26.9	28.4	—	—	11,742	
			1970 June	75	52.9	15.5	31.5	—	—	12,474	
35	35	Moray & Nairn 45,000	1974 Oct	75	9.7	41.2	40.0	9.1	—	367	Winifred Ewing (b.1929, e.Feb.1974) — SNP
			Feb	75	7.0	49.3	43.7	—	—	1,817	
			1970 June	72	22.8	27.8	49.4	—	—	6,109	
13	83	Motherwell & Wishaw 52,000	1974 Oct	75	44.6	31.8	18.2	2.9	2.4C	4,962	Jeremy Bray (b.1930, e.Oct.1974) — Lab
			Feb	77	46.7	20.0	30.6	—	2.7C	6,313	
52	22	Orkney & Shetland 28,000	1974 Oct	67	12.4	17.2	14.2	56.2	—	6,852	Jo Grimond (b.1913, e.1950) — Lib
			Feb		15.4	—	22.6	62.0	—	7,305	
			1970 June	66	21.1	—	31.9	47.0	—	2,532	
21	66	Paisley 64,000	1974 Oct	72	41.8	33.1	15.6	6.5	—	5,590	John Robertson (b.1913, e.1961)—Scottish Labour Party
			Feb	71	48.4	21.2	30.3	—	—	8,897	
			1970 June	72	54.1	7.3	32.4	6.2	—	10,197	
33	42	Perth & East Perthshire 62,000	1974 Oct	74	13.6	40.8	38.9	6.7	—	793	Douglas Crawford (b.1941, e.Oct.1974) — SNP
			Feb	78	15.1	27.2	47.3	10.4	—	8,975	
			1970 June	74	23.8	16.9	52.1	7.2	—	11,888	
67	28	Renfrewshire East 64,000	1974 Oct	78	20.8	23.2	41.4	14.6	—	8,710	Betty Harvie Anderson (b.1915, e.1959) — Con
			Feb	81	20.1	10.4	50.6	18.9	—	15,486	
30	59	Renfrewshire West 73,000*	1974 Oct	80	38.5	28.6	26.8	6.1	—	5,300	Norman Buchan (b.1922, e.1964) — Lab
			Feb	80	40.2	15.2	35.4	9.1	—	2,668	
44	33	Ross & Cromarty 34,000	1974 Oct	70	16.8	35.7	38.9	8.6	—	663	Hamish Gray (b.1927, e.1970) — Con
			Feb	75	19.8	23.0	36.1	21.1	—	2,871	
			1970 June	72	26.0	11.7	33.2	29.1	—	801	
34	43	Roxburgh, Selkirk & Peebles 59,000	1974 Oct	79	8.9	20.0	27.4	43.7	—	7,433	David Steel (b.1938, e.1965) — Lib
			Feb	86	6.2	8.0	33.7	52.0	—	9,017	
			1970 June	81	9.6	6.8	41.1	42.2	0.3	550	

Party Percentages

%OO	%CT	Constituency	Date	% Turnout	Lab	SNP	Con	Party Percentages Lib	Other	Maj	Member of Parliament
36	55	Rutherglen 49,000	1974 Oct	79	44.4	25.3	24.0	6.3	—	7,356	Gregor Mackenzie (b.1927, e.1964) — Lab
			Feb	82	47.6	15.2	37.2	—	—	4,153	
24	68	Stirling, Falkirk & Grangemouth 66,000	1974 Oct	79	43.2	39.8	14.1	2.9	—	1,766	Harry Ewing (b.1931, e.1971) — Lab
			Feb	82	41.9	34.5	23.6	—	—	3,849	
			1971 Sept (by-election)	60	46.5	34.6	18.4	—	—	4,488	
21	71	Stirlingshire East & Clackmannan 66,000	1970 June	73	50.7	14.5	34.8	—	—	7,230	George Reid (b.1939, e.Feb.1974) — SNP
			1974 Oct	82	36.3	50.7	10.5	2.5	—	7,341	
			Feb	83	36.4	43.5	19.5	—	0.6C	3,610	
21	70	Stirlingshire West 56,000	1970 June	76	50.7	15.5	38.2	5.6	—	10,551	Dennis Canavan (b.1942, e.Oct.1974) — Lab
			1974 Oct	81	39.0	38.2	18.4	4.4	—	367	
			Feb	83	40.8	29.7	29.5	—	—	4,844	
71	20	Western Isles 23,000	1970 June	79	48.9	21.4	29.7	—	—	7,419	Donald Stewart (b.1920, e.1970) — SNP
			1974 Oct	63	24.7	61.5	8.3	5.5	—	5,232	
			Feb	67	19.1	67.0	6.9	—	6.8	7,200	
15	77	West Lothian 83,000*	1970 June	65	38.4	43.1	18.5	—	—	726	Tam Dalyell (b.1932, e.1962) — Lab
			1974 Oct	79	45.3	40.9	10.0	3.4	—	2,690	
			Feb	81	45.3	34.9	19.0	—	0.7C	6,422	
			1970 June	77	52.9	28.1	18.1	—	0.8C	13,744	

THE SCOTTISH GOVERNMENT YEARBOOK 1976-7

ed. by M. G. Clarke and H. M. Drucker

CONTENTS

REFERENCE SECTION

THE SCOTTISH GOVERNMENT YEARBOOK 1978
ed. by H. M. Drucker and M. G. Clarke

CONTENTS

APPENDICES